A MEASURE OF
Faith

A MEASURE OF
Faith

MAXINE BILLINGS

A MEASURE OF FAITH

A New Spirit novel published by Kimani Press in 2007

First Published by BET Publications, LLC in 2004

ISBN-13: 978-0-373-83072-5
ISBN-10:   0-373-83072-6

© 2004 by Maxine Billings

www.kimanipress.com

Printed in U.S.A.

This book is dedicated to my mother:

Annie Ruth Nelson

Mama, you taught me by your example what true love is all about. You set boundaries, which helped to make me a better person. As I've grown older and wiser, I've come to love and appreciate you more. Thank you for the sacrifices you made for me. I'm so glad that you're my mother.

ACKNOWLEDGMENTS

My Heavenly Father, Jehovah: Thank you for granting me the privilege of serving you and being able to write this book. Because of you and your Son, Jesus Christ, I can wake up each day and look forward to a brighter future.

My husband, Tony: Thank you for your ongoing love and support. The genuine love you showed for me when we first met is what drew me to you. I cherish our years together and the years to come.

My daughter, Tasha: I admire your strength and character. Each moment we share makes me stronger. Thank you for being such a wonderful inspiration.

My son, Stefan: Thank you for the loving concern you show for me. You always lift me up when I need it the most. Your kind heart and gentle spirit help keep me going.

My stepfather, Jimmy Nelson: Thank you for being a father to me.

My father-in-law and mother-in-law, Charlie and Agnes Billings: Thank you for treating me like a daughter and always being there when my family needs you. Your love and support are appreciated.

My first cousin, Jacquelin Thomas: I owe you a debt of gratitude for all you've done for me. You did so many things to help make this book possible. Thank you for having such a kind and giving spirit.

My editor, Glenda Howard: Thank you for the faith you showed in me by allowing me this wonderful opportunity to share my stories. Your patience and input make it a pleasure to work with you.

My agent, Pamela Harty: I don't know what I'd do without you. Thank you for choosing to work with me. You're always there when I need you. Thanks for all that you do. You're the greatest.

My dear friend, JoAnn Turner: Your love and encouragement have helped me through some stressful moments. Thank you for always being there when I need you.

My copy editor and production editor: Thank you for the hard work you put into editing my story. I realize that you put much effort into it, and I really appreciate all you did. I feel that I have learned a lot from you.

Special thanks to Dr. David Helton and his nurse, Kim White: Thank you for the information you shared with me so that I could write what I hope is a realistic story regarding a health issue that many women face today.

There are many other people in my life who I could include on this page. Although your name is not mentioned here, please know that your love and support mean so much to me. You helped me to write this book, also.

Chapter 1

The sound of wheels screaming filled Lynnette Montgomery's ears. She stomped her foot on her brake as hard as she could, but it was too late. There was a loud crash. The truck seemed to have come out of nowhere.

As her silver 2000 Land Rover came to a screeching halt, Lynnette eyed the two young boys in the old pickup truck who had just smashed into her. The driver looked at her and pounded his fists on the steering wheel. He seemed to be muttering something, but she couldn't make out the words. The expression on his face caused her to swell with anger. *Who does this little weasel think he is?* She nearly fell down trying to get her petite frame out of her vehicle. She intended to give him a piece of her mind.

As Lynnette approached the boys, they got out of the truck. She walked up to the one who had been driving and lit into him like a firecracker. "Don't be looking like you're mad at me! *You* hit me!"

The boy didn't say anything. The other one asked her, "Are you all right?"

Lynnette snapped, "I'm fine, but look at my car!" She pointed to the long scratched-up dent on the driver's side that went from the front all the way to the back.

The young driver finally spoke. "I'm sorry. I didn't see you."

"Didn't see me!" Lynnette snapped again. "What are you? Blind?"

At that moment, a police car pulled up and stopped. The officer exited his vehicle and walked over to them. After he obtained both versions of what had transpired, he wrote down Lynnette and the other driver's license and automobile insurance information. Lynnette was even more outraged to learn that she and the teenager were both being charged for failure to yield the right of way. Even though he hit her, she had gotten in her turning lane too soon.

"What am I supposed to do about getting my car fixed?" she asked the officer.

He politely replied, "You'll need to contact your insurance company. The accident report should be ready in two to three days."

As Lynnette grabbed the citation from the officer's hand, she couldn't help but feel that life wasn't fair. *I get hit by another car while I'm in my turning lane minding my own business, and I'm at fault? This is a bunch of baloney!*

As she climbed back into the Land Rover, Lynnette's thoughts drifted to how she'd snapped at the teenagers. She overreacted too quickly and felt bad about being so harsh to them. *How could I have talked to them like that?* If someone had talked to her seventeen-year-old son, Joshua, or her sixteen-year-old daughter, Miranda, in that manner, she would be ready to whip somebody.

Since her reaction was one not typical of her, she reasoned that it had to be hormonal. Having recently left her doctor's office, she had been given some of the most devastating news of her entire life. She was stressed to the limit. She winced at the pain she felt in her abdomen.

It was an unusually warm day for the middle of January; however, this was typical of the south. Today, it felt like spring. The sun was shining radiantly with the temperature close to seventy degrees. Who would have thought that just a couple of weeks ago the city had gotten its first snowstorm one week and an ice storm the following week? Despite the beautiful weather, Lynnette felt absolutely miserable. She'd had a rotten day.

With her fortieth birthday just two weeks away, she was already feeling blue. Now, to top it off, she'd been told that her life was over. At least, that's how she felt. And as if that wasn't enough, she'd had the accident on her way home. She felt like crawling under a rock, never to return.

It was five o'clock when Lynnette pulled into the empty space beside the family vehicle, a white Chevrolet Suburban, in the four-car garage of their three-story brick home. Her husband, Robert, wasn't home yet as his company truck was not in the garage, but the kids were home. Miranda's compact-size car was in the garage, and Joshua's pickup was in the driveway.

Lynnette needed desperately to talk to Robert. She turned off the ignition, but her feet wouldn't allow her to leave the vehicle. Suddenly her arms encircled the steering wheel and in the next instance, she was bawling uncontrollably. Her mind began to digress back to her visit at the doctor's office when he delivered the news to her.

Dr. Mandell looked at her apprehensively as he spoke. "You mentioned that you've been having some pain in your abdomen. During your examination, I found fibroid tumors on your uterus."

She was bewildered. "What are fibroid tumors?"

The doctor explained, "Uterine fibroids are growths that develop from the cells that make up the muscle of the uterus. They're also called leiomyomas or myomas."

She shook her head, wondering, leio myo who?

Dr. Mandell continued, "Fibroids can be treated by removing them with surgery either through a myomectomy, which is removing the fibroids and leaving the uterus in place or a hysterectomy in which the uterus is removed."

Her head started to throb as her brain attempted to absorb all he was telling her. "If I just have the fibroids removed, is there a possibility they may grow back?"

The doctor advised her, "Yes, they may develop again even after the procedure. If they do, more surgery is needed in twenty to forty percent of cases."

Lynnette was so emotionally distressed she didn't even hear Robert's truck when he pulled into the space beside her. She heard someone tapping on her window. Startled, she looked up and saw Robert leaning down. She quickly wiped her face with her hands, grabbed her purse, and forced herself to climb out of the vehicle.

At forty-five, Robert Montgomery didn't look a day over thirty. He had short jet-black hair with just a hint of gray and long, gorgeous eyelashes for which any female would die. He sported a neatly trimmed moustache that Lynnette found very attractive.

Glancing at the dent on the car and then back at Lynnette, Robert asked, "Honey, are you okay? What happened?"

Lynnette tried to keep the tears from flowing again. She

wrapped her arms around his waist and buried her face in his chest, her tears soaking his shirt. Robert put his arms around her and held her tight.

She attempted to explain. "Dr. Mandell…" She couldn't finish.

"What is it?" Robert asked consolingly as he rubbed his hand up and down her back. "Did the doctor give you some bad news?"

Lynnette endeavored to get the words out a second time. "Dr. Mandell…"

She was scaring Robert. "What is it? Is it *that* bad?"

"I may need sur-ge-ry-ry-ry-ry-ry," she wailed.

Robert didn't understand. "Surgery? What kind of surgery? Are you all right? What's wrong?" He realized he was hurling too many questions at her all at once, but he needed some answers.

Lynnette clung to him tighter. "Dr. Mandell said I have fibroids on my uterus," she said, sniffling.

Robert had never heard the term before. "What are fibroids?"

"Tumors. They're probably what's causing the pain in my abdomen. He recommended that I get tested to rule out other causes. He said I may need to have a hysterectomy."

"These tumors—are they cancerous?" Robert wanted to know.

"We hope not. But in very rare cases, they can become cancerous. Oh, Robert, I don't want anybody cutting on me," Lynnette cried.

"Calm down," he said gently. "Didn't you say all he told you is that you *may* need the surgery?"

"Yes," Lynnette answered through her tears.

"So you don't know for certain. When do you have to go back to see him?"

"In a month."

"It'll be okay," Robert assured her. "Even if you do have to have the surgery, people have operations all the time."

Lynnette leaned back and stared at her husband. She repeated, "People have operations all the time. Is that all you have to say? Why is this happening to me?"

"Honey, calm down," he kindly reminded her. "At least you don't have some dreaded disease."

Lynnette pushed Robert's hands away from her. "Don't tell me to calm down." She'd had an awful day. What she needed was sympathy and understanding. She was disappointed in his response because he seemed to downplay her news.

"I come home from a horrific day, and you're acting like it's no big deal. And look at my car!" She turned and pointed. "On top of my life practically being over, I got hit on the way home by a couple of careless kids. And the police say it was my fault, too, because I got in my turning lane too soon. Have you ever heard such nonsense?"

Robert looked at the Land Rover, then back at Lynnette. "I'm sorry you had a bad day. As for the car, we'll get it fixed."

"Get it fixed!" Lynnette ranted. "Is that all you're worried about? Never mind whether or not I got hurt."

Robert put both hands on her waist. "Didn't I just ask you a minute ago if you're okay? Besides, I don't see any scrapes, scratches, or bruises."

That's it! Lynnette shoved Robert's hands off her once more and headed inside. "Never mind. I should've known you'd respond this way. Nothing is ever a big deal to you!"

"Lynn!" Robert called after her. "Wait a minute!" But she was already gone. *Well,* he thought, *I may as well go in and face more of the wrath of Lynn.* He knew it was coming.

Robert grabbed his lunch box out of the truck and went

through the kitchen door following in Lynnette's path. Joshua and Miranda were setting the table for supper.

Robert put his lunch box on the kitchen counter. "Hi, kids. How was your day?"

Miranda looked up and smiled as she placed silverware on the table. "Hey, Daddy."

Joshua put a plate on the table. "Hi, Dad," he said, grinning.

"I had a great day," Miranda said, beaming. "How was yours?"

"Okay," Robert answered. "Pretty busy," he added. He patted his son on the back. "Josh, what about you? How'd you do on that history exam?"

"Pretty good. I got an A." Joshua answered.

"That's great, son." The two males of the family held their hands up as Robert exclaimed, "High five!" and slapped their hands together.

Miranda smiled and shook her head. "You two are so silly."

Joshua responded, "We're not silly. You're just too serious."

"Whatever. Daddy, what's wrong with Mama? She said she was going to lay down. You know how upset she gets if we don't eat supper together."

The family eating meals together was one of Lynnette's pet peeves. It was her way of keeping the lines of communication open. During dinner, they always shared the day's experiences and enjoyed a lot of laughs.

"She had a bad day, honey. She'll be okay. You two go ahead and start. I'll be back in a minute."

Robert walked up the long, winding dark mahogany staircase. He found Lynnette in the bedroom laying down. He went over and sat down on the king-size bed beside her. There was a box of Kleenex on the nightstand and a crumpled-up tissue in her hand.

"Honey, are you okay? I'm sorry if I upset you. Do you want to talk about it?"

"No," Lynnette said, sniffling. "I've already tried to talk to you, and that didn't work. I just want to be left alone."

"Lynn, I'm just as shocked about this as you are. I don't know what it is I'm supposed to say except if you need the surgery, have it. I just want you to get better."

She sniffled again. "I came home today with some of the most devastating news of my life. Somebody wants to take away a part of what makes me a woman, and I don't want to give that up. I needed you to be there for me, but you made light of the whole situation. I feel as though you don't care about what I'm going through."

"I *do* care. You know I do. I just don't understand. I'm sorry if I made light of it. Will you come down and eat with me and the kids? You and I can talk some more later tonight, and you can tell me everything the doctor told you."

"No, you go ahead. I'm not hungry. I think I'll soak in the tub for a while. Tell Josh and Randa I'll be down in a little while."

After Robert left, Lynnette didn't get up right away. She didn't feel like moving. She didn't even feel like going downstairs, but no matter how bad she felt, she had to be there for her family.

Joshua and Miranda had just finished loading the dishwasher and were straightening up the kitchen when Lynnette came downstairs. She walked in on them as they were thumping soapsuds at each other.

Lynnette stood in the doorway with a smile on her face, examining her two children. They were a mere fifteen months apart and had a very good relationship.

She and Robert were not planning to have any more children at this stage in their lives, but how could she allow someone to take away such a precious part of her anatomy? It was a gift from God, where her babies had developed and been protected until she had given birth to them. *No, I won't allow it!* a voice yelled inside her head.

Lynnette walked up between her children just as Joshua was taking his turn at flicking suds at Miranda. He missed her and got Lynnette instead, smack on her right cheek. "Oops. Sorry, Mom. Didn't see you," Joshua apologized.

Lynnette put her arms around them as Joshua wiped her face with a dish towel. She gave them both a peck on the cheek. "What are you two up to? Goofin' off?"

Miranda answered, "Josh is, as usual."

"You started it," Joshua cut in. "Mom, are you feeling better? You want me to fix you a plate? Randa made some corn bread so I better forewarn you. Eat it at your own risk."

Miranda reached behind Lynnette and popped the back of Joshua's head.

Lynnette attempted to paste a smile on her face. "You two are silly. I'm okay, but I'm not hungry. Thank you though. How was school today?"

"Fine," they answered.

Joshua exclaimed, "I got an A on my history test."

"That's great, honey." Lynnette rubbed the back of Joshua's head. "I'm sorry I barged through this afternoon. Is there anything either of you need to talk to me about?"

"No," they replied.

Miranda wanted to know, "Are you sure you're okay? Daddy said you had a bad day."

"I'll be fine. You two got your homework done?"

"I've got some reading to do," Joshua told her.

"I did mine at school." Miranda stuck her tongue out at Joshua.

"Randa, how many times have I told you not to stick your tongue out at your brother? That's rude. Josh, you better go do your reading. Where's Dad?"

"I think he's in the den," Miranda replied, "talking on the phone to Aunt Carla."

Joshua and Miranda went upstairs to their rooms. Lynnette settled down at the kitchen table to work on some of her home improvement designs for Rose Johnson. Rose was a very distinctive woman. She was sixty-seven years old. Her late husband, Thurgood, had been very wealthy and had bequeathed her an abundance of money and possessions. One of the commodities she had acquired was an immense one-hundred-year-old manor near the historic district of Carrollton, Georgia. Her plans were to have it restored and made into a home for foster children.

When Lynnette and Robert had met with Rose the previous week in the dilapidated building, they had been reluctant to take on the project. Robert cautioned Rose that for what she would disburse in renovating it she may as well have it bulldozed and rebuilt. No, she wouldn't dream of doing that. It had been a gift from her dearly departed Thurgood. Besides, Rose had apprised them that R & L Builders and Designs by Lynn had come highly recommended as being the prime choice for the proposal. She had likewise related that she had heard about how they had worked together as a husband-and-wife team and designed and built their own home. She'd even seen pictures of it in *Southern Homes* magazine, and she was considerably impressed.

Yes, Lynnette and Robert had come a long way since they had first met twenty-one years ago in Chicago. They had scraped and saved every penny they earned to start their own businesses and make a better life for their family. Ever since having Robert and the children in her life, Lynnette had always considered herself happy. That is, until today.

Chapter 2

Robert's voice was low as he spoke into the telephone. "Carla, if your doctor said you needed to have a hysterectomy, would you have it?" He needed another woman's perspective even if it had to come from his own sister.

"I beg your pardon," Carla Sinclair said, gasping.

"Let me rephrase the question: If your doctor said you possibly needed a hysterectomy, how would you feel about it? Would you have it?"

Carla answered, "I probably wouldn't want to have it unless I had no other choice. Even then, it would probably be difficult. I don't know. I'd probably get a second opinion. Why on earth did you ask that?"

"Lynn went to the doctor today."

"Yeah, I know. That's why I called. To see how she is. She told me she hasn't been feeling too good." Carla gasped. "Oh no. She's not having a hysterectomy, is she?"

"I don't know. She may have to. She doesn't want one. I don't understand. If having a hysterectomy will help her, why won't she have it?"

"Robert, you don't understand because you're a man. A woman's heart is passionate. There's emotional pain involved. The human body is uniquely designed. A woman being able to get pregnant, have her baby grow inside her body, and then give birth are precious moments she will never forget. James and I can't have children. I can't tell you the number of times I've cried about it. Still, I don't think having a hysterectomy would be an easy decision for me to make either."

Robert's heart went out to his forty-year-old sister and her husband, James, forty-two. He knew how much they wanted children. He confided, "She's pretty upset with me right now. Lynn felt I wasn't supportive. I just want her to have the surgery and get better. It was a shock to me just like it was to her."

"Don't worry about it too much," Carla consoled her brother. "You'll just have to educate yourself a little and learn how to help her through it. You'll have to be patient and understanding."

"I guess you're right. Well, I better go. I promised her we'd talk."

"Okay. Tell her I'll call her tomorrow. Don't worry. She'll be okay."

When Robert hung up the telephone, he thought about what his sister had told him. He agreed he needed to be extra patient and caring where Lynnette was concerned. If ever she needed those things from him, she needed them now. It was already evident to him that he was going to have to dish out a huge helping.

He was about to enter the kitchen when he saw Lynnette still engrossed in her designs. He stopped in his tracks and simply stood there gazing at the love of his life. Every time he looked at her, she took his breath away. She was the most beautiful creature on which he'd ever laid eyes. He admired the way she held her head to one side. The short feathered hairstyle she wore made her facial features even more appealing.

When he finally joined her, Robert pulled out a chair and sat beside her. He prudently removed the pencil from her hand, placed it on the table, and took both her hands in his as he looked into the depths of her eyes.

His words were delayed, yet tender in affection. "Baby, I love you. You're my world, and I will do anything for you. I'm so sorry about this afternoon. I'm just as scared about this as you are. I know my choice of words didn't help matters. I'm here for you, and I'll be by your side every step of the way, no matter what you decide. You can count on that."

Lynnette smiled as she pressed her hand flat against Robert's cheek. "I know, baby. You've always been there for me. I'm sorry, too. I let my emotions get the best of me. I took my pain out on you, and that was wrong of me. I know you're in my corner. I've known that ever since we first laid eyes on each other twenty-one years ago. Do you remember?"

"Of course, I do." Robert grinned. "I couldn't stop thinking about you. You were so beautiful. You still are. Even more beautiful than the day I met you."

They talked and laughed despite the fact that deep down inside they were both terrified about the recent turn their lives had taken.

It was two in the morning. The news about the surgery and the pang of discomfort in her abdomen would not allow Lynnette any slumber. She was cuddled up on the window seat underneath the big Palladian window in the den looking up into the starry heavens. She felt terrible about the way she had treated Robert the day before. He was still very caring toward her and had been since the day they met.

Their trip down memory lane caused her to recall the very first time they ran into each other in Chicago in the department store where she worked. Her mind began to form mental pictures of the day she would never forget. She smiled as she replayed the scene in her head.

"Hi. I'm looking for a pin for my mother. She has so many. I want something different. Do you have any suggestions?"

Whoever this charming, good-looking gentleman is, *she thought,* he sure is a sight for sore eyes, with those long, beautiful eyelashes. *She would have given anything to have lashes such as those. It wasn't fair. Most women had to buy them or paint them on.*

She smiled at him as she reached down to open the glass case. "Here's one I think you might find to your liking." She took it out and handed it to him. It was in the shape of a heart surrounded by a cluster of ten-carat rubies with a diamond at the top in the center.

"She'll love it!" he exclaimed. "I'll take it."

When she handed over his change, their hands touched for a fleeting moment.

Lynnette smiled again at the memory of their next meeting. She had thought about him the remainder of the evening. She thought they'd never see one another again, but the next day, they nearly knocked each other down at the door of the department store. She was in a rush. She had to be at her afternoon class at five o'clock.

Images started playing in her head again as she relived what happened.

" 'Cuse me," she said without looking up.

"Oh no. Excuse me." He held her arm. "Are you okay?"

She looked him in the face then. "I'm fine."

Their eyes met. "Hey, you were here yesterday. You sold me a pin for my mother."

She remembered him. How could she forget those eyelashes? "Yes. Did she like it?"

"She loved it. We're visiting her sister. We're leaving in a few days, and I came by to let you know how much I appreciate your help."

"You're welcome. I'm glad she liked it."

"I can see you're in a hurry. I wanted to show my gratitude by taking you out to dinner before I leave."

Now, he was nice and all with those gorgeous eyelashes, but she didn't know him from a man on the moon. "That's not necessary. I was merely doing my job."

"I'm sorry. I didn't mean to be so presumptuous. We only saw each other for the first time yesterday, and here I am asking you out, and I haven't even introduced myself." He held out his hand. "My name is Robert Montgomery. Most people call me Rob."

She shook his hand. "I'm Lynnette Alexander. Everyone calls me Lynn."

They smiled at each other. He asked for her phone number. She didn't hesitate in giving it to him. Then she was on her way.

Lynnette shook her head to bring herself back to the present. She had wanted to go to dinner with him so bad. She didn't dare tell him that though. She didn't want to appear desperate.

After their brief acquaintance, Robert had gone back home to Georgia, and Lynnette had remained at home in Chicago. She had expressed to him how vital it was for her to complete her education before making any life-altering changes. He had been so loving and patient. They talked on the telephone and took turns visiting each other for two years until she had gotten her bachelor of fine arts degree in interior design, at which time she consented to be his wife.

Now her mind was back on her present situation. Life was so unfair sometimes. You live a few years and acquire everything of which you have ever dreamed and more. Then one day life throws you for a loop, and your whole world comes tumbling down. She was so happy and content with her life until the day before. Now her thoughts were ricocheting around in her head like Ping-Pong balls.

Lynnette surveyed the room under the glow of the floor lamp. She glanced up at the mahogany ceiling fan, the pale yellow walls, and cozy furnishings beneath the vaulted ceiling. Of all the rooms, she treasured this one the most.

Tucked in the corner beside the window seat and French doors stood a built-in bookcase that she had designed and Robert had built with his own two hands. Its companion was on the opposite side of the seat. They had even put cabinets and drawers on the front of the window seat on which she was resting. A massive Oriental rug covered the pine hardwood floor. Some of the furniture consisted of a floral-patterned wing chair and ottoman, a burgundy leather chair, and a cherry desk.

Lynnette was still scanning the room when Robert strolled over and joined her on the seat. "Stomach cramps keeping you awake?" he asked. He remembered many a night he'd found her suffering in silence. He was so glad he'd finally convinced her to go to the doctor.

"No," Lynnette lied. "I'm fine."

Robert didn't believe her but decided against voicing his feelings since he didn't want to upset her further. "I forgot to tell you I talked to Carla. She said she'll call you today."

He felt the need to reinforce what he'd told her earlier. He reached over and took her hand in his. "Lynn, I can't begin to imagine what you're going through, but I want to help you in whatever way I can," he reiterated. "I'll try to be patient with you, but I need you to be patient with me, too."

Lynnette squeezed his hand. "I know, honey. I'm trying not to be sad, but every time I try to look on the bright side, I only see darkness. I'm sorry I took my frustration out on you. I just hoped you'd be more understanding."

"It's hard to understand something that someone else is going through when you're not the one who's actually undergoing it. Carla says a woman's heart is passionate. Women respond more emotionally to things than men. Maybe I was making light of what the doctor told you because I thought if I did, you would, too. I realize it's a serious matter and one not to be taken lightly.

"I have something to tell you, and I want you to listen good because I mean it. No matter what life throws at us, I'll always love you, and you'll always be as attractive to me as you were when we first met. So don't think that if you have the surgery it will make you less of a woman to me because it won't. We're in this together. You don't have to go it alone."

Robert leaned closer as they wrapped their arms around each other.

Lynnette whispered, "Thank you, honey. I needed to hear that. I love you so much."

Robert turned off the lamp, and they walked away hand in hand. He yearned to wrap himself up inside Lynnette's thoughts so he could begin to glean her every emotion and be in a better position to comfort her.

Chapter 3

Rose realized Lynnette had not heard a word she had just spoken. "Lynn, honey, what's the matter?"

The two women were sitting at Rose's kitchen table. Lynnette had a vacant expression on her face. "Hmm? Oh, I'm sorry. What were you saying?"

"Honey, are you all right?" Rose inquired. "You look like you're in another world."

"I'm okay. I didn't rest well last night."

The last thing Rose wanted was for Lynnette to consider her a nosy old lady, but she looked so distraught. She put her hand on Lynnette's. "I'm not trying to get in your business, but do you want to talk about it?"

As soon as Lynnette and Rose had met, they had spontaneously clicked as though they had been lifelong friends despite their age difference. As much as Lynnette fancied her, however, she could not share her dilemma. "No, but thank you for asking. What were we discussing?"

"Floors," Rose answered.

"Oh yes. Well, Robert was telling me that some of the wood floors can be salvaged by sanding them down and re-sealing them. You mentioned that you want to refurbish as much of the old flooring as possible. I think that's a good idea. Not only will you save money, but I feel you'll be more than happy with the finished results."

"Would you like some more coffee, dear?" Rose asked politely.

"No, ma'am. I've got to go by the store to check on some things, and I have a couple of other clients to see today."

Rose's face lit up. "My, my," she said, "you're a busy lady. You sure do keep on the go. You're very good at what you do."

"Thank you, Ms. Rose," Lynnette said, standing. "Be thinking about what you want in the way of trim and molding for the walls. I'll see you in a few days. If you need anything, call me."

Rose stood and walked Lynnette to the door. "Okay, dear. Thank you."

"You're welcome. I'll see you later."

On the drive to her store, Lynnette's mind was still a jumble. She had been trying since the day before, without success, to snap out of her gloom. The harder she tried, the more discouraged she became. Robert was trying so hard to bring her back to life. She realized that she had to be dragging him down with her, but she felt so miserable.

As she journeyed through town, she admired how much it had grown since she and Robert had moved to the area. They lived in Faithe, a small community between Sand Hill and Carrollton. Small indeed compared to Chicago. She had come to love this region of Northwest Georgia and the surrounding counties as well. Atlanta was nice, too, but since departing Chicago Lynnette had gotten accustomed to the smaller towns. When deciding on a location for her store, Robert had discovered the building one day when he was on a job site in Carrollton. He purchased it, fixed it up, and surprised her with it on their second wedding anniversary.

When Lynnette got to the store, Beverly Smith, her assistant, was on the telephone with a customer. Lynnette went to her office, grabbed some documents off her desk, and carefully stuffed them inside her portfolio. As she reentered the store's facade, she heard Beverly saying, "All right, Mrs. Livingston, I'll tell her. Okay. You, too. Bye now."

"Hi, Beverly," Lynnette greeted her.

"Hi, Lynn, that was Mrs. Livingston. She really liked the bed ensemble she purchased. Now she wants the window treatments *and* the accent pillows. I told her we're expecting another shipment in a few days."

"That's wonderful. I thought she might want them. I'm gonna meet Carla for lunch. Why don't you join us?"

"I'd love to," Beverly replied, "but I've already made plans. Maybe next time."

"Okay, sure. Well, you know the routine. Just put the sign on the door. I probably won't be able to come back by the store after lunch. I have a couple of clients I need to see."

"Okay," Beverly said as she put the clock sign on the door and locked it. As they walked to their cars, Beverly asked, "How's that project with Ms. Johnson coming? Everybody's talking about it. It seems it's the biggest thing to hit Carroll County in a while."

"It's going fine. We're still in the planning stages. She's a very witty lady. She knows exactly what she wants, and she's got it all laid out."

"That's great. Well, have a good lunch. I'll see you tomorrow."

"Thanks, Beverly. You, too. See ya."

As Lynnette made her way to her vehicle, she smiled as she considered what a spectacular woman Rose was. She hoped if she lived to be Rose's age that she would be so full of life. Immediately, her mind drifted to thoughts of the surgery, and her smile disappeared.

"How are you, girl? Are you feeling any better?" Lynnette's sister-in-law, Carla, asked her over lunch at Valentino's.

It was evident that Robert and Carla were related. Their eyelashes intrigued Lynnette. She and Carla had been like sisters since the moment they met. Lynnette had also bonded with their mother. Lillian was one of the sweetest women Lynnette had ever known, the kind of mother she wished she'd had. Growing up without a mother left a terrible void in Lynnette's life. When Lillian died, Lynnette felt as though she had lost her own mother again.

"I wish I could say I was, but in all honesty, I'm not. I never expected anything like this to happen. I want to get over it and get on with my life, but I can't. I just don't feel normal anymore. When Dr. Mandell told me, my emotions just went haywire, and I feel I can't control them any longer." Lynnette felt herself getting frustrated. "Let's talk about something else."

Carla touched her sister-in-law's hand. "I'm sorry, Lynn. I wish there was something I could do to make you feel better." Then Carla's face lit up. "Hey! Why don't you, me, James, and Robert get together this weekend and do something? Maybe it'll take your mind off things and help you feel better."

Lynnette hesitated. "I don't know."

"Aw, come on. Why don't we go to Helen or Pine Mountain?

You know, they both have all those arts and crafts shops. You might even find some things for your store. Come on. What d'you say?"

It did sound good, but Lynnette couldn't. She just wasn't in the mood. "It sounds wonderful, Carla, but we can't." She placed her hand on Carla's and added, "Thanks though. I appreciate your thoughtfulness."

Carla was undoubtedly disappointed. "Yeah, yeah, yeah," was her reply. She teased, "You know, lately you're just not much fun. I love you though, and I'm here for you."

"Thanks, Carla. I love you, too, girl."

Carla put forth her best efforts at keeping Lynnette entertained while they ate. She had a million questions to ask regarding the surgical procedure but realized that for now she would have to respect Lynnette's desire not to discuss it.

Lynnette struggled to keep her mind focused on her conversation with Carla, yet her thoughts were far, far away.

When Lynnette arrived home, she was accosted by a quiescent solitude. She turned on the oven, went over to the refrigerator, and took a glance at the calendar they kept there to keep up with their family's busy schedules. Joshua and Miranda had opted not to participate in any extracurricular activities this school year. She was thankful that they were still doing a good job of jotting down their schedules at the fast food restaurants where they worked. They both were working until nine o'clock so they would probably be home around nine-thirty. Robert had informed Lynnette that morning that he would be home around seven.

She removed a casserole from the freezer that she had prepared a week ago and placed it in the oven. She had almost a full hour to herself before Robert got home. She was still feeling down in the dumps so she decided to take a soothing, hot bubble bath.

She strolled up to the master bath, turned on the water in the deep whirlpool tub, and added her favorite bubble bath under the hot running water. She lit several scented candles and placed them on the side of the tub near the lush green potted plants.

Lynnette eased into the hot, bubbly water in the glow of the candles and leaned her head back against the bath pillow. She closed her eyes and allowed her mind to wander. She felt powerless to raise herself from the abyss of sadness in which she was so totally consumed.

Her thoughts drifted heavenward. *Oh, God, why is this happening to me? Have I done something so awful that I deserve this? This is serious. This is major surgery we're talking about.*

Lynnette's mind immediately digressed to her childhood, to the time when one of her foster mothers had gone into the hospital for routine surgery and had died on the operating table.

That could happen to me. I could die during surgery; then if I do make it, my life as a woman is over. I love being a woman. I can't let anybody take that part of my body away from me. I can't do it. I just can't do it. I don't want to feel like a shell of a woman.

"Lynn!" Robert exclaimed as he approached her.

Lynnette's eyes flew open, and she jumped at the sound of her name. "What? What is it?"

"Hey," he said breathlessly. "I'm sorry. Did I scare you?"

Lynnette had her hand to her chest. "Goodness, yes. What is it? What's wrong?"

"Nothing. I just didn't know where you were." Robert moved over a couple of candles and a plant before sitting down on the side of the tub. *All these candles and plants,* he thought. Sometimes he felt like he was in a jungle instead of a bathroom. "How are you? Better?"

"No, not really. I was just sitting here thinking."

"Wanna talk about it?" Robert dared to ask.

"Why don't you take your shower, and I can tell you over dinner? What time is it?"

Robert looked at his watch. "About ten past seven," he answered.

"Good," Lynnette said. "It's time for the casserole to come out of the oven. By the time you shower and get dressed I'll have it on the table."

The water was so soothing to her tense body. Lynnette detested having to abandon her warm, bubbly cocoon. There, she could shut out the rest of the world and focus only on herself and what she was going through. *Is that selfish?* she wondered. She didn't care. This was the second hardest thing she'd ever come up against. The first, being abandoned by her mother when she was four years old, still hurt like it was yesterday.

"Oh, before I forget, we're putting your car in the shop next Thursday and picking up your rental," Robert told Lynnette while they ate supper.

"That's fine," Lynnette replied, "as long as I can get something equivalent to the size of my Land Rover that allows me to sit up high. And I don't want some little bitty car that I can't get my merchandise in either." She was aware that she had a bit of an attitude. She was in a terrible mood, and she did not care who knew it.

Robert sensed her mood. He was tired of her moping around, behaving as though she was dying. *What she needs to do is just have the surgery and get it over with.* It was as simple as that. Why couldn't she see that?

"That's no problem. I already explained that to the car rental company. You know, you *can* just forget the rental car and drive the Suburban."

When she didn't respond, he asserted, "I see you're still in a bad mood." As soon as the words were out of his mouth, he knew he'd messed up big time. He had not meant to comment on her attitude. It came out before he could stop it.

"I don't want to drive the Suburban. It's too big. And I'm not in a bad mood," Lynnette snapped. "I just have a lot on my mind. Everything was fine until I went to the doctor."

Robert looked up from his plate and studied Lynnette's face. He was trying not to lose his patience with her. "Maybe you need to seek psychological help."

Lynnette stared at him. She was deeply hurt and offended by his statement. "Robert, I have a medical condition. I'm not crazy. How could you even say something like that?"

"I'm not saying you're crazy. All you've been doing since yesterday is moping around. This isn't like you. I've never seen you like this before. Maybe you need some professional help in order to deal with the way you're feeling."

Lynnette wished he wouldn't say that. "What I need is for you to be a little more understanding."

Robert was frustrated. "Lynn, I'm trying to be understanding. Why can't you just have the surgery and get on with your life so we can all get on with ours? Why do you insist on making yourself and the entire family miserable?"

Lynnette glared at him. "Oh, is that what I'm doing? Making everybody miserable?" She stood and backed away. "Do you think I *want* to feel this way? I can't help it. Am I supposed to walk around here all jolly just to appease you?"

Robert hung his head and shook it slowly from side to side. "Lynn, that's not what I meant. I don't want you to pretend to be happy if you're not. I just can't stand seeing you like this. I wish you would just snap out of it."

"Robert, I wish I could just snap out of it. Honey, I've tried, but I can't," Lynnette replied. "I know you can't understand completely, but I've got all these thoughts and emotions going through my head. Sometimes I can't get one thought finished before there's another one taking its place."

Robert felt like a whipped dog. He got up, went over to her, and took her by the arm. "I'm sorry. Come on. Sit back down." He led her back to her seat. "Let's finish dinner." Instead of going back to his chair opposite hers, he sat down beside her. "We're gonna get through this. If I ever stop saying the wrong thing, we'll get through it. It's just that I want to help you, and I don't know how. The harder I try, the more I mess up."

Lynnette looked at Robert with teary eyes. "I know you're trying, baby, and I love you all the more for it." She gently cupped his face with her hands and kissed him. She leaned her forehead against his. "It's just that this is a major decision in my life. I'm so scared, and I don't know what to do."

Robert had not comprehended until that moment just how frightened his wife was. He took her hands in his and gazed deep into her eyes. "I'm scared, too. I love you so much. If anything ever happened to you, I don't know what I'd do. I want to protect you from everything that hurts you, but I can't. I feel so powerless."

Lynnette felt a lump the size of a fist in her throat upon hearing her husband's heartfelt sentiments for her. She knew with all her heart exactly how much he loved her, but at that moment, hearing it made her feel more complete.

* * *

It was three o'clock in the morning and another sleepless night for Lynnette. She had so much on her mind, and the pain in her abdomen wasn't helping matters. She was again at her favorite spot in the den. As she glared up into the sky, she attempted to pray. This time, however, no words came.

She leaned her head back and let the tears flow. Suddenly she felt someone touch her shoulder. Startled, she opened her eyes to see Joshua standing there in his pajamas.

"Mom, what's wrong? Why are you crying?" Joshua wanted to know.

Lynnette hastily wiped her face with her hands and tried to fake a smile. "I'm fine, honey. Go on back to bed. You shouldn't be up. You've got school tomorrow."

Joshua sat down on the window seat and gazed at his mother, concern in his eyes. "Mom, you're not fine. What's wrong?" He started to rise. "Do you want me to get Dad?"

Lynnette stopped him from getting up. "No. I've just got a lot on my mind. That's all."

"What is it?" he questioned her.

Joshua was pushing her, trying to get her to open up. She couldn't get mad at him though because it was a trait he had inherited from her. She did the same thing whenever she sensed distress and wanted her family to confide in her.

"Nothing, honey. Go on back to bed. I'm coming," Lynnette said as she rose.

As they walked upstairs, Joshua told her, "Mom, you know, I'm not a child anymore. I know something's bothering you. I don't like seeing you sad."

They reached the top of the stairs and stopped. "Thank you. I know you're concerned, and I appreciate it. Don't worry. I'll be fine." Lynnette kissed Joshua's cheek. "Now go to bed." She smiled. "Good night."

"Good night."

When Lynnette slid into bed beside Robert, he stirred. Although he already knew, he asked sleepily, "Where have you been?"

"Downstairs. I couldn't sleep. Dr. Mandell's talking about taking away a part of what makes me a woman. I don't want to feel empty inside. I don't want you to look at me differently."

"Com'ere." Robert raised his arm so Lynnette could scoot next to him.

His voice was warm and soothing against her ear. "Your anatomy is not the only thing that makes you a woman. I love you for the wonderful woman you are. I love you for your mind, your personality, and your incredible spirit. You know what you need to do?" he asked, not waiting for her to answer. "Relax your mind and your body and leave all your worries with God. Don't rely on your own strength. Rely on God. When you're weak, He'll make you strong. When you're broken at heart, He'll stay close to you and help you through."

Lynnette's tense body began to relax. It was comforting to know that the Almighty Creator would stay by her side. It also gladdened her heart to have been blessed with a wonderful, caring husband such as the one laying beside her.

Chapter 4

As Robert sat at his desk in the den, his mind reflected on what he had just read in the pamphlets spread out on the desk before him. Now he was beginning to get a clearer understanding of why Lynnette was so depressed about the possibility of having a hysterectomy.

It's major surgery. The risks include blood clots, bleeding after surgery, severe infection, anesthesia-related problems, bowel blockage, urinary tract injury, and the most frightening one, death. Some women even experience an emotional reaction to the loss of the uterus.

Fibroids occur more often in black women than in white women. They seem to occur at a younger age in black women and to grow more quickly. They're most common in women aged thirty to forty. Twenty to twenty-five percent of all women will get fibroids.

Robert was still attempting to soak all this information into his brain when Lynnette walked up behind him.

"Whatcha doing?" she asked. She placed her hands on his shoulders, leaning over as she attempted to see what had his attention. She saw the pamphlets Dr. Mandell had given her spread out on the desk.

Robert turned his head slightly to look at her, his reading glasses resting on his nose. He reached his right hand back to gently pat her hand, which rested on his left shoulder. "Just reading. I found these on your dresser. I'm trying to get a clearer understanding of what it is you're going through and find ways I can help you through it."

"That's really sweet, honey."

"Next weekend, I was thinking I'd take you to Apple Mountain. You know Ron, one of my crewmen?"

Lynnette nodded.

"He and his wife, Amy, won't be able to use their timeshare and said we could use it. How does that sound?"

"Okay, I guess."

Lynnette didn't sound very enthusiastic. "Look." Robert turned slightly in his chair. "Com'ere," he told her as he took her hand and pulled her around to sit on his lap. He pushed a tiny strand of hair out of her eye. "You're under a lot of stress. Maybe doing something different will help. You need to get away for a while to relax your mind. Let's go away for a couple of days. Leave all our worries behind us."

Lynnette politely interjected, "They'd only be waiting for us when we get back."

"You're right, but if you're going to get through this, you've got to let me help you. I'm not going to let you mope around the house depressing yourself. I'm your husband. I love you. Let me help."

Lynnette smiled, kissed Robert's cheek and whispered in his ear, "Okay, Eyelashes."

Robert leaned back a little and inquired, "What did you just call me?" It had been a long time since she'd called him by the nickname she'd given him.

"You heard me, Eyelashes."

Robert put on a wide grin. He was thrilled she seemed to be in a good mood for a change. "You haven't called me that in a long time. Are you flirting with me?"

"Maybe I am, maybe I'm not." At that, Lynnette jumped up and ran as fast as her legs would carry her.

Almost instantaneously, Robert was after her and chasing her, both of them laughing through the house and up the winding staircase.

As Lynnette maneuvered her compact SUV over the highway, she said, "Randa, honey, before we go shopping I need to take a catalog to Ms. Rose. It's on the way. We won't be long."

Ever since Lynnette had opened her store she'd upheld her resolution not to operate the business on the weekend. Everyone had warned her that she was making a mistake and would not be in business very long with that rule, but business was still booming. It was Saturday, and the store was closed.

"Okay, Mama. Is this the lady who's building the children's home?"

"Yes, it is."

"That's really nice of her to provide a home for children who don't have one."

Lynnette looked at her daughter and smiled. "Yes, it is. She's a very sweet lady. I want you to meet her."

Discussion of the children's home made Miranda ask her

mother, "Mama, do you ever think about your mama and where she might be?"

Lynnette answered, "When I was younger I did, but I don't think much about her now."

"You really don't remember anything about her?"

Lynnette shook her head and tried to keep her tears inside. "N-no," she said, her voice cracking. "I was very young."

All Lynnette knew about her parents was what she had been told by other people. When she had gotten older, she learned from Illinois's family and children's agency that her father had died in an automobile accident when she was four. Soon thereafter, her mother had left her. Being shifted from house to house, her life had been void of any stability.

Miranda recalled some pieces of information that her mother had been able to share with their family. "Maybe if your daddy hadn't died, she wouldn't have left. I know that's not an excuse, but maybe it's the reason."

Lynnette felt her eyes becoming moist with tears. So many times she had yearned for her and her mother to have the close relationship that she and Miranda had. Maybe this was one of the things she so desperately needed—for her mother to be by her side to help her through this agonizing phase of her life. *Robert doesn't understand. He's trying, but he can't. Not like a mother would.*

Miranda heard a sniffle. When she looked at her mother, Lynnette was wiping her face.

"Mama, I'm sorry. I didn't mean to make you cry." Miranda felt terrible. Sometimes she chose the wrong thing to say at the wrong time. She didn't know her mother would get so upset. Talk of her mother's mother usually did not affect her in this way.

Lynnette attempted a smile. "It's okay. It's not your fault. I've been really sad lately anyway."

"Yes, I know. What's wrong?"

"Well, I may as well tell you. I can't keep it from you forever. You're a young woman now."

Miranda's eyes grew large with apprehension. "What's wrong, Mama? You're not sick, are you?"

"When I went to the doctor, he told me that I have fibroid tumors on my uterus. I may need to have a hysterectomy."

Miranda stared at her mother. "Are the tumors cancerous?"

"Probably not." Lynnette did not want to frighten her daughter; therefore, she refused to mention that in very rare cases—far less than one percent—changes could occur in the fibroid tissue that could cause it to become malignant. "I can have the tumors removed or have a hysterectomy where my uterus will be removed."

"Well, why don't you just have the tumors removed?"

"Well, I could, but they may grow back and I'd have to have more surgery."

"So you're having the hysterectomy?"

"I haven't decided what I'm gonna do. I'm still thinking and praying about it. Right now, I'm not feeling very good about myself. I'm thinking about turning forty. I guess I'm starting to feel old and unattractive."

They approached an intriguing white two-story country cottage with green shutters. Flowers were scattered throughout the yard and on the spacious front porch.

"I'll pray for you, too, Mama," Miranda assured her mother. "And don't feel bad about turning forty. Everybody still thinks you and I are sisters."

Lynnette looked over at her daughter and smiled. "Thanks, sweet pea."

Rose had her front door open before Lynnette and Miranda made it to the steps. She grabbed Lynnette and hugged her.

Eyeing Miranda, she inquired, "And is this pretty young lady Miss Randa?"

Miranda was impressed that the sweet stranger knew her name. She looked at her mother and blushed as she held out her hand to Rose. "Yes, ma'am. I'm Randa. It's nice to meet you."

Rose accepted Miranda's hand and concurred, "It's nice to meet you, too, Randa. I'm Rose."

"Ms. Johnson to you," Lynnette reminded her daughter.

Rose continued, "Handshakes are nice, but I like hugs. May I have one?"

Lynnette stood there, smiling as she watched them hug. Rose was so outgoing and energetic. Nobody was a stranger to her. Lynnette wanted to be just like her.

Rose put her arm around Miranda's tiny waist and told them, "Come on inside, you two."

Lynnette spoke as she followed them into the foyer of Rose's grand house. "We can only stay a few minutes. We're going shopping. Here's the antique furniture catalog I promised you."

Rose accepted the book from Lynnette and clutched it to her bosom as though it was some prized possession. "Thank you, Lynn. You're such a dear. I can't wait to look through it and find some antique pieces for the living room."

Rose escorted them to the den where they sat down. Miranda was simply captivated with the grandeur of the room. Her eyes were open wide as they soaked in the charm of the area. The room had an array of every color of the rainbow and exquisite Chippendale furniture throughout. Two large built-in bookshelves contained enormous quantities of reading material. Rose had her own personal library. She obviously enjoyed reading. So did Miranda. This was something the two had in common.

"Ms. Johnson, your house is beautiful," Miranda commented.

"Thank you, dear, but it doesn't compare to yours. I've seen it in magazines. I bet you and Josh are real proud of your mama and daddy for having created such a magnificent home for you, especially one so full of love."

Lynnette and Miranda glanced at each other and smiled.

"Yes, we are. We know they worked very hard. Ms. Johnson," Miranda continued, "Mama says you're building a home for children."

Rose nodded. "Yes, I am. Your parents are fixing it up for me."

"I think that's very special of you since so many children don't have a family or home to go to. I wish you'd been around when Mama was a little girl and didn't have anywhere to go." As soon as Miranda said the words, she realized she probably should not have uttered them. She had gotten caught up in the moment and perhaps shared a little too much information.

Upon hearing Miranda's words, the pain in Rose's heart was so intense she felt as though she'd just been stabbed.

Lynnette was touched at Miranda's comment. She patted Miranda's knee and told her, "That's sweet, honey. We better go if we want to catch the sales before everything gets gone."

"All right, Mama." Miranda hated to leave. She really did like Rose.

Lynnette and Miranda stood. Rose hooked her arm in Miranda's as she walked them to the door. "I wish you didn't have to go so soon." Then she had a brilliant idea. "Lynn, I know it's short notice, but I'd love to have you all over for Sunday dinner tomorrow. Can you come?"

Miranda didn't give Lynnette an opportunity to answer before she begged, "Oh, can we, Mama, please?" Then she hugged Rose and exclaimed, "I like Ms. Johnson."

Rose leaned the side of her face against Miranda's and replied, "I like you, too, Randa."

Lynnette finally answered, "Let's check with your dad. If he doesn't have anything planned he hasn't told me about, we'll see." Then she told Rose, "I'll call you later this afternoon and let you know. Thank you for inviting us."

"Oh, it's my pleasure."

Lynnette said to Rose, "Why don't you come to morning service with us tomorrow? We can pick you up."

Rose was caught off guard by Lynnette's invitation. She stuttered, "I c-can't tomorrow. Maybe another time."

Lynnette smiled. "All right."

After Lynnette and Miranda had gone, Rose started to consider what she would fix for dinner the next day. She wanted everything to be perfect. After all, these were special people she was having over.

Sunday morning, Robert could not believe his eyes when he caught sight of Lynnette dressed and ready for morning service while he and their two teenagers were still romping around attempting to get ready. He almost bumped into her as he was entering their bedroom.

"You're ready early," he observed.

"Yeah," Lynnette said, sighing. "I think I'll drive myself. I want to be there when Henry and Josephine unlock the doors. Maybe see if they can pray with me before service begins. I've got so much on my mind."

"I wish you'd told me earlier so I could go with you." Robert was disappointed. He needed to be there with her.

"It's okay, honey. I'll be fine. I'll see you and the kids there." Lynnette stood on her tiptoes and kissed Robert once on the lips.

"Okay. Be careful."

"I will," Lynnette declared over her shoulder as she headed out the bedroom door.

As she drove, Lynnette reflected on the turn her life had taken. Her mental faculties weighed down with apprehension, she sensed her need and desire for a safe haven, a place of refuge. She always felt totally secure in God's house.

As she pulled her SUV into the parking lot, she spotted the Dotsons' silver Cadillac. She parked, got out of her vehicle, and walked up to the double doors of the massive building. She opened the door and went in.

Henry and Josephine Dotson were sitting in the front center row chatting away. They were two of the oldest members. They were deeply respected by everyone in the congregation and the community. Henry was a church elder. Due to various health problems, Josephine was somewhat limited as to how much she could do in a physical sense. However, she was very supportive of her husband, and despite her limitations, always had a kind word for everybody and would do whatever she could to offer assistance.

The couple were in their late eighties but looked to be only in their sixties. Although married for more than half their lives, they still displayed a deep love and respect for each other. Lynnette admired them and hoped and prayed that her and Robert's marriage would stay as concrete as theirs.

Lynnette looked around admiring the architectural design of the building. Ceiling fans hung from the high-vaulted ceiling. On the walls hung huge pictures in gold-trimmed frames with gardenlike scenes. One picture on the back wall embodied a scene comparable to the Garden of Eden with a capacious waterfall flowing in the background. As she stood there staring at the expressive piece of art, she could see herself in the picture running through the garden, playing with the animals and rejoicing with her family.

As she walked toward the couple, she admired the shiny gold banner in the sanctuary that bore the year's scripture text from Romans 8:31: *If God be for us, who can be against us?*

Lynnette was not in the habit of arriving so early. The air was placid except for the Dotsons' light chattering. She glanced around at the empty seats. Soon they would be full of parishioners desiring to hear the Word of God. She cleared her throat as she neared the Dotsons. They smiled when they turned and realized it was her.

Henry stood and hugged her. "Sister Montgomery, it's so good to see you. How are you?"

Lynnette smiled. "Good morning, Brother Dotson. I'm okay. How are you?"

"Just fine," he answered.

"Sister Dotson," Lynnette acknowledged, "how are you?"

Josephine stood and the two women hugged. "I'm fine, sugar. How's the family?"

"They're fine. I left them at home getting ready. They should be here shortly."

"Have a seat," Josephine said.

Josephine sat back down beside her husband, and Lynnette sat beside her. Josephine turned to face Lynnette and took her hand. "Dear, is everything all right? You don't sound like yourself today."

"Well, actually I came early hoping to find the two of you here. I'm going through some things, and I wanted to talk to you and ask you to pray with me before the service starts."

Josephine queried, "Lynn, what's wrong?"

Lynnette informed them that she possibly needed surgery, but she was afraid.

"Brother Dotson, could you lead us in a prayer?" Lynnette pleaded. "I feel so burdened down. I don't know what to do."

"Sure I will. Let's go back to the library."

The three of them went to the library and sat down. They held hands as Henry led them in prayer.

"Heavenly Father, we approach you this morning on this beautiful day that you allowed us to wake up to. We're thankful for the many wonderful blessings you bestow upon us each and every day that we live. At this time, we need to offer a special prayer to you for our beloved sister, Lynn.

"Her heart is heavy with a burden she cannot carry alone. Her doctor has told her she may need surgery, and she's scared. Please help her to gather information about the surgery she faces so that she can make a decision that gives her peace of mind. Help my wife and me and the entire congregation to be a pillar of support, strength, and encouragement to our dear sister and her family, not just during this period but for always.

"We love you so much, Father. We realize many times we sin and fall short of your righteous requirements. For the times we do, we beg your forgiveness. And we offer this prayer in Jesus' dear name. Amen."

Lynnette and Josephine repeated, "Amen."

Lynnette was so deeply touched by Brother Dotson's heartfelt prayer that she was moved to tears. So was Josephine. The three stood and hugged. Lynnette was in much better spirits, and her burden felt somewhat lighter. As they made their way from the library, more people were arriving and congregating with one another. When Lynnette spied her trio coming through the door, she went to greet them, a smile beaming across her face.

Robert smiled and took her hand in his as they made their way to their seats. "You look like you're feeling better," he whispered.

"I am," Lynnette said. "My spirit has been lifted."

Robert was alert to his wife's happier mood as she chatted with the sister on the seat in front of them. Now perhaps they could get on with their lives and things could get back to normal.

Sunday afternoon, the Montgomery clan sat around Rose's dining room table partaking of sweet and savory food and enjoying laughs and lively conversation. Robert had baked one of his scrumptious homemade pecan pies and brought it along even though Rose had instructed them not to go to any trouble.

After Robert had put away his last bite of food, he leaned back in his chair, rubbed his belly, and boasted, "Ms. Johnson, that was deeee-licious. Your cooking reminds me of my mama's."

Rose, proud of her knack for putting together delicious meals, beamed as she responded, "Thank you, Robert. I'm glad you enjoyed it. Greg always complains when he visits that I'm going to make him fat. Funny thing is, while he's grumbling out one side of his mouth, he's busy stuffing food in the other side."

Everybody burst out laughing.

"Is Greg your son?" Joshua inquired.

"Yes."

"Where does he live?" Joshua asked.

"Pennsylvania."

Miranda frowned and shivered. "Oooh, it's cold there."

"Not always," Rose remarked. "They have warm weather like we do here, but when it's cold, it's really cold."

"Is he married?" Miranda wanted to know.

Robert and Lynnette looked at each other and smiled. "Whoa," Robert intervened, holding up his hand. "You two keep popping all these questions at Ms. Johnson. She can't answer one question before you throw another one at her."

"That's okay, Robert," Rose said. "They're inquisitive. I like that. That's how we learn. I don't mind. To answer your question, Randa, he's not married yet, but he will be later in the year. He has a really sweet fiancée."

"What's her name?" Miranda inquired.

Lynnette and Robert eyed each other again. Robert had always told Lynnette that Miranda had her mouth. They both loved to talk. They could talk a person's head off. Robert poked Lynnette with his elbow. "It's obvious she's your daughter."

Lynnette didn't say anything. She playfully elbowed Robert in his side.

"Her name is Sheree," Rose answered.

Joshua declared, "I'd like to meet them. When are they coming to visit?"

"Well, they're going to be the directors of the children's home when it's completed. They'll be moving here sometime before the end of the year, but I'll keep you informed."

It was apparent to Lynnette and Robert that their offspring were not going to allow them any conversation with Rose. They simply sat there listening and enjoying the interchange among the threesome.

The next thing they heard was Miranda saying, "So how did Greg and—what's her name again?—oh yes—Sheree meet?"

Lynnette noticed how drawn to Rose her children were. *What is it about this woman? She's so unique.* Joshua and Miranda had not taken to another woman in such a way since their grandmother Lillian had died. In the same manner, Lynnette felt herself being drawn to Rose.

Chapter 5

The following week seemed to go by too fast. At least for Lynnette it did. She reasoned it was because in another week she'd be forty. She was in no hurry to get there. Any other time, the week would have dragged by. The closer her birthday got, the more depressed she became. She was beginning to have second thoughts about the trip to Apple Mountain.

She and Robert had managed to get her vehicle to the shop and pick up her rental car earlier that afternoon. A Ford Taurus station wagon was not what she wanted. It was roomy, but after being accustomed to driving an SUV, she felt like she was sitting on the ground. *Somebody needs to tell that car rental company that a station wagon and a sport utility vehicle are not even closely related.* She would have told them herself if it hadn't been for Robert almost dragging her out of the place.

Later that night, Lynnette was quiet as she and Robert got ready for bed. She was sitting at her vanity going through her nightly ritual of creams, lotions, and moisturizers when Robert emerged from the bathroom.

As he pulled back the covers on the rice-carved four poster bed, he told her, "I may quit work a couple of hours early tomorrow afternoon so we can hurry and get on the road. How does that sound?"

Lynnette looked in her vanity mirror for some sign of Robert's reaction as she told him, "I changed my mind. I'm really not in the mood to go." She saw him in her mirror as he let the covers drop onto the bed. He leaned on the bed and stared at her in disbelief.

"You're kidding, right?"

"No, I'm serious. I'm not going."

Robert stood up rigid. "Lynn, we discussed this last week. When were you planning to tell me? After we had loaded up the truck and were pulling out the driveway?"

"I'm sorry. I know I should have told you sooner. I thought I would get over this feeling, but I haven't."

Robert turned around and plopped down on the bed. "Lynn, I'm trying to be patient and understanding, but ever since last week you've been moping around. I thought you were feeling better. You're acting like somebody died."

Lynnette spoke from her heart. "I feel like a part of me *is* dying."

"Lynn, you've got to get over it. Other women have had the same thing. They had the surgery, and they're doing just fine. What good will it do for you to sit around depressing yourself about it?"

"Robert, I know what you're saying makes sense, but I can't help it. I'm trying. I really am, but it's still haunting me."

"Do you plan to just stop living your life now? Moping around all the time? What about me, Josh, and Randa? What are we supposed to do while you dig a hole for yourself? Do you expect us to sit and watch? I'm telling you now I won't do it."

Lynnette caught Robert's image in the mirror again. Was he threatening to leave her? "Exactly what are you saying, Robert?"

"I'm saying I'm not putting my life or our children's on hold because you can't face reality. We will not sit around here moping with you. And I'm not cancelling the trip. If you don't want to go, fine. Stay here. Josh and Randa like the resort. If they don't have plans, I'll take them. If they do, I'll go by myself."

Lynnette felt as though her heart had been pierced with a knife. Robert had never spoken to her in such a manner. Why was he doing this? And now of all times. He knew what she was going through. "Well, I think that's a very selfish attitude for you to have," she murmured through tears.

Robert knew his words had hurt her to the core. What was he supposed to do? He had feelings, too. "Call it what you want. I mean it. I'm not going to let you drag us down with you." Robert got up and started to get into bed.

Lynnette didn't like his attitude one bit so she shot at him, "Well, if that's the way you feel, maybe you should just sleep in one of the guest rooms tonight."

He was tired of always having to give in to her. "I'm not going anywhere. If you want somebody to sleep in the guest room, you go."

They had never argued like this before. Lynnette yanked herself up off the bench and went to an unoccupied bedroom down the hall.

As she laid restlessly in bed, she was still thinking about Robert's attitude. Why was he so angry at her? She thought about it for a moment. *Perhaps it's because he should be.*

After all, he truly had been trying to sympathize with her and help her. He'd sat down with the pamphlets and read them to get a clearer understanding on the matter. A lot of husbands wouldn't have done that. He'd even planned the trip she had just thoughtlessly cancelled at the last minute.

Lynnette began to cry. *What have I done? I have a wonderful husband, and I've been behaving so irrationally. I don't want to feel sad and depressed for the rest of my life. I can't go on like this.*

When Lynnette got up the next morning, Robert was already gone. He was obviously still very upset with her.

Beverly had requested the morning off to go to a doctor's appointment so Lynnette was keeping the store open until she got there to relieve her. She was glad it had been a busy morning with customers, salespeople, and telephone calls so she didn't have a lot of time to dwell on her and Robert's disagreement. She was on the telephone with a customer when she heard the door chime and saw Rose walk in. Lynnette waved at her.

"As you know, Mrs. Thomas," Lynnette uttered into the receiver, "the bed is the focal point of any bedroom so your bedding selections are significant to the entire design of the room. When people stay at your hotel, you want them to feel at home. You want them to keep coming back. I would like to suggest that you use a few accent pillows. They can be inexpensive while adding balance to the colors and patterns of the room."

Lynnette ceased talking and listened intently as the woman on the other end of the line spoke.

"Yes, ma'am," Lynnette answered. "You think about it and let me know what you decide." There was a pause. "All right. You have a good day, too, Mrs. Thomas. Good-bye." She placed the cordless telephone back in the stand and turned her attention to Rose.

"Good morning, Lynn," Rose's smile gleamed across the width of her face. "I didn't know you were here. I didn't see your car. I thought I'd come in and browse. How are you?"

Lynnette tried to appear lighthearted. "Morning, Ms. Rose. My car's in the shop. I'm driving a rental. I'm fine and you?"

She clearly had failed at her cheerful attempt for Rose replied, "I'm doing well, but you sure don't sound as good as you say you are." Without thinking, Rose inquired, "What's the matter, dear?"

Lynnette truly did like Rose. She had come to adore her but didn't think it wise to share anything on a private level with her. She had to keep her personal life separate from her professional one. She supposed, though, that she'd already broken that rule, since she and her family had recently eaten dinner at Rose's house.

For some reason, she felt she could confide in Rose. So she said, "Robert and I had a disagreement last night. I think he's still upset with me. He was gone when I got up this morning. He's never done that before."

This sounded serious. Lynnette seemed terribly worried. Rose did not want to give her the impression that she wanted to get in her personal affairs; however, she was genuinely concerned so she repeated her usual line, "I'm not trying to be nosy, but do you want to tell an ol' lady about it?"

Before Lynnette realized it, everything was coming out. "I'm turning forty next week. And on top of that, I found out recently that I have fibroid tumors on my uterus, which means I might have to get a hysterectomy. I've been really down lately. Robert and I were supposed to go out of town this weekend. We were going to leave this afternoon, but I told him last night I'm not going. He got upset and told me that he and the kids aren't going to put their lives on hold because I can't face reality."

Rose looked at Lynnette, understanding in her eyes. She yearned to make all of Lynnette's troubles disintegrate like a puff of smoke. Seeing her in so much mental and emotional pain made her own heart ache. "I'm so sorry."

"Ms. Rose, I don't know what's wrong with me. I don't know why I can't let go of this dreadful feeling. I try to be happy, but deep down inside, I'm not. Is this normal?"

"Considering what you're going through, dear, yes, it's very normal. Our bodies start to go through numerous changes as we get older. We view life in a different manner than when we were younger. In a way, we become different people. Petty things we used to consider important aren't such a big deal anymore. Things that didn't used to mean a hill o' beans mean so much more to us.

"We don't understand it at first because we're not used to feeling that way. Think about it. I bet when you were younger and you thought about all the things women have to go through—periods, childbirth, menopause—you probably couldn't wait to be set free from the things that make us so unique from men."

Lynnette thought about it. She certainly had felt that way.

Rose went on, "Now that you're older and somebody wants to take away that precious part of you, you want to run in the opposite direction."

Lynnette admitted, "That's exactly how I feel. When I was younger, I couldn't stand the things I had to go through as a female. I feel different now though, but it's kind of a weird feeling. Sometimes I feel like I don't know who I am anymore. Does that sound crazy?"

Rose sympathized, "Not at all. Being a different person doesn't have to be looked upon as something bad. View it as a time to do different things with your life. Find new interests, new hobbies."

"I don't know if I can do that."

"You can if you try. When I found out I was going through menopause, I didn't think I could either. But one day, I said to myself, 'Rose, either you're gonna beat this or you're gonna let it beat you.' That's when I made up my mind that I was going to make the best of it."

"Did you still have bad days?" Lynnette desperately wanted to know.

"Yes, I did, but I had more good days than bad. Whereas, before it was the other way around. I'm not trying to scare you, but honey, when you turn forty, that's when the creepy toes set in."

Lynnette managed a giggle. Rose sure had a way with words. "What's the creepy toes?"

"That's when everything associated with getting older starts slowly creeping up on you from all angles. Before you can get rid of one thing, here comes something else. Lynn, just remember that how we deal with things that happen in our life is all about how we perceive them in our mind and how we allow them to affect us."

Lynnette was quiet.

Rose said, "I know you're familiar with the saying 'what doesn't kill us makes us stronger.' "

"Yes," Lynnette said, "but what I'm going through now feels like it's killing me."

"You feel that way now, but don't forget that the worst kind of pity is self-pity. If we go around feeling sorry for ourselves all the time, life will always drag us down and keep us there.

I guess I sound like I'm lecturing you, and I don't mean to. It's just that I'm quite fond of you, and I'd hate for you to continue to let this drag you down."

Rose's words of encouragement soothed Lynnette's spirit. She wrapped her arms around Rose and squeezed her tight. "Thank you, Ms. Rose. I really appreciate your concern for me."

Rose hugged her back. It felt so good. She did not want to let go. "You're welcome." She clung tighter until Lynnette lovingly broke their embrace. "Oh." Rose reached into her large handbag, pulled out the catalog she had borrowed, and handed it to Lynnette. "Here's your catalog."

Both women began to wipe the tears away from their faces and smiled at each other.

Rose said, "I marked the items I want with those little yellow sticky things. What are they called?"

Lynnette smiled. "Post-its."

"I bet whoever invented those things made a lot of money. They sure come in handy."

Lynnette laughed. "They sure do. Ms. Rose, you're a hoot. I'll let you know when your items come in."

"All right, dear. Have a good day."

"Thank you. You, too. And thanks for cheering me up."

"You're welcome. Bye, dear."

Lynnette actually felt better after talking to Rose, who always seemed to know just what to say at exactly the right time. Lynnette felt a strong connection to her.

Later that afternoon, the house was quiet with Joshua and Miranda out with some of their friends. Lynnette and Robert would have been on their way to Apple Mountain at this very moment, had she not cancelled their plans. Lynnette could still feel the tension between them. She felt he was avoiding her.

She decided to go in search of him. Just as she was heading out the bedroom door, they bumped into each other.

Lynnette hastily announced, "I'm sorry for the way I've been acting lately. You've tried to help, and I've rejected it. Please don't be mad at me."

Robert had been on his way to apologize to her. He had not been able to concentrate all day. He felt terrible about their argument. He'd had to correct several mistakes he'd made on the job. He couldn't afford to do that in his line of work as a builder. "I'm sorry about our argument last night, and I feel bad that we went to bed angry with each other. That's something we should never do. If something happened to one of us, we'd have to live with it for the rest of our lives.

"And I'm not mad at you. I'm mad at myself. I know this is a time when I should put your needs ahead of mine. The trip would have been for me as well as you. You were right. I was being selfish. It's okay if you don't want to go, and there is no way I'd leave and go without you."

"Thank you, honey. All I ask is that you be patient with me. Just give me a little more time."

Robert felt dreadful about the things he'd said to Lynnette the night before. "I promise I'll try, but I need you to be patient with me, too."

"I will," Lynnette said. "I love you."

"I love you, too." Robert still had a desire in his heart to do something special to cheer her up. "So what do you want to do tomorrow?"

As Robert held her, Lynnette buried herself deeper within the security of his arms. "Nothing. I'm tired. I just want to stay home and relax."

He was disappointed in her response. The last thing she needed was to be lying around depressed. "Okay, but next weekend, we'll spend all day Saturday together, just the two of us. No laying around the house. We need to do something."

"That sounds wonderful. You know what I'd like to do?"

She was smiling. It was good to see her smile. He asked, "What would you like to do?"

"Go bike riding."

"That's a good idea. We haven't done that in a while."

The following Friday night, Robert and Lynnette were lounging on the sofa when the telephone rang. Lynnette answered the call and screamed at the top of her lungs. "Simone!"

Robert looked at his wife as though she had lost her mind. *Simone!* he thought. *Not Simone Kirkland,* he prayed. To his knowledge, Lynnette hadn't talked to her in years. He began to get a bad feeling in the pit of his stomach. He decided to make his exit. When he walked past Lynnette, she was laughing so hard he thought she was going to explode. As he made his way upstairs, he could not help but wonder why her girlfriend could bring her out of her depressed state, but he, her own husband, could not.

Lynnette was deeply engrossed in her conversation with Simone. "Girl," she said, "we haven't talked in ages. How long has it been?"

"I don't know," Simone answered. "What? Five years? So how are you?"

"I'm okay. I'm going through some things," Lynnette confided in her long-time friend, "but I'll be all right."

"What's wrong?" Simone wanted to know.

"I don't want to talk about it now. I'll tell you later. So what made you call out of the blue?"

"Well," Simone said, "tomorrow's your fortieth birthday. I just got my hands on two tickets to see Jeffrey Osborne in concert tomorrow night at the Atlanta Civic Center. I know how much you love Jeffrey. I know it's last minute, but I just got into town today. A friend of mine who lives in Atlanta got them for her and her husband. She had a death in her family, and they had to go out of town so she gave the tickets to me. So what d'ya say?" Simone asked in a melodious tone, "Can you woo woo woo?"

Lynnette laughed. "Girl, you're still crazy. Marshall doesn't want to go with you? I bet the two of you would have a great time."

Simone laughed. "Girl, I got rid of him three months ago."

Lynnette gasped. "You're not divorced, are you?"

"Yes, honey. I had to get rid of him."

"Oh," Lynnette said, moaning, "that's so sad. I'm so sorry. Are you okay?"

"Don't be sorry. I'm fine. Never been better."

Lynnette thought about Simone's daughter. "What about Samantha? She doesn't want to go?"

"She's away at school. I get to see her every weekend except she has plans of her own this weekend."

"Oh, what school does she go to?"

"University of Georgia."

"Oh, how nice. How'd she end up there?"

"They offered her a scholarship."

"That's nice."

"Listen," Simone said, "I'm gonna be in town all next week. I'll be looking at some houses I found on the Internet. My accounting firm just opened an office in Atlanta, and I'm moving to the area."

"Oh yeah? That's great. Where do you wanna live?" Lynnette inquired.

"Atlanta most likely. You know me. I love the city. I'm not

a country girl like you. 'Course you didn't used to be either 'til you met Robert and he swooped you off your feet."

Lynnette hated it when Simone whined about Robert and how different she was because of him, but she ignored her friend's comment as she usually did. "That's great. You'll be closer to Samantha, and we'll be closer to each other. Where are you staying?"

"My friend who gave me the tickets—she and her husband are letting me stay at their house."

"Well, that's no fun, being by yourself. You can stay with us."

"Now, Lynn, you know Robert and I aren't the best of friends," Simone reminded her. "Besides, I was hoping you'd come with me tomorrow to the concert, and we can just spend the night at my friend's house. I could bring you home Sunday."

"I can't, Simone. Robert and I already made plans. We're just gonna spend a quiet day together tomorrow, just the two of us."

Simone was disappointed. Lynnette just did not know how to have fun anymore. Robert had turned her into a homebody. Before he came along, she and Lynnette partied and stayed out late. "Aw, come on, Lynn. Robert can't let you outta his sight for two minutes?"

Sometimes her friend could be really irritating. Lynnette wasn't going to let this one slide. "Simone, don't start on Robert. He doesn't have me on a chain."

"Yeah, that's what you say. That's why I got rid of Marshall. He thought I was gonna stay at home all the time. I told him I'm still young and can get around. Don't have kids at home to tend to, and I'm gonna enjoy life. Tomorrow's your birthday. You should go out somewhere and have some fun, have a party. Leave Grumpy at home."

Lynnette did not appreciate all the negative vibes coming from Simone, but she was her dearest and oldest friend. They grew up together in Chicago and went through grade, elementary, and high school together. Simone was like a sister to her. Her mother had always treated Lynnette like a daughter. Simone had her faults, but she had always been there when Lynnette needed her.

Lynnette was not going to let Robert down again. She had already cancelled their trip to Apple Mountain last week. Much to her own surprise, she boldly stated to her friend, "No, I can't. I'm spending the day with Robert."

Without pausing to allow Simone an opportunity to argue further, Lynnette added, "So will you come Sunday afternoon and stay with us while you're here? Do you remember how to get to the house, or do you need directions?"

Simone was disturbed that Lynnette was permitting Robert to control her life. However, she decided to let the subject rest—for the moment. Abruptly, she said, "Okay, give me directions."

Lynnette gave Simone the information; then they said their good-byes.

When she went upstairs, she found Robert in his recliner in their bedroom reading. As expected, he did not appear happy.

He flatly asked, "Was that Simone Kirkland?"

Lynnette sat on the bed facing Robert. "Yes. She's gonna be in the area for about a week, and I invited her to stay with us."

Robert felt his blood pressure rising. Yet he forced himself to remain composed. "When will she be here?"

It was obvious to Lynnette that Robert was upset about Simone staying with them. He would just have to get over it. After all, Simone was like a sister to her. "Not 'til Sunday afternoon. I told her we're spending tomorrow together. I'm tired. I'm going to bed. You coming?"

Robert was extremely agitated. He probably would not get a wink of sleep that night or the next several days. "Not right now," he answered. He got up. "I'm gonna go downstairs and watch TV for a while."

"Okay. Good night."

"Good night."

When Robert walked out of the room without so much as a good-night kiss, Lynnette ascertained that he would be in a bad mood the whole while Simone was staying with them. She wished the two of them could put aside their differences and at least try to get along.

There was nothing worth looking at on television so Robert went to the bottom floor to the exercise room. There he lifted weights in order to release the frustration he felt rushing throughout his body.

Lord, I'm really going to need your help over the next several days. I'm already trying to deal with my dismal wife and now she's invited her meddling girlfriend to stay with us for a whole week. Give me strength.

Chapter 6

Saturday morning, Lynnette was in bed when the aroma of food tickled her nose. She opened her eyes. There stood Robert with a tray of some of her favorite breakfast foods—bacon, grits, scrambled eggs, fresh strawberries, and orange juice. In a corner of the tray stood a tall bronze-colored vase filled with a dozen yellow roses. She sat up, and he placed the tray down gently in front of her.

"Oh, honey, what a wonderful surprise to wake up to."

He leaned in closer so they could share a kiss. Then he removed the flowers from the tray and placed them on the nightstand.

"Thank you, honey." Lynnette smiled.

"You're welcome," Robert said. "Josh and Randa helped."

There was a knock on the door. Lynnette answered, "Come in."

The door opened slowly, and in came Joshua and Miranda.

The grin on Lynnette's face grew wider. "Good morning, you two." She couldn't help but notice the huge gift basket that Miranda was carrying. Through the clear cellophane wrapping, Lynnette spied various items she could use to pamper herself.

The two teenagers greeted their mother as they stood beside the bed. "Good morning."

Miranda said, "This is for you. It's from Josh and me." She glanced at her brother and turned back to face Lynnette.

Joshua added, "We know you haven't been feeling good lately so we wanted to give you something to help you relax."

"How sweet," Lynnette said, through tears. "I love it." Then she looked at Robert and asked, "Honey, can you take this tray a minute?"

"Sure," Robert answered.

Joshua and Miranda stood aside so their father could remove the tray. Lynnette got out of bed, removed her basket from her daughter's arms, placed it on the bed, and hugged her children. "Thank you so much. You guys are incredible. I love you."

"We love you, too," Joshua and Miranda said, in unison.

Lynnette asked, "Are you gonna stay and have breakfast with your dad and me?"

"No," Miranda said. "We already ate."

Joshua said, "Yeah. We'll let you and dad enjoy it. We'll see you later."

"Okay," Lynnette concurred.

Before Joshua and Miranda shut the door, Lynnette waved good-bye.

Lynnette put the basket on her dresser and climbed back into bed. Robert placed the tray back in front of her, clapped his hands, and rubbed them together. "Let's eat."

First, they said the blessing. They talked as they ate. Lynnette bit off a sweet, juicy chunk of strawberry and offered the rest to Robert. She put the last bite in his mouth and licked her fingers.

"Ooh, honey," Lynnette bragged, "this is so good. You know, you'd make a great chef. You're a wonderful cook. Don't you ever wish you'd finished cooking school?"

"Sometimes, but I like building things."

"Well, cooking is kind of like building things," Lynnette protested.

"Yeah, but once somebody eats it—poof." Robert gestured with his hands in the air. "It's gone. You don't see it anymore. I can still go places and see things I built. Who knows? One day I may go back."

"Honey, you should. That's a great idea."

Robert looked at his wife. "Are you serious? I was just kidding."

Lynnette answered, "Yes, I'm serious."

Robert's mind sauntered back to the night before when Simone had Lynnette laughing at the top of her lungs. He was not pleased that her friend could cheer her up, but he was powerless to do so. His voice took on a sad, solemn tone. "I'm satisfied with my life—with *our* life. I wish you were."

Lynnette didn't say anything. She simply looked away. She wished he wouldn't insinuate that she wasn't content with what they had. She was. She was just going through a very difficult period in her life, but there was just no way he could understand that.

Robert asked, "What can I do to make you happy?"

Lynnette looked at him. "Will you stop? I *am* happy."

"No, you're not. Not the way you used to be. You used to have me cracking up all the time. I miss your sense of humor.

Now the only time I see you really laugh—I mean belly-roll laugh—is when you're with other people."

"That's not true," Lynnette denied. Then she smiled. "I bet I can still make you laugh."

Robert stared his wife dead in her face and challenged her. "I don't think you can."

"Yes, I can."

"Then do it." Robert refused to take his eyes away from Lynnette's face.

"Well, you gotta stop staring at me first."

Robert kept staring. "I'm waiting."

Lynnette began to laugh. "Robert, stop. You're making me nervous."

Robert wouldn't take his eyes off her. "What? I'm not doing anything."

"If you don't stop staring at me," Lynnette warned, "I'm going to stare right back at you."

"Okay, go ahead. Let's see who can stare the longest."

"Okay, let me move this tray." Lynnette lifted the tray and put it on the floor beside the bed. She attempted to stop laughing and stared into Robert's face.

They stared at each other for several seconds. Neither one could keep a straight face. They burst out laughing and fell back onto the bed.

"I told you I could make you laugh," Lynnette declared.

Robert was still laughing. "You're crazy, you know that?"

"Yeah, crazy in love with you."

"Oh yeah?"

"Yeah."

Lynnette felt wonderful. Robert still knew how to make her feel good even when she was feeling at her worst. He wanted her to be the way she used to be. He just didn't understand that no matter how hard she tried, she couldn't. The old Lynnette was gone. He would just have to get used to the new one.

Later in the day, Lynnette and Robert went bicycle riding.

"Hey, that's not fair. You cheated!" Lynnette yelled at Robert as she pedaled behind him on her bike.

They were grateful that the springlike weather was still holding up, thereby allowing them the opportunity to enjoy their bike ride. They used to ride together all the time. Lynnette had forgotten how invigorating it was. She had felt like a little girl as they rode along with the cool breeze sweeping across her face.

Robert turned to look at her trailing slowly in his path. "I said on the count of three."

"On the count of three means after you say three, not before. That's okay. If cheating is the only way you can win," Lynnette teased, "be my guest."

"You wish," Robert said, laughing, as they parked their bikes in the garage. "Have you worked up an appetite yet?"

"Yes. I'm famished."

"Good. Let's get cleaned up. Then I'll get the grill fired up."

After they had showered and changed, Robert put the chicken breasts he had marinated overnight on the grill. Lynnette had managed to find some beautiful sweet ears of corn in the supermarket the day before, and he put them on the grill, too. She also made a salad, baked beans, and rolls. They would wash it all down with a big pitcher of lemonade made from freshly squeezed lemons.

It was dusk when they plopped down at the patio table on the deck to savor the works of their hands. Three large candles on the table and tier lights in the yard and along the deck rails provided all the light they needed.

Lynnette felt as if she was in paradise. "Honey, thank you for a wonderful day. You made turning forty fun."

"You're welcome. You deserved it. You know, days like today don't have to stop here. Josh and Randa are becoming more and more independent, which means you and I will have more time to spend with each other."

"I know. By the way, where are those two?"

"They went to eat and see a movie."

"I'm so glad they still enjoy doing things together. A lot of brothers and sisters aren't like that when they get older. Do you think they'd be as close as they are if they were farther apart in age?"

"I don't know. Sometimes I wonder. Carla and I are almost five years apart, and all we did was fuss and fight when we were younger. We couldn't stand each other, but as we got older that changed." Robert grinned. "When Josh moves out on his own, he may have to take Randa with him. Either that or we'll have to give her a shot of morphine to calm her down."

Lynnette giggled. She grew quiet as she began to contemplate the future of her children. "Where did the time go? It seems like only yesterday they were both babies," she reminisced. "Can't we just lock 'em up in their rooms and not let 'em out 'til they're like thirty?"

Robert laughed. Knowing Lynnette, she would do just that if she could. "If only it were that easy."

Lynnette's face took on a sullen expression. "You know, I just want them to always be as close as they are now. I want them to always be there for each other, especially if something happens to me." She added, "Or you."

Robert's heart went out to his wife. He was aware that she was contemplating the surgery and something going wrong if she decided to have it. He wished she wouldn't think that way, but he supposed she couldn't help it.

"Josh and Randa will be fine," he assured her. He had to get her mind on to something else. "Now, enough about the kids. I want to talk about us. We haven't been on a vacation alone in years. Since Josh and Randa can barely fit us into their busy schedules now, I'd like to take you someplace special. Wherever you want to go. Whatever your heart desires."

Lynnette's face lit up. "Honey, that's sweet. You know where I want to go?"

"No, tell me."

"Disney World."

"Disney World?" Robert repeated. He grinned. "Honey, I think you're a little big for Disney World. That's for kids."

"It's not just for kids. It's for anyone who wants to have fun. I've never been, and I'd love to go. You said anywhere I want to go. You're not reneging on your promise, are you?"

"Oh no. Of course not. If you want to go to Disney World, then Disney World it is."

Lynnette bounced up and down in her seat, clapping her hands like an excited three-year old. "Oh, I'm so excited." She leaned over and kissed Robert. "Thank you, honey, for making what I thought would be one of the worst days of my life so special. I love you."

"You're welcome. I love you, too."

Robert was pleased that at least for one whole day he had been able to bring some sunshine into his wife's life. *Maybe now she'll bounce back to her old self,* he thought.

The next morning, Robert was flabbergasted to see Lynnette still in bed asleep after he had come from downstairs. He and the kids were dressed and ready for Sunday morning service.

He strolled over to the bed, leaned down, and shook her gently. "Lynn, wake up. We've got to leave in thirty minutes, and you're still in bed."

Lynnette slowly regained consciousness as she rubbed her eyes with the back of her hands. "I'm not going," she mumbled.

Robert was taken aback. "What do you mean, you're not going? Are you sick? What's the matter?"

Why did he have to ask so many questions? He was acting like she was committing a crime. "I just don't feel like going today. I'm tired. You and the kids go on. I'll be okay."

Robert was not pleased; however, he didn't want to upset her so he left her alone.

That afternoon, Lynnette and Miranda were cleaning up the kitchen after dinner when they heard a car pull into the driveway. Lynnette knew it was Simone because she had telephoned about ten minutes earlier and given Lynnette her exact location.

Lynnette hastily dried her hands on a towel and tossed it onto the dish rack before racing out the kitchen door. She ran to the driver's side of Simone's rental car and flung open the door. As soon as Simone was out of the car, the two women grabbed each other and hugged as if they were holding on for dear life, all the while laughing. Then they stood at arm's length for one to observe the other.

Simone was very attractive in a sunflower-yellow double-breasted pantsuit. Simone, who was three months older than Lynnette, had a tall, slender figure and looked as though she had just stepped off a modeling runway. Lynnette admired her friend's reddish-brown layered shoulder-length tresses.

"Look at you," Lynnette bragged. "You look terrific. And you still got the same neat, trim little figure you had when we were in school."

Simone swatted Lynnette's arm and threw her head back

in laughter. "Thanks. Look at you. You've had two kids and don't even look like it. What *is* your secret?"

Lynnette laughed. "Girl, there is no secret. I just eat all the potato chips and oatmeal pies I want and stay active."

Simone laughed. "Don't tell me you're still doing that. I remember when you'd spend the night with me. I'd eat my snacks during the day, and you'd be hoarding yours. I'd wake up in the middle of the night and hear you rattling paper, sounding like a big rat."

Lynnette burst out laughing. "I had to sneak and eat 'em. If I didn't, I always ended up giving you half. Girl, you were just greedy. Eat yours now and eat mine later."

Simone laughed. "Girl, you wrong."

Lynnette grabbed Simone's hand and headed toward the house. "Come on inside. Randa can't wait to see you."

Miranda met them at the door and stepped back for them to enter. "Hi, Ms. Kirkland," she said.

"Hi!" Simone's voice rang out as she grabbed Miranda and squeezed her tight. "You're still just as pretty as ever."

Finally, they let go of each other, and Simone exclaimed, "Randa, it's so nice to see you again."

"It's nice to see you, too," Miranda said.

Looking around the room, Simone asked, "Where are Robert and Josh? I know Robert's dying to see me," she joked. "He probably didn't sleep a wink last night from all the excitement."

"Simone, stop." Lynnette gave her friend a playful jab of her elbow in her side. "You'll see them later," she advised her friend. "They're at the gym playing basketball." She tactfully pulled Simone by the arm. "Come on. Are you hungry? Thirsty?"

Simone followed. "No, I'm fine."

Miranda left her mother and Simone to themselves in the den. The two were dying to catch up on old times.

"Did you find someone to go to the concert with you?" Lynnette inquired.

"No."

"I'm sorry you didn't get to go."

Simone giggled. "Oh, you don't have to be sorry, girl. I still went. By myself."

Sometimes Lynnette admired how outgoing Simone was. She didn't allow anything to stand in her way and keep her from enjoying life. "Well, tell me about it. Was it good?"

"Honey, yes." Simone's face was glowing. "When Jeffrey sang 'The Woo Woo Song' he came into the audience and let different ones sing the song."

"No, he didn't!" Lynnette exclaimed. "Did you sing?"

Simone acknowledged, "You know I did."

"Ooh, girl, it sounds like you had a terrific time."

"I did. Now don't you wish you had come?"

"I won't lie," Lynnette confessed, "I like Jeffrey, but Robert and I had a wonderful time yesterday. I wouldn't trade it for the world, not even for Jeffrey." She sensed her friend about to make a smart-aleck comment so she put up her hand and playfully demanded, "Don't even go there."

Simone pretended ignorance. "What?"

Lynnette mocked her. "What?" Then she changed the subject. "So tell me about your new office."

Simone relaxed against the soft plush sofa with her hand across the top as she faced Lynnette. Her face beamed with pride as she spoke. "Well, it's nice and spacious and located in the heart of downtown. I have a big office all to myself. Everything's great."

Lynnette gave Simone's knee a light tap. "That's good, Simone. You always did like working with numbers. Do you like being a CPA?"

"I love it. I may even open my own firm one day. Now that I don't have Marshall breathing down my neck like a fiery dragon, I should be able to do it."

Lynnette's heart went out to her friend. She looked at Simone with genuine tenderness in her eyes. "Oh, Simone, I feel so bad about you and Marshall. What in the world happened?"

"Girl, he was too needy for one thing. And overly demanding for another. You know how I've always been about my space. He acted like I had to be under his nose all the time. I couldn't do anything without him checking up on me. I got tired of it so I told him to hit the road."

Lynnette propped her elbow on the back of the sofa and pressed the side of her face against her hand. "You couldn't work things out with him? Marshall adored you."

"No, there was nothing to work out. The damage was beyond repair. For the first time in years, I feel like I can breathe. I *love* my freedom. Marshall was smothering me. He knew when he married me that I wasn't a homebody. I may never get married again. I love being single."

Lynnette rolled her eyes heavenward. "Yeah, that's what you say now, but I know you, or have you changed that much since high school?"

Simone faked ignorance again. "What are you talking about, Lynn? I only hung out with you."

Lynnette playfully scoffed, "Yeah, right. I can't even begin to tell you the number of times you called me at the last minute to break our plans because you had met the guy of your dreams."

Simone laughed. "Well, it's not my fault they all turned out to be total nightmares."

Lynnette laughed. "You're crazy."

Simone desperately wanted to hear what was happening with her friend. "Now tell me what's going on with you," she demanded. "You said on the phone you're going through some things. What's the matter? Is it Robert? Has he gotten on your last nerve?"

"No, Robert's good to me. He's a wonderful husband and father."

Simone just could not fathom Robert being as captivating as Lynnette professed. There wasn't a man on earth who was. "Well, what is it?" she pressured her friend.

"I found out recently that I have fibroid tumors on my uterus, and I may need to have a hysterectomy."

Simone's mouth flew open. "Are you serious?"

"Yes, but I haven't decided if I'm going to have the surgery."

"Well, I've heard that a lot of hysterectomies that are performed nowadays are really unnecessary and that other treatment options can be done in lieu of them. Have you considered that? You know, a lot of these doctors just want a bunch of money in their wallets. I wouldn't do it if I were you."

Lynnette had forgotten how opinionated her friend could be at times. Now she was wishing she had not even opened her mouth and confided in Simone. She did not need to hear all this negative feedback. She was stressed out enough as it was. She was about to tell Simone so when Joshua walked in calling out over his shoulder, "They're in the den, Dad!"

Simone stood, smiling, and walked over to greet Joshua with her hand extended. "Well, hello, Josh."

Joshua returned Simone's smile. "Hi, Ms. Kirkland."

Simone said, "Lynn, he's still the spitting image of you."

Lynnette smiled. "That's what everybody says." She looked on as Simone and Joshua talked. Robert walked in and took a seat on a nearby chair.

Joshua excused himself, and Simone turned her attention to Robert. She grinned. Knowing that he was not particularly fond of her, sometimes she did things just to touch his nerves. "Robert!" she cried out, holding out her arms.

Robert stood and hugged her. "Hey, Simone. How are you?"

"I'm fine. What about yourself?"

"Great. Long time, no see."

"Yeah, I know." Simone decided to play with him. "Miss me?"

A small snicker involuntarily escaped Robert's mouth. "Well-l-l, I wouldn't exactly say that."

Simone threw her head back in laughter. "Robert, I can say one thing about you. I never have to guess where I stand with you. You just whack me over the head with it and go about your business."

Robert grinned. "Well, wouldn't you rather me whack you over the head than stab you in your back?"

"Good point. At least we know where we stand with each other, don't we?"

Lynnette grinned from her spot on the sofa. "Y'all need to quit. Don't get started 'cause I'm not gonna be refereeing your lil' fights."

"We're not fighting," Simone told her friend.

"Not yet," Robert mumbled under his breath.

Lynnette and Simone laughed at Robert's tidbit of humor. Simone sat back down on the sofa beside Lynnette, and Robert returned to his seat. They talked some more. After a brief moment, Robert politely excused himself and went upstairs. When he finally went to bed around eleven o'clock, Lynnette and Simone were still downstairs talking and laughing.

Lynnette was a totally different person around other people. Why couldn't she be as happy with him as she was with everybody else? He felt he was no longer fulfilling his role as her husband. If he was, she wouldn't be so sad all the time. He knew she'd had a hard life. His only hope was that God would give him enough strength to see them through this crisis.

Chapter 7

On Monday afternoon, Lynnette and Rose discussed the renovation project.

As they walked through Rose's living room, Lynnette advised her, "It looks like Robert and his crew will finish up the jobs in front of yours ahead of schedule. If so, they can probably start on the renovation in a few months. He knows how important this project is to you and the community."

"I appreciate that, but tell him not to rush," Rose said. "It's obvious from his work that he's a master at what he does, and I know his services are in high demand."

Lynnette smiled, full of pride. Robert was very good at his job. "I'll tell him."

As they crossed to the other side of the room, Rose pointed to an empty corner and said, "This is where I'm going to put the grandfather clock I had you order for me. How do you think it'll look here?"

"Oh, it's the perfect spot for it. I think it'll look wonderful. Have you given any thought to the style of furniture you'll want for the home once it's finished?"

"Well, I don't want everything to match exactly. What I mean is I want to be creative and mix and match different styles and colors together in the same room in a way that none of the pieces look out of place." Rose looked at Lynnette. "Do you understand what I'm saying?"

Lynnette nodded. "Sure. You know, you can save a lot of money if you shop flea markets and yard sales. That's where I got several of the pieces in our house. You may even be able to find some beds and other furniture. With a little work, you and I can fix them up like new, and it'll be fun, too."

As Lynnette and Rose left the room, Rose said, "Lynn, you're such a dear. You really enjoy what you do, don't you?"

Lynnette was grinning from ear to ear. "Yes, ma'am, I sure do."

They entered the den and sat down.

"Ms. Rose, may I ask you a question? It's kind of personal."

"Sure. You can ask me anything."

"Out of everything that you've done in your life, do you have any regrets about anything that you perhaps should or shouldn't have done?"

Rose was quiet for a moment. It scared Lynnette. Maybe she had reopened some old wounds that had not completely healed. Perhaps she had gone too far. Just because she and Rose had become good friends that didn't give her the right to go digging around in her personal business.

Lynnette reached over and gently touched Rose's hand. "I'm sorry. I shouldn't have asked you that. It's none of my business. I just—"

"No, it's okay. I was just thinking. I do have regrets, and

there are some things that if I could do them over again, I would do them differently. What made you ask?"

Lynnette said, "Well, for the past few weeks, I've been feeling so down about the surgery. Robert's always kidded me about being such a heavy thinker. He says I think too much. That my brain stays on overload." Lynnette and Rose let out small snickers.

Lynnette continued, "This is so different than anything else I've experienced, but now I realize I have to keep forging ahead despite what I'm going through."

"I think that's very well said," Rose agreed. "You go, girl."

After Lynnette had gone, Rose's heart swelled with elation at Lynnette's positive change in attitude. *Lynnette's strong-willed. She's gonna make it through this. Her faith is strong. She has a loving, supportive family, and I will be there to help her every step of the way.*

On Wednesday evening, the house was quiet as Robert sat at his desk in the den carefully reviewing the floor plans for the children's home. Only two more days and Simone would be out of his hair—that is, what he had left. He was pretty sure he'd lost a handful just in the four days she'd been staying with them. He had to admit though that the two of them seemed to be getting along pretty well, but perhaps it was mainly due to the fact that he was purposely steering clear of her.

Sometimes Robert felt guilty for not taking more of a liking to her, especially since Lynnette was constantly praising Simone and her mother for being a family to her when no one else wanted her. Simone had too much of an independent spirit. The funny thing was that when he had first met her, he found her to be a likable individual. However, as time went on, their personalities began to clash. For Lynnette's sake, he attempted to be peaceable with Simone.

He heard someone enter the room. Expecting to see Lynnette, he looked up with a wide smile on his face but lost it when he saw his rival. His steer-clear tactic wasn't working too well that night. He'd been trapped.

Simone responded cheerily to the irritated look on his face. "My goodness, Robert, you don't have to look so disappointed. You look like you just bit into a lemon."

Robert offered an apathetic apology. "Sorry. I thought you were Lynn."

"She's upstairs taking a bath. You and I haven't had a chance to talk much so I thought I'd come down and bug you for a few minutes."

Bug me is right. We haven't had a chance to talk much because I've been avoiding you. Robert was positive Simone realized it. "I've been trying to stay out of your and Lynn's way so you can catch up on old times."

"Whatever you say," Simone replied.

Robert decided against responding.

Simone went on. "I'm worried about Lynn. I hope you're not gonna let her have that surgery. I told her I wouldn't do it if I were her."

Robert really did not wish to discuss this with Simone. However, he had to set her straight. He glared at her. "I can't tell her to have it or not have it. And you don't need to be telling her what to do either. It's tough enough for her as it is. If it'll help, I want her to have it, but the ultimate decision is hers. Whatever she decides, I have to support her."

Simone could not believe her ears. She placed her hands on her slender hips and stared at Robert. "Robert, I don't understand you. You run every other aspect of her life, and you're not gonna try to talk her out of having this surgery?"

Robert's eyes shot daggers at Simone. He did not appreciate her innuendo about his and Lynnette's marriage. Nevertheless, he remained composed when he spoke. "Simone, don't test me. I try to get along with you for Lynn's sake because I love her, and I know how she feels about you. As for your little comment about me running her life, I'm not going to dignify that with a response because you are in my house, and I don't have to answer to you." He had not meant to throw his hospitality in her face, but she had pushed him too far.

Out of all the years Simone and Robert had contended with each other, he had never once lost his temper with her until that moment. Even now, he did it so firmly yet politely that she began to feel a tiny morsel of regret for deliberately pushing his buttons. She dropped her hands from her hips. "You're right. I'm sorry. I overstepped my boundaries. I'm just worried about her. She doesn't want to have this surgery. I know it. If she did, she would have already decided."

"Simone, when people have to make major life decisions, they can't just make them on the spur of the moment. They have to give it prayerful consideration. It takes time. So she's doing the right thing by taking her time. And when she does make a decision, I think it will be one that she can live with."

Lynnette's cheerful voice interrupted their conversation. "Hey, what are you two doing?" she asked.

Simone answered, "Just talking about you."

"Something good, I hope."

Robert looked at his wife and smiled. "What else is there?"

Lynnette strolled over to Robert and leaned down to kiss his cheek. "Oh, honey, you're too sweet."

Simone was struck by the love the two shared. She envied

them. It made the loneliness she felt more evident in her heart and mind.

Friday morning, Lynnette was quiet as she got ready for work. Robert was convinced she was upset about Simone's departure. Simone had her quirks, but she also had a way of bringing to the fore a liveliness in Lynnette that even he was unable to bring about. He envied her ability to make his wife come to life in such a way.

He noticed Lynnette, still in her robe, standing barefoot in her closet just staring at her clothes. He came up behind her and wrapped his arms around her. He tried to lighten her mood. "Are you thinking about me or Simone?"

Lynnette turned her head slightly to look at Robert. "Hmm?"

"Nothing. Never mind."

Lynnette complained, "I can't find anything to wear."

Robert stared at the long line of clothes and stepped beside her. He reached up and grabbed a black-and-white pinstriped pantsuit and handed it to her. "Here you go. This looks great on you. It makes you look very professional. I bet if you stick one of those sparkly silver doohickeys right here—" he fingered the front of her hair on her right side and continued "—you'll really be styling then."

Lynnette looked at Robert and smiled. "Sparkly silver doo-hickeys," she repeated. "Honey, they're barrettes, not doohick-eys." She put her arms around him and hugged him. "You're sweet. I don't know what I'd do without you."

"Same here." He kissed the top of her head. "Get dressed so you can see Simone before she leaves." His grin was huge.

Lynnette playfully popped his hand. "You don't have to sound so excited that she's leaving."

Robert's grin grew bigger.

Finally, the whole Montgomery family was downstairs bidding good-bye to Simone.

Simone hugged Robert. "Thanks for letting me stay. I know I get on your nerves at times."

Robert looked at her, raised his eyebrows, and smiled.

Simone giggled. "Well, all the time. I really appreciate your hospitality."

"You're welcome. Bye, Simone. Have a safe trip." Robert turned to Joshua and Miranda. "See you two this afternoon. Have a good day in school."

"Bye," Miranda and Joshua replied in unison.

Robert gave Lynnette a warm hug and kiss before heading out the door.

"Bye, Ms. Kirkland," Joshua and Miranda declared.

Simone waved as she smiled. "Bye. See you guys later."

As Lynnette walked her children to the door, Simone stood in the distance relishing in their heartfelt love and devotion to one another. She would give anything to have what Lynnette had.

Buzz-z-z-z!

"That's it!" Carla shouted. "We win again."

James Sinclair, Carla's husband, was confused. "What do you mean, you won? I was in the middle of giving my clue. Why did you buzz me?"

Carla proceeded to gather the cards and game pieces. She put them in the box and replaced the lid. "James, you know how to play Taboo. You know you're not supposed to say the words on the cards. Sorry, hon." She patted him on the back as she stood.

James laughed and looked at his brother-in-law. "Rob, I believe we have just been bamboozled."

Robert nodded in agreement. "And by our own wives."

Lynnette commented, "We won fair and square."

"Lynn," Carla said, "come help me with dessert." As the two women headed toward the kitchen, Carla yelled at their husbands, "Sore losers!"

In the kitchen, Lynnette and Carla scurried about filling glass bowls with a light, creamy fruit dessert.

"So how are you?" Carla asked.

"Okay. I'm just taking one day at a time. I have good and bad days."

A pitiful look washed over Carla's face. The thought of her sister-in-law whom she loved like a sister having surgery petrified her. There were so many risks involved. "What about the hysterectomy? Are you gonna have it?"

"I don't know. I'm still thinking about it."

Carla nodded.

"Do me a favor," Lynnette implored.

Carla would do anything for Lynnette. "Sure. You name it."

"Pray for me. I'm so scared and confused. I don't know what to do. One minute, I decide to have the surgery. The next minute, I'm against it. Please keep me in your prayers," Lynnette beseeched. She added, "Pray for Robert, too. I know I'm about to drive him crazy. He's trying to help, but most of the time I get all emotional on him."

"You got it."

"Thanks, Carla. I love you." Lynnette hugged Carla.

"I love you, too."

They placed spoons in the desserts and grabbed one in each hand. Carla said, "Let's go cheer up our big babies."

"Yeah. They're probably still pouting."

Lynnette and Carla giggled.

"Here you go, honey," Carla told James as she handed him his dessert.

"Thank you, baby."

Lynnette gave Robert his. "Here, sweetie. This will make you feel better."

"Thanks, babe." Robert put a spoonful of the creamy mixture in his mouth. "Sis, this tastes great. Did you make this?"

"Yes. I'm glad you like it. I got the recipe from one of my coworkers."

"Yeah, baby," James added, "this is good."

"Thank you. Since you like it so much, I'll make it for you again one day."

Lynnette asked, "Are you two gonna be ready for another game of Taboo when you're finished?"

"Sure," James answered. "Are you two ready to be whipped?"

"Excuse you," Carla told her husband.

"Don't talk junk now," Lynnette admonished James.

Robert grinned. "We'll see who's talking junk."

As the four of them laughed and talked, Robert wondered how long Lynnette's present mood would last. He never knew what to expect anymore. Sometimes it was like walking on eggshells around her. For the moment though, he would enjoy her pleasant mood.

Chapter 8

One week later, Lynnette and Robert sat in the waiting room of Dr. Mandell's office for her follow-up appointment. Lynnette was a ball of nerves as she pretended to look at a magazine. What she was really doing was eavesdropping on two older women's conversation. They were only a few feet from her and Robert so she had no problem hearing every word they said.

Lynnette heard the dark-haired woman say, "I'm here with my daughter. She had her second child six weeks ago."

"Oh," the other woman said, "how nice. What did she have?"

"Another boy. He's so sweet. He's such a good baby," the proud grandmother bragged. "Do you have grandchildren?"

"Yes. One. A little girl two years old by my daughter. She and her husband wanted to have one more, but she had to have a hysterectomy."

"Oh, I'm so sorry. How is she?"

"She's fine." They heard a door open. The woman glanced toward the door. "Here they are now."

A stunning couple walked toward the two women. The woman who had last spoken stood. "Are we ready to go?" she asked them.

"Yes," her daughter answered.

The woman turned back to the woman with whom she'd been conversing. "This is my daughter and her husband."

The lady with the dark hair smiled and said, "Hello."

"Hello." The couple returned her smile.

"Okay," the lady told her daughter and son-in-law. "I'm ready." To the other woman, she said, "It was nice talking to you."

"You, too."

As they walked past Lynnette, she could not help but feel a tinge of jealousy. Mothers and daughters together during good and bad times. That's what being a mother was all about. Laughing with your children when they're happy. Crying with them when they're sad.

Lynnette's thoughts digressed to her own mother. The mother she didn't remember. The mother she never got to know. *Mama, why'd you have to leave? I need you so bad.* Before she realized what was happening, tears were streaming down her face.

When Robert turned his head to speak to her, he beheld her tear-soaked face. He immediately pitched the sports magazine he'd been examining onto the table in front of them. "Honey, what's wrong?" he tried to whisper. He grabbed a tissue from a Kleenex box on the table and wiped at Lynnette's face.

Lynnette gently withdrew the tissue from Robert's hand and wiped her face. He grabbed another tissue and handed it to her, and she blew her nose.

"Nothing," Lynnette was finally able to answer. "I'm fine."

She did not want to discuss it at the doctor's office. People were already starting to stare.

Robert could not imagine what had upset his wife so. He was still trying to figure it out when a nurse called out Lynnette's name.

Dr. Mandell looked consolingly at the couple from behind his huge cherry oak desk. "Well, Lynnette, it's been a month since I last saw you. As I told you before, drug therapy is not a long-term solution."

Robert queried, "What exactly does the drug do?"

The doctor answered, "It shrinks the fibroids. However, it's used as a preparation for surgery since it reduces the amount of estrogen in the body. Unfortunately it causes all the symptoms of real menopause. There are medications that can reduce the menopausal symptoms. But again, drug therapy for the fibroids is only a temporary treatment in anticipation of menopause or surgery. Of course, I would also like to suggest some tests to rule out other causes for your pain."

Lynnette's head was spinning. She did not care to hear anymore. For the moment, she would deal with the physical pain from the fibroids as best as she possibly could until it got to the point where she could take it no longer.

Dr. Mandell continued, "So, Lynn, it's your call. What do you want to do?"

Robert prayed she would agree to the surgery or at least to the tests.

Lynnette attempted to put her thoughts into words. "At this point, I still don't want the surgery, and I don't want to go through any tests. I'll just tough it out and see how it goes."

Tough it out! Robert thought. He simply could not understand why she would choose to suffer in pain instead of seeking the help she needed so this could be a thing of the past.

On the way home, Robert remained quiet. He would never understand women. Not even if he lived a million years. *Just have the surgery!* his inner voice screamed.

Lynnette knew he was upset. She interrupted his thoughts. "You're not talking. What's the matter?"

Robert had no desire to discuss the matter with her. In addition, he was angry at Simone. He felt like she had some influence on Lynnette's decision during her recent visit; however, he knew if he told Lynnette what was on his mind, they'd have an argument so he lied. "Nothing."

Lynnette did not believe him so she prodded him. "I know something's bothering you. What is it?"

Robert did not say a word. He didn't want to upset her. He had to stay quiet for the moment. He was in a terrible state of mind and preferred to discuss this with her after he'd had time to calm down.

"You're upset because I told Dr. Mandell I don't want the surgery, aren't you?"

Still, Robert refused to answer.

"Robert, talk to me. We've always been able to talk, no matter what. What is wrong with you?"

Why was she pushing him? She knew very well that he was upset and why. He finally spoke from behind the steering wheel. His voice was not argumentative. "Lynn, I don't want to argue with you," he warned her. "Let's just drop it for now."

Lynnette turned slightly in her seat and stared at him. "I will not drop it. I want to talk."

Why couldn't she just be quiet and leave him alone? Why was she being so pushy? It was as though she wanted to argue with him. Who was she mad at? Him? Herself? Who?

This time Robert's voice was stern. "Why do you want to

talk, Lynn? You don't pay any attention to anything I say. Just drop it. I told you I don't want to talk about it now."

Robert's tone told Lynnette that he meant exactly what he said so she complied against her will and dropped the subject. Her feelings were so hurt that in order to keep her composure she had to force herself not to look at him. She stared out her window as she tried with all her might to hold back her tears.

Robert had to get away to a quiet place all to himself so he could think and pray. After dinner he grabbed his Bible, went downstairs to the bonus room, and tucked himself in a chair in the corner. He was so angry at Lynnette, but he knew in his heart that God was not pleased with his attitude. He opened his Bible and turned to the book of Colossians. He flipped over one page to chapter three and read verse nineteen: *Husbands, love your wives, and be not bitter against them.* That's exactly how he felt. Bitter. Angry. He hated feeling this way. His spirit felt crushed. He decided to pray for a few minutes.

Afterward, Robert pulled himself up from the chair and maneuvered his way to the downstairs bathroom. He turned on the cold water, cupped his hands under the running water, and splashed the cool liquid onto his face a couple of times. He grabbed a towel and slowly dried his face. Then he neatly folded the towel in half and placed it back on the rack. Since turning his pain over to God, he was beginning to feel a little better. He decided it was time to talk to Lynnette and went upstairs where he found her in the den watching television. He walked over to the sofa where she sat, but he didn't sit down.

"Can we talk?" he asked her.

"Sure," Lynnette answered. She picked up the remote off the sofa and turned off the television. "Wanna sit down?"

Robert joined her on the sofa. He looked into her eyes as he spoke. "I'm sorry. I got so angry at you this afternoon at the doctor's office when you told Dr. Mandell that you don't want the surgery. All along I've been saying how I'll support you no matter what you decide, and I didn't do it. I just want you to be all right. That's all that matters to me. That you're okay. Are you?"

Lynnette could still see the pain in her husband's face. She knew he was truly concerned about her, and this touched her deeply. She took his hands in hers. "I'm okay. I'm sorry, too. I knew you were upset, yet I kept pushing you to talk when I should have just let it rest until we'd both had time to cool off. I know you want me to have the surgery, but I'm so scared, and I can't go through with it feeling this way."

"I know you're scared. I am, too."

"But you don't understand," Lynnette said.

"I know I don't understand what you're going through because it's your pain."

"That's not what I mean."

Robert gave Lynnette a serious look. "What do you mean then?"

Lynnette began to relive another painful childhood memory. "When I was little, one of my foster moms went into the hospital to have routine surgery. She never made it home. She died on the operating table."

"I'm sorry," Robert apologized. "You never told me."

Lynnette went on. "That could happen to me. I can't take that chance. Please try to understand."

"It's okay," he assured her. "It's your decision, and you've made it. I'll be by your side no matter what."

Lynnette could tell that he was still worried. "You know how you're always telling me I think too much? Well, you worry too much. I'll be fine."

Robert could only say, "Okay."

In the middle of the night, Robert heard painful cries emanating from Lynnette.

"No-o-o. Mama, please don't leave. Please, Mama, don't go."

Robert shook her. "Lynn, wake up. Honey, you're dreaming. She opened her eyes.

"Com'ere," Robert instructed as he pulled her into his arms. "You were having a bad dream."

Lynnette's mind wandered back to their visit to Dr. Mandell's office the day before. Ever since she had seen and heard the two women talking about their families, she had been thinking about her mother.

She finally confessed to Robert, "Yesterday at Dr. Mandell's office, I overheard these two women talking. One was talking about her daughter who had just had a baby. The other one was talking about her daughter who had a hysterectomy. Seeing them and hearing them made me start thinking about my own mother and how nice it would have been if she hadn't left me so she could be with me now. I just don't understand why she left."

Her crying at the doctor's office was starting to make sense to Robert now. "Is that what had you crying?"

"Yeah. I just couldn't tell you then."

"Maybe there's a part of you that still wants to find her."

Lynnette was both shocked and disturbed that Robert could even conceive such an outrageous idea. She pulled back from him and raised her voice an octave as she spoke. "I don't want to find her. She hasn't thought enough of me in all these years to find me so why would I want to find her? She's nothing to me, not even a memory. I hate her for leaving me."

Robert pulled Lynnette closer. *"Hate's* a pretty strong word."

Lynnette jumped up and sat on the edge of the bed. "That's easy for you to say. Your mother didn't abandon you. Your mother died. It wasn't her choice. Mine had a choice."

Robert sat up and touched Lynnette's shoulder. "I don't want to upset you, but perhaps there were circumstances beyond her control that kept her from staying."

Lynnette turned to stare at her husband. "How can you say such a thing? There is no excuse for leaving your own child. I don't care what the circumstances were. I was only four years old. How would you feel if the shoe was on the other foot? If it was you who had been abandoned? Would you be so understanding then, or would you be angry?"

"I don't know how I'd feel," Robert admitted.

"Exactly," Lynnette snapped. "So unless you've gone through it yourself, don't tell me how to feel."

Robert moved across the bed so that he was sitting beside Lynnette. He put his arm around her. "I'm sorry. I'm not trying to tell you how to feel. Let's not argue again. We just made up. Come back to bed."

Lynnette leaned her head on Robert's shoulder. "I'm sorry. I'm not mad at you. I'm mad at her, and I guess I'm taking it out on you. I'm not sleepy. You go on back to bed. I'm going downstairs. Maybe if I do some reading, it'll make me sleepy."

"Okay, but don't stay up too long."

As Lynnette departed the room, Robert hoped that he could be a source of great strength and encouragement to his wife in her time of need.

Chapter 9

Saturday afternoon, Robert and Joshua were doing some work on the exterior of the house when Lynnette pulled into the garage so fast she almost knocked down the trash can. She jumped out of the vehicle wearing sunglasses and a scarf on her head. She dashed into the house.

Joshua looked at his father. "What's wrong with Mom?"

"Beats me." Pointing to the loose bricks the two of them had been working on, Robert added, "Finish those. I'll go check on her."

Robert found Lynnette in the master bath in front of the mirror, combing her hair and crying. Her hair had been cut short and cropped to her head. He was shocked. "Honey, what's wrong? What'd you do to your hair?" He walked closer until he was standing behind her.

Lynnette kept combing through her hair as she attempted

to explain. "I thought a new hairstyle would help me feel better, and…just look. I look like a man."

Robert didn't know what to say. "You don't look like a man. It's short, but it'll grow back."

"Look at it," Lynnette demanded as she held up a short strand of hair. "I can't roll it. I probably won't even be able to style it. What was I thinking?" she wondered out loud.

Robert tried to choose his words carefully. "Well, honey, when did you decide to get it cut?"

"This morning at the beauty shop."

Robert gulped. "Did the stylist cut it the way you asked her to?"

"Yes, but now I hate it. I wanted to be spontaneous so I thought a new hairstyle was the thing to do. When people see me looking like this, they're gonna think I've flipped."

Robert stepped beside Lynnette. "Calm down." He took the comb from her hand and placed it on the sink. "It's not so bad." He took her by the hand and escorted her out of the bathroom. "The more I look at it, the more I kind of like it," he added.

"You're just saying that to make me feel better."

Robert snickered. "I think you know me better than that. I admit I'm surprised that you got it cut so short. I've never seen it this short before, but I think it looks good on you."

Lynnette did know her husband, and he had no problem being open and up front with her. She felt in her heart that Robert was being truthful with her. However, she still could not believe she'd gotten all her hair whacked off. Talk about a midlife crisis. She was really going through some changes.

"Girl, I love your hair," Carla exclaimed as she retrieved a large glass bowl of tossed salad from the Montgomerys' refrigerator.

Lynnette slowly rubbed her hand over her neatly trimmed hair. "Do you really? You don't think I went overboard?"

"No. It's you." Carla smiled as she formed a mental picture of the look on her brother's face when he had seen it. He adored the way Lynnette wore her hair previously. "What did Robert say?"

Lynnette quickly grabbed two bottles of salad dressing from the refrigerator. "Well, he said he likes it. You don't think—"

"I know what you're going to ask," Carla interrupted. "I think you know him better than I do by now. You've been married to him for all these years. If he doesn't like it, he wouldn't have told you he does."

"You're right. It's just that lately I haven't been feeling very good about myself, and I guess my self-esteem is a little low right now."

The two women started toward the dining room. "I know," Carla said, "but cheer up. Things will get better."

Lynnette strolled over to the living room entrance, peeked her head in, and announced that dinner was about to be served.

Rose got up from her seat where she had been chatting with Robert and James. "I wish you had allowed me to help. I don't feel right not doing anything."

"Ms. Rose," Lynnette told her as she showed Rose to her chair, "you are a guest, and I want you to just relax and enjoy yourself. Now you have a seat right here."

After everyone was seated, they held hands as Robert said the blessing. They said Amen and began passing around platters of mouthwatering food.

"Robert," Rose said as she bit into a hush puppy, "you and Lynn have a very beautiful home. And to think, the two of you designed and built it yourselves."

"Thank you," Robert replied. "We knew what we wanted, and we just did it."

Lynnette added, "As you can see, Robert's very good at what he does."

"Indeed, he is. You're both extremely talented." Rose turned to Carla. "Carla, your husband tells me he's an air traffic controller. Do you work outside the home, too?"

"Yes, ma'am," Carla answered. "While James is keeping our skies safe, I'm helping to rehabilitate people suffering from diseases and disabilities."

"Ahh." Rose nodded. "You're a physical therapist."

Carla nodded.

Rose continued, "You all have such interesting careers, and you seem to really enjoy what you do."

They all nodded in agreement that they were indeed happy with their chosen professions.

Carla popped a morsel of catfish into her mouth. "Ms. Johnson, I think your children's home is a wonderful contribution to this county. You'll be able to make such a huge difference in the lives of children."

Rose let her hand rest on the table. "I have to tell you, Carla, I'm very excited about this project. I only wish my Thurgood could be here to see it when it's completed."

James asked, "Was Thurgood your husband?"

"Yes." Rose smiled. "He passed on two years ago. When I learned he had left me the house, the one Robert and Lynn are working on, I couldn't think of anything better to do with it than fix it up for someone who needs it more than me."

"That's very generous of you," Robert said. "It's good to help others, especially those less fortunate."

"Well," Rose added, "I've been blessed with an abundance, and I want to share it."

As they ate, talked, and laughed, Lynnette could not help but feel happy and blessed. The only thing missing in her life was her mother.

"Mama, please don't leave. I need you. Don't go," Lynnette mumbled in her sleep. "Why, Mama? Mama-a-a-a-a."

Robert shook Lynnette gently. "Lynn."

Lynnette continued to moan. "Mama-a-a-a."

Robert shook her again. "Lynn. Honey, wake up. You're talking in your sleep."

She scooted over into Robert's arms and whispered as she spoke. "I can't seem to get her out of my head."

Robert's voice was soothing. "Maybe it's been building up over a period of time. And you've been under a lot of stress lately."

Lynnette agreed. "You're right. Ever since I found out about the fibroids and the surgery, everything's been going downhill. I hate feeling this way. Why is this happening to me? What have I done to deserve this? Am I being punished? Wasn't it enough that my own mother walked out on me? Now I have to suffer more dreaming about her leaving. It's not fair, Robert." She began to cry. She felt wretched.

Robert spoke consolingly. "You did nothing wrong. You know that. That's the way life is sometimes. God is not punishing you. This is a test, just like all the other tests you've been through and passed. Your faith will help you through this. All it takes is a measure of faith. What does the Bible say about faith? Remember Jesus said if we have faith the size of a mustard seed we can move mountains. Imagine what you can do. Your faith is so much bigger than that.

"What your mother did was wrong, but look at you. You could have turned out like her, but you didn't. You're a wonderful mother to Josh and Randa. You're a wonderful wife, and I love you. Aren't you the one who's always telling us when life gives us lemons to make lemonade? Now that's what you have to do. Don't do it for me. Don't do it for the kids. Do it for yourself."

Lynnette knew she should listen to Robert. Everything he said made sense, but it was easier said than done.

Chapter 10

Lynnette slept late the next morning. The dreams and the pain in her abdomen had robbed her of a peaceful night's sleep.

When Robert came out of the bathroom, he was disappointed to see that she was not up. *Here we go again,* he thought. He felt she wasn't taking her spirituality seriously by neglecting spiritual activities.

He walked around to her side of the bed and looked down at her. "What's wrong? Aren't you coming with us today?"

Lynnette didn't dare look at Robert. She didn't want to see the disappointment on his face. "No, I don't feel well."

Robert came close to voicing his disapproval but decided against it. After all, she'd had a dreadful night, and he had no desire to add to her stress by getting her upset. "Do you want one of us to stay home with you?"

Lynnette batted her eyes. "No, I'll be fine."

He leaned down and kissed her lightly on her cheek and left.

As she laid in bed, all Lynnette could think about were the tumors. *Maybe they are cancerous. Cancer could be spreading through my body right now. Maybe I should have the surgery. No, I can't. I want to enjoy life. Have a little fun.*

Finally, she drifted off to sleep. A couple of hours later, she got up and took a shower. She wanted to cook dinner for her family, but she just didn't feel up to it. She felt guilty but not enough to prepare a meal. She was looking through the kitchen cabinets in an effort to find something in a can that she could just heat up and serve when her threesome walked in. They were carrying bags of Chinese food. Lynnette could smell it as soon as they walked through the door.

As they set the bags on the table, Robert said, "Since you're not feeling well, we stopped and got Chinese." He closed the cabinet, gently took her by her arm, and guided her to the table. "Come sit down. I know you're probably hungry. You need to keep up your strength."

Lynnette obeyed. Joshua and Miranda grabbed some plates, glasses, and silverware. After everyone was seated, Robert said the blessing and they began eating. Lynnette was quiet as her family talked. She attempted to eat but did not have an appetite. Finally, she ceased picking at her food, dismissed herself, and went upstairs.

A few minutes later, Robert followed her. She was laying on the bed. He sat down beside her. "Lynn, what's wrong? You were quiet during dinner. You barely touched your food. You need to eat."

"I'm not hungry," she stated.

"Are you still thinking about your mother?" he asked.

"I'm thinking about a lot of things."

"Like what?"

Lynnette didn't respond.

"Tell me," he gently prodded.

He won't understand, she thought.

"Why won't you talk to me? Tell me what's bothering you."

Lynnette still did not say anything. She closed her eyes.

Robert needed to know what was on her mind, but he didn't want to pressure her. He decided that she would talk when she was ready. He got up and walked away.

Thirty minutes later, the telephone rang. Lynnette opened her eyes. She saw Robert with his back to her as he stood with the telephone to his ear. She could hear him whispering.

"She's asleep," she heard him say. "She's not feeling good."

Quickly, Lynnette raised up. "Who is it?" she inquired.

Robert turned to face her yet gave her no answer.

She repeated, "Who is it?"

Robert frowned. "Simone."

Lynnette reached for the phone. "I'll talk to her."

He begrudgingly handed her the phone. He stood there for a few minutes simply staring at her. He didn't understand her. All she seemed to want to do was lay around, but as soon as Simone called she perked right up. He walked away.

Robert was in the den when Lynnette came to inform him that she was going out for a while. He stared at her in disbelief. Was she serious? She hadn't felt like joining them for service that morning. Now here she was announcing to him that she was going out.

He said, "Oh. Where are you going?"

Lynnette showed no emotion as she spoke. "I need to go out for a while. I'm just going for a drive."

Robert got up. "I'll go with you."

"No," Lynnette said. "I want to go alone."

Robert sensed that she was not being totally honest with him. "It's Simone, isn't it? You're going out with her."

"Just for a little while. I won't be long."

Robert sighed. He had to remind himself that she needed his patience. "Okay. Have a good time."

After Lynnette left, Robert was still sitting there wondering what had just happened.

"Did you have a good time?" Robert inquired as Lynnette locked the kitchen door. She jumped. He was sitting in the dark at the kitchen table.

She threw her hand to her chest. "Whew, you scared me."

"Do you realize it's eleven o'clock? You've been gone all day and half the night. I've been trying to call you, but you didn't answer your cell phone or return my call. I was worried something had happened to you."

Lynnette switched on the light. When she saw the look on Robert's face, she wished she'd left them in the dark.

"Honey," she began her explanation as she walked over to join him at the table, "I know you're upset. I'm sorry. I should have called."

"Where have you been? You said you were going out for a little while."

Lynnette answered, "I went to Simone's house. You know she lives in Atlanta now. We got to talking, and the time just got away from me." She realized her nervousness was causing her to talk much too fast. She sat down beside Robert and placed her hand on his. She spoke slower this time. "Honey, I'm sorry. I should have called. My cell phone was off. I was having such a good time I didn't even think about it. I'll make it up to you. Please don't be mad."

Robert got up. He couldn't hold his feelings in any longer. "Lynn, what's wrong with you? You've never left me hanging like this before. I've been sitting here all evening long worrying about you. You don't have time for God or your family. You wouldn't even come with us this morning. You were laying around like somebody had died. But as soon as Simone called, you perked right up and was out the door. I don't understand you."

Lynnette didn't appreciate the way Robert was talking to her. "What is wrong with me doing something I want to do for a change? Don't I deserve some time for myself?"

"I want you to have time for yourself, but that doesn't mean you have to stay out half the night."

Lynnette stood and started to walk away. "I'm not going to argue with you. I'm a grown woman, and I'm not under a curfew. I'm going to bed. I'll talk to you after you've had a chance to calm down, but you needn't think I'm going to bow down to you."

Why was she angry at him? She was the one who had been gone all day and half the night and had come waltzing in at eleven o'clock. Robert caught up with her and stopped in front of her. "Listen," he pleaded, "I don't want us to go to bed angry with each other. I want to talk. I just don't understand what's going on with you. Ever since last month, you've been acting so strange."

Lynnette was tired of his whining. "You know, Robert, I really don't understand you. You complain when I mope around the house, and the one time I go out and enjoy myself without you, you get all emotional on me. What is it you want from me?"

"Try to understand what I'm saying. I want you to have a life outside of me and the kids, but I don't want you to shut me out. We said that when Josh and Randa got older and more independent we'd spend more time together. When I wanted to take you to the mountains last month, you cancelled at the last minute."

"So you're pitching a tantrum because I changed my mind and you didn't get your way," Lynnette stated.

Robert threw his hands in the air. "Lynn, this has nothing to do with me getting my way. Forget it." He walked off and left her standing there.

Lynnette felt awful. Why had she insisted on arguing with him? He had every right to be upset with her, but when he would not let the subject rest, she had gone on the defensive. He was right. They shouldn't go to bed angry. She would apologize. She went upstairs. Robert was standing in front of the huge bay window in their room staring out into the night sky.

She walked slowly up behind him and placed her hand on his back. "I'm sorry. I didn't mean to argue with you. I felt so carefree today. I guess I wasn't in a hurry to get back home. Don't take that the wrong way. I love you and the kids, but lately, I've been feeling like something's missing from my life. I'm getting older, and I want to enjoy what time I have left."

Robert continued staring into the moonlit sky. "You're talking like you're on your deathbed. You're still young. You just turned forty is all. You've been acting so different lately. You're not the Lynn I fell in love with. I miss her."

Lynnette stepped in front of Robert. "That's just it, honey." She placed her hand on her chest. "I'm not the same. I'm different. People change. You have, too."

Robert shook his head. "Maybe I have but not like you. I feel as if we're growing apart. The closer I try to get to you, the farther you pull away." He paused, then added, "And Simone. I know she's your friend, but you know I'm not crazy about her. With her back in your life now, you tend to push me away."

"I'm sorry you feel that way. You know I love you with all my heart. Simone is a very dear friend. She's like a sister to

me. You know that. I didn't mean to make you feel neglected.
I'll try to do better."

Robert and Lynnette put their arms around each other. He
apologized. "I'm sorry I've been giving you such a hard time.
I'll try to do better, too."

I'll try, Robert thought, *but it won't be easy. Why'd Simone
have to move here? Why couldn't she have stayed in Chicago
or wherever she was?*

March brought warmer temperatures and spring in full
bloom. The weather was perfect for shopping at yard sales.
As Lynnette and Rose strolled around the yard of the last
house for the day, their eyes meticulously skimming every
item, Lynnette noticed a Colonial-style table covered with
paint. "Ms. Rose." She motioned for Rose to follow her.

Lynnette ran her fingers gingerly across the table. "Isn't it
lovely? We can strip it and stain it. And look at the price. Only
three dollars."

"Three dollars," Rose repeated. "Let's buy it."

Miranda was quiet in the stall of the girls' restroom in the
sophomore building. Sheena Long, a tenth-grade beauty
whom all the boys at school flocked over, entered the restroom
talking loudly. Her friends followed closely behind. The girls
apparently thought they were the only ones there. When
Miranda heard them talking, she stood on the toilet to keep
from being seen.

She heard an unfamiliar voice say, "So, Sheena, have things
gotten hot and heavy with you and Josh Montgomery yet?"

Sheena laughed. "Not yet, but they will."

Another voice Miranda didn't recognize asked, "Well,
everybody knows he's still a virgin so how can you be so sure?"

"Well, look at me," Sheena bragged. "All the boys like me. He won't be able to resist."

The first girl spoke again. "So are you gonna dump Craig when you and Josh get together?"

"What for?" Sheena wanted to know. "I won't need Josh after I get what I want from him. He'll be history."

The second girl added, "He won't know what hit him."

All three girls were laughing as they left the restroom.

When Lynnette arrived home, she heard Joshua and Miranda in the kitchen. It sounded like they were arguing.

"I don't believe you," Joshua was saying. "You're lying. You're making this up because you're jealous."

Miranda asked, "Josh, why would I make up something like this?"

"I told you. You're jealous."

Lynnette stood between her two children, holding out her arms to distance them from each other. "Whoa! What's going on here?"

Joshua answered, "Randa's making up lies about Sheena."

Lynnette asked, "Who's Sheena?"

"Her name is Sheena Long. She's a girl at school. Mama, I'm not lying. I overheard her and some of her friends talking about Josh today at school. She was saying after she goes to bed with him, she's going to dump him."

Lynnette took each one by the hand and walked them over to the kitchen table. "Come on. Let's sit down and talk about this. Randa, are you sure you're not mistaken about what you heard?"

"Yes, Mama, I'm sure. I heard them."

"She's lying, Mom. Sheena and I are friends. She wouldn't say that."

Lynnette held up her hand. "Wait, Josh. You know your

sister better than that. You know she wouldn't make up something like this."

"Why not, Mom? You know how she acts sometimes. Like I don't have a life outside of her."

"Listen, you two. I don't like you arguing like this. You're brother and sister. Are you going to let some outsider come between you?"

They hadn't heard Robert come in. "What's all the commotion in here?"

Miranda started to get up. "Daddy..."

"Randa," Lynnette warned, "sit back down, please. You can talk to your dad from here."

Miranda returned to her seat. "Daddy," she went on, "I overheard this girl telling her friends at school today that she's going to dump Josh once she gets him to go to bed with her. When I told him, he got angry with me. He says I'm making it up."

"Dad," Joshua said, "she's just jealous. She needs to stop being nosy and mind her own business. She's nothing but a busybody."

"That's enough," Robert said in a stern voice. "You're both angry right now. I want you to wash up for supper, and after we eat, we're going to sit down and discuss this calmly like sensible people."

Robert was distressed that his family seemed to be arguing more and more lately. Him and Lynnette. Now Joshua and Miranda. Everyone seemed to be under so much stress.

Chapter 11

At breakfast the next morning, Joshua was passive. Although they had a family discussion the night before and had seemed to clear the air, Miranda sensed that he was still upset with her. While their parents chatted away, Joshua picked at his food while Miranda tried to figure out a way to prove to her brother that she was not lying about Sheena. She had to do something to make him believe her.

After breakfast, Miranda went upstairs to her room to retrieve the item she would need to prove her case. When she came back downstairs, Joshua had gone without her. They had planned to ride to school together in his truck since neither of them had plans that afternoon. She knew now without a doubt that he was still miffed at her.

Lynnette was wiping off the kitchen counter when Miranda approached her. "Mama, he's still mad at me. We were supposed to ride to school together, and he left without me. Why doesn't he believe me?"

Lynnette's heart went out to her daughter for she knew how close the two were. Now that they were getting older, they seemed to be adversaries instead of friends. She could see how painful it was for Miranda. Lynnette stopped wiping the counter and looked at her.

"Maybe a part of him does believe you, and another part just doesn't want to because he's hurt. Just give him some time. He'll come around. You'll see."

When Miranda got to school, she pulled into her assigned parking space in the back of the building. She stepped out of her car onto the dark asphalt. The brick building loomed ahead of her as she made her way toward it. Many other students were arriving for school and were walking with their friends as they talked and laughed. She was in a hurry. She didn't have time to talk this morning. She threw her hand up at a couple of people she knew and continued walking.

She was familiar with Sheena's morning routine of stopping by the restroom to primp before class. That's where she intended to put her plan into action. She scurried past people moving quickly in the halls, turned the corner, and headed for the sophomore building.

Her steps became faster after she opened the door and went inside. As she maneuvered her way through the other students, she spotted Sheena and slowed down. When Sheena dashed into the restroom, Miranda quickened her pace. She had no intentions of beating around the bush. She would get straight to the point and hoped it went as well as she had planned.

Miranda followed Sheena into the girls' restroom. "I heard what you said about my brother yesterday, and I don't appreciate it."

Sheena stopped primping long enough to turn and glare at Miranda. "What are you talking about?"

"You know what I'm talking about," Miranda spat out. "I heard you and your little buddies in here talking yesterday. I was hiding in the stall. I heard every word you said. You think you're going to get Josh to have sex with you and then you're going to dump him for Craig. You think you're hot stuff, don't you? I wonder what Josh will say when I tell him what you're planning."

"And do you think he's going to believe you? He likes me."

"So. I'm his sister. Why don't you leave him alone? You think sleeping with somebody you care nothing about makes you somebody special, don't you?"

Sheena grew hot with anger. She had heard people talk about Miranda's grit. "You know what? You talk too much. You wanna know something else? The only reason I even gave your brother the time of day is 'cause everybody knows what a pair of Goody Two-shoes you two are. A lot of girls at school like Josh, but he won't talk to them. So I started talking to him one day just to prove that I can go to bed with him."

Miranda angrily walked off. As she sped down the hallway, she removed the mini tape recorder from inside the pocket of her jacket and shut it off. She had gotten Sheena's confession on tape just as she had planned. *Now all I have to do is play it for Josh.*

Lynnette took a bite of pepperoni pizza. "Carla, have I changed?"

"What do you mean?" Lynnette's sister-in-law wanted to know.

"Well," Lynnette answered, "Robert says I act different now."

Carla took a sip of tea. "In what way?"

"He feels like I'm neglecting him. I visited Simone recently. We got to talking, and I didn't get home until eleven o'clock that night. He was upset."

"Yeah, I know. He called me. You know, I've heard that men go through some sort of midlife crisis. Perhaps his age is getting to him and he wants to spend more time with you like he did when the two of you were younger."

Lynnette started laughing. "Get outta here." When she saw that Carla was not sharing her laughter, she asked seriously, "You think so?"

Carla nodded. "It's possible."

Lynnette stared at Carla.

"What?" Carla asked.

"Did he tell you that? What's he been saying?"

"No, he hasn't said anything. I'm just saying maybe that's it."

"Maybe you're right. That never entered my mind."

Carla changed the subject. "Are you still having those dreams?"

"Yes. Off and on."

Carla was genuinely concerned. "Do they scare you?"

"No. Confuse me is more like it. You know, when I was younger I used to dream about her. I hadn't really thought about her in years though 'til last month."

"Maybe it's because you've been so stressed out lately."

"I don't know. Maybe."

"Lynn, I know life hasn't been easy for you. Just remember you have a family who loves you."

"I know," Lynnette said.

When Lynnette arrived home that afternoon, she found Miranda setting the table alone. She gave her daughter a quick peck on the cheek. "Hey, sweet pea. How was your day?"

"Okay," Miranda replied dryly.

"You don't sound like it was okay. What's wrong? You and Josh still upset with each other?"

Lynnette and Miranda sat at the kitchen table while Miranda relayed to her how she had gotten Sheena's confession on tape. She tried to get Joshua to listen to it, but he refused.

"He yelled at me to stop sticking my nose in his business. He said I'm jealous and that he's going to keep seeing her. Mama, I had to do it. She's making a fool out of him, and he can't even see it. I did it for him. He's so angry at me though I guess I should have butted out."

Lynnette reassured her daughter, "You couldn't have butted out. He's your brother, and you love him. You saw someone trying to take advantage of him, and you did something about it. Everything will be okay. You'll see." She stood and rubbed her hand over her daughter's hair. "Your dad will be home soon. I'm going to talk to Josh. After we eat, maybe we can all go get some ice cream. That is, if you and Josh aren't too embarrassed to be seen in public with your parents."

Miranda attempted to smile. "Okay."

Lynnette found Joshua lying on his bed with his headphones on. He sat up and removed them as she entered the room. She sat down beside him. "Randa told me about the tape."

Joshua looked at his mother. "Why can't she just mind her own business? She's just jealous. She can't stand it if everybody's attention isn't focused on her. I'm tired of it."

Lynnette didn't recall ever seeing Joshua as upset with his sister as he was at the moment. In an effort to smooth things over between them, she said, "I know you're upset with her right now, but she loves you. You two have always been close."

"I know, but she's got to understand that I have a life outside of her."

"So how serious are you about this girl?" Lynnette needed to know.

Joshua felt a lecture coming. "Mom, we're just friends. I like her, and I think she's pretty. But I'm not ready for a relationship."

"Well, when you are ready, I trust you'll be selective about who you choose."

"I will."

Lynnette and Joshua talked a few more minutes before she headed back downstairs. The pain she felt in her abdomen reminded her of the surgery she had decided not to have. At this point, even with the pain she was experiencing, she was glad she had said no. Her family needed her. She couldn't go through with it. Not when there was so much tension among them.

Chapter 12

"I saw you talking to Sheena today," Miranda expressed disapprovingly to Joshua as she was passing his room. She stopped in the doorway.

Although he had told her the day before that he would continue seeing Sheena, when Miranda had seen the two of them talking at school earlier in the day, she had almost gone into shock. She was seething with anger. She shook her head as a frown covered her entire face. "How can you have anything to do with her after what she said about you?"

Joshua looked up from the homework assignment on which he was working. He was tired of his sister trying to boss him, and he didn't feel he had to explain anything to her. Nevertheless, he said, "She was upset about something."

Miranda folded her arms as she leaned against the doorjamb. "What?" she demanded.

"Craig broke up with her, and she was upset."

"Humph." Miranda twisted her mouth and jolted her shoulders as she let out the expression. "Serves her right."

Joshua did not understand his sister. Sometimes she could have such a negative attitude. "Randa, why do you have to be so mean?"

"I'm not being mean. She treated you like you're nothing. Don't you have any self-respect? You need to stop being so naive."

"I'm not being naive. I was just trying to be a friend and cheer her up," Joshua said. "Besides, what business is it of yours anyway? You're not the boss of me."

"Humph," Miranda said again as she turned to go to her room. She hadn't meant to make her brother angry. It was just that when she had seen him talking to Sheena, she had wanted to scream at the top of her lungs. Why was she being so irrational? She and Joshua had always been the best of friends. Now all they did was argue. He believed she was jealous of Sheena, and perhaps she was. She felt horrible. She went back to Joshua's room.

When Joshua saw her, he gazed at her impatiently and dropped his pencil onto his paper. "What is it now?" he asked indignantly.

"I'm sorry. I shouldn't have talked to you that way. I guess a part of me is jealous of all the time you spend with your friends."

"Randa, you know I always take time out for you no matter what. I'm not going to let anybody come between us, but you've got to understand that sometimes I need my space. You have your friends, too."

Miranda shook her head. "Not like you. You're so outgoing. Everybody likes you. I can't make friends like you."

Joshua half-smiled. "Well, you do kinda take yourself too seriously. You're very outspoken, and everybody who knows you knows it. Loosen up a little. I'm not saying pretend to be something you're not. Just let people see the real Randa, the person you are inside.

"For example, I know you love to laugh and have fun, but you very seldom let other people see that side of you. Most of the time when I see you at school, you've got a look on your face like you're ready to put somebody in a headlock."

Miranda couldn't help but giggle. Embarrassed, she hung her head. "I do not."

"Randa," Joshua teased, "if you were walking down the street and a mugger approached you, once he saw the look on your face, he'd give you his wallet."

They both broke into laughter.

Miranda hated to admit it, but she supposed Joshua was right in his opinion of her. She could have a boisterous attitude at times, but she had to keep up her guard. When people catch your guard down, that's when they aim for the kill. Isn't that what had happened to Joshua? She wished she could be more like him. She resolved to try to improve her attitude.

On Saturday, Lynnette was feeling buoyant, and her mood felt incredibly lighter. She was about to head out when Joshua came downstairs.

"Mom, you going out?"

"Yes. Wanna come?"

"Where are you going?"

"Sport Shoe. I need some walking shoes. I'll probably get some lunch first though. You coming?"

"Yes." Joshua headed back upstairs as he spoke over his shoulder. "Just let me wash off real quick."

Lynnette teased him. "Wash off nothing. You better get your big, rusty self in the tub."

Joshua stopped in the middle of the stairs and turned to look at his mother with a half-grin on his face. "Mom," he pleaded.

"You heard me. Haven't you been playing basketball? You're not coming anywhere with me smelling all sweaty and musty. You could probably get away with that wash off stuff when you were younger but not now." Lynnette waved her hand at him. "Go on. I'll wait."

Thirty minutes later, Joshua was ready to go. Lynnette rubbed her hand over his head. "You know I was just playing around with you, don't you?"

Joshua blushed. "I know."

As they got near the Land Rover, Joshua begged, "Can I drive?"

Lynnette stepped back with a shocked look on her face. "Drive the Rover?" she teased. "I don't think so."

"Aw, Mom, come on. I'll be careful. It's not like you won't be with me."

"*Hmmmm.*" Lynnette pretended to ponder it over. "Okay." She gave Joshua the keys.

As they were about to get into the vehicle, Joshua stopped and grinned. "Mom, why'd you put me through all that drama when you knew you were gonna let me drive?"

Lynnette shrugged. "I don't know." She smiled. "I guess I just felt like harassing you. I don't get to do that like I used to." She jumped into the vehicle.

Joshua grinned and shook his head.

As they rode down Highway 27, one of Lynnette's favorite songs, Billy Ocean's "Caribbean Queen," came over the radio. She grabbed a hairbrush from the console and used the handle as a microphone as she mimicked the words and danced from side to side.

Joshua laughed. He hadn't seen his mother have this much fun in a long time.

When they had to stop at a red light, Joshua declared, "Mom, I think you're drawing attention to yourself."

Lynnette kept bobbing her head from side to side. *"Hmm?"*

Joshua leaned back out of sight and pointed to the vehicle beside his mother. Lynnette turned to look, never missing a beat, and looked directly into the face of a young girl staring and smiling at her. Lynnette simply waved and continued dancing and singing. The girl smiled and waved back.

The light turned green, and Lynnette and Joshua were off again. At Applebee's, they were seated promptly. While they waited on their food, Joshua filled Lynnette in on how things were going at school. A few minutes later, their food arrived. They bowed their heads, and each said their own silent prayer of thanks for their food.

Lynnette smiled and took a bite of salad. She was delighted that she and Joshua were able to spend the afternoon together. Every now and then, she liked having some one-on-one time with her children. Joshua had started to fill her in on some of the latest songs.

Suddenly, out of the corner of her eye, she caught a glimpse of a young girl staring intently at them from a table on the opposite side of the restaurant. "Don't look now," Lynnette warned, "but I think *you've* captured someone's attention this time."

Joshua continued eating. "Where?"

"Don't look now," Lynnette cautioned him again. "To your right at that table by the window in the middle. Okay, now you can look."

Joshua quickly stole a peek across the crowded restaurant and turned back to his food. He didn't say anything.

Lynnette was curious. "Well, do you know her?"

Joshua appeared uninterested. "Yes."

"My goodness," his mother teased. "This is like pulling teeth. She's pretty. What's her name?"

Joshua's answer was delayed in coming. "Sheena Long," he murmured.

"Sheena Long," Lynnette repeated the name slowly. It sounded familiar. Then she remembered where she'd heard it. She couldn't believe her ears. She dropped her fork onto her plate. "Isn't she the girl who Randa heard talking about you in the restroom at school?"

"Yes." Joshua knew his mother well. "Mom, please don't start."

Lynnette rolled her eyes at Sheena.

"Mom, are you okay?" Joshua inquired.

Lynnette answered but kept her eyes focused on the girl. "Yeah. Sure. I'm fine." She paused, still not taking her eyes off Sheena. "You want me to beat her up?"

Joshua knew his mother wouldn't hurt a flea so he decided to play along with her since she seemed to be in such a good mood. His eyes lit up. "Would you?"

Lynnette stared at her son in disbelief. "I'm kidding."

Joshua couldn't keep a straight face. "I know. So am I."

Lynnette lightly tapped Joshua's hand. "You are so bad."

Just then, Lynnette saw the girl walking in their direction. Lynnette was shocked. She asked, as though to no one in particular, "Is she coming over here?" Then she answered her own question with an attitude. "I know she's not coming over here."

The next thing Lynnette and Joshua knew, the girl was standing beside their table. Sheena looked at Joshua and smiled warmly.

"Hi, Josh. I saw you sitting here, and I wanted to speak with you before I left. How are you doing?"

"I'm fine. How are you?" Joshua returned her smile.

"Fine." Sheena looked shyly at Lynnette, then back at Joshua.

"Sheena, this is my mom, Lynnette Montgomery. Mom, this is Sheena Long."

"Hello, Mrs. Montgomery."

Joshua just knew his mother was about to go berserk. He lightly tapped her foot with his underneath the table.

Lynnette looked at Joshua, then Sheena. She was boiling on the inside. She thought she might lose her religion and go off on the girl. Instead, she managed to say, "Hello." The two females shook hands.

Lynnette and Joshua saw Sheena look at two girls standing near the exit. "Well, I have to go. Josh, thanks again for talking to me the other day at school. And I'm really sorry about everything that's happened. I'll see you later. Bye."

"You're welcome. Bye."

Sheena waved and was gone.

"What was that all about?" Lynnette inquired.

Joshua shrugged. "Nothing really. I found out that what Randa said about Sheena was true. Some of the kids at school backed up what Randa said. I asked Sheena about it. She denied it at first, but she finally admitted it. When her boyfriend found out, he broke up with her. She was upset. I talked to her and tried to make her feel better."

"I'm so sorry. Are you all right?" Lynnette asked.

"I'm fine, Mom. Except for feeling like a complete idiot, I'm fine."

"I know you're hurting. I want you to remember something. You are a very unique person. You are a young man of admirable character. Your father and I raised you and Randa to have high moral standards. Some people don't appreciate that and characterize it as a weakness, but don't let that get you down because God is pleased with you, and He's smiling down on you."

"Thanks, Mom. I'll be okay."

Lynnette looked at her son with admiration. "You're really something. Do you know that?"

"Why do you say that?" Joshua humbly inquired.

"After all that girl put you through, you still have a kind heart toward her."

"Well, like you said, it's the way you and Dad raised us."

Lynnette chose the moment to shed some humor on the matter. As she spoke, she moved her head from side to side. "Yes, and it's a good thing we did, too, since we have to set a good example. Otherwise, I would've snatched her up by those braids and swung her around this restaurant 'til she couldn't see straight."

Joshua snickered as he covered his mouth with his hand. "Mom, you need to quit."

Lynnette laughed. "You know I'm just kidding."

"I know." Joshua knew what a caring individual his mother was. She was the best.

She stopped laughing. "I'm just letting off a little steam. Trying to make myself laugh. I'd never do any of that stuff. My bark is worse than my bite."

Joshua agreed. "You don't have to tell me. I know."

Lynnette and Joshua enjoyed the rest of their meal together. She relished the time she spent with her family. The time would come one day when they wouldn't be able to be together like they were now. Eventually, Joshua and Miranda would leave home and go off to live lives of their own. It was a bittersweet thought.

Chapter 13

The next couple of weeks were substantially better for Lynnette. With April came rainy days and warmer temperatures. She had started taking advantage of the warm weather by taking long walks in their neighborhood as a source of much-needed exercise and refreshment.

Carla yelled after her sister-in-law. "Wait up! You're killing me!"

Lynnette glanced over her shoulder at Carla and shouted, "Come on, slowpoke!" She turned into the driveway and stopped to wait on Carla and give her some encouragement. "Come on. You can do it. There you go. Just a few more feet."

At last, Carla made it into the driveway. She took deep breaths as she leaned over with her hands on her bent knees. "Girl...where do you...get all...that energy?"

Lynnette wiped her perspiring face with the towel that hung around her neck. "You're just outta shape." She proceeded to tease her sister-in-law. "And what is it you do for a living again?" She tapped her index finger on the side of her face as a pretense that she was in deep thought. "Oh yeah. Physical therapy." She laughed.

Carla swiped at Lynnette with her towel and missed. She started laughing. "I'm gonna get you for that."

"You'll have to catch me first," Lynnette declared as she took off running toward the house.

"Don't think I can't," Carla exclaimed as she chased Lynnette into the house.

"Hey! Hey! What's going on?" Robert inquired as the two women ran through the kitchen door.

Lynnette stopped to stand behind Robert where he sat at the kitchen table with James. She told James, "Your wife's after me. She wants to hurt me real bad because I walked faster than her." Then she playfully trembled behind Robert and begged him, "Honey, please save me."

Carla plopped down in the chair beside James. She told Lynnette, "If I wasn't so tired, I'd come over there. Yeah, hide behind your husband. You must have forgotten how I used to beat him up when we were little. Isn't that right, Robert?"

Robert looked at James, shook his head, and made a twirly motion with his fingers. "They've really flipped this time."

Robert was glad Lynnette was in such a good mood. He loved seeing her so alive. It reminded him of their younger days. He had no concept of how long her pleasant nature would remain, but he would enjoy it while it lasted.

"What time will you be home?" Robert asked Lynnette over the telephone.

"I don't know. We're just going to get a manicure and a

pedicure." Lynnette added, "And probably a massage. I need to pamper myself."

"Do you have to do this today? It's Friday. You know Friday's our night out with James and Carla."

"Exactly. Robert, I want to do something different for a change."

He didn't remember her mentioning who she'd be with, but he had a pretty good idea. "Who are you going with again?"

"Simone."

He knew it. *Every time Lynnette's around that woman, she forgets who she is and that she has a family at home.* Robert involuntarily let out a heavy breath. "Lynn, you know how I feel about Simone."

Lynnette was losing her patience. "Robert, do we have to argue about this? You suggested that I do something different, and now that I want to, you're giving me a hard time."

"I don't mind if you do some things you want to do. I just don't want you doing them on time that we've set aside for each other and our family."

Lynnette was not going to give in to Robert. "Will it hurt this one time if I cancel our Friday night out to do something I want to do?" She breathed deeply. "I'm wasting valuable time arguing with you about it."

Robert sighed. "Go ahead. What time can I expect you home?" Before Lynnette could answer, he added, "And don't pull that stunt you did last time."

She glanced at her watch. "It's four-thirty now. I'll try to be home around nine o'clock. If not, I'll call you."

Robert reminded Lynnette, "I'm not kidding. I expect you home at a reasonable hour."

She had to go. She wasn't going to stay on the telephone

debating this with him. "I heard you. I'll see you later tonight. Bye."

She hung up the phone before he could say anything else. Lynnette was furious at Robert. Who did he think he was telling her what time to be home? He wasn't her father. She was a grown woman. And she wasn't under a curfew. She'd show him. She'd come home when she was good and ready. And another thing. She wasn't making any telephone calls to check in with him either.

Later that night, Robert stood staring out the bedroom window. He was furious. Lynnette was being selfish and unreasonable. Did she think she was going to put him last on her list of priorities and he would accept it? He had tried to be patient with her and understanding of her emotional state, but this was getting ridiculous. He was going to put an end to her foolishness. He was relieved that Joshua and Miranda were spending the night with friends so they wouldn't have to witness the interchange between him and Lynnette. The longer he stood at their bedroom window watching for her, the more annoyed he became.

At five minutes before midnight, Robert heard Lynnette coming up the stairs. He was sitting in his recliner in the bedroom when she came in.

He stared at her and asked, "What is it you're trying to prove?"

"What do you mean? I'm not trying to prove anything," was Lynnette's curt reply.

"You deliberately stayed out late after I asked you not to."

"I don't know what you're talking about," Lynnette lied.

"Yes, you do. You said you'd be home at nine o'clock, but if you weren't, you'd call."

Lynnette tossed her purse on the bed. "Robert, I'm not a child. You were talking to me like I'm a child, and I don't appreciate it. And you didn't ask me not to stay out late. You told me not to."

"Ever since this thing with the surgery, you've become a different person, and I'm not liking what I'm seeing."

"Well, this thing with the surgery, as you put it, has made me a different person. You and the kids have always been the focal point in my life. I take my responsibility as a wife and mother very seriously. I've made sacrifices for my family. Is it wrong for me to want to do something for myself now?"

"No, it's not wrong, but the way you're going about it is. I'm not saying you've got to spend all your free time with me. I want you to have other interests, too, but please don't shut me out. And don't shut out the rest of the family either."

"I'm not shutting anyone out. I just want to live my life."

"What am I supposed to do while you're off living your life? Sit around and wait until you're finished? We promised that we would spend more time together once Josh and Randa got older. We both work hard all week long. The weekends are the only time we have together. Now you want to take that away."

Lynnette went to her dresser and yanked out her nightgown. "Robert, I'm too tired to argue with you. I'm going to bed."

"You should be tired after staying out half the night," he snapped.

Lynnette didn't respond. She went into the bathroom and shut the door. A few minutes later, she reappeared. Robert was still in his chair. He said, "You know, the sad thing is you don't even feel you're wrong."

Lynnette sat down on the side of the bed. "So I'm supposed to feel guilty now? I'm just as upset with you right now as you are with me." She got up. "I'll sleep in one of the guest rooms tonight. I know we said we wouldn't go to bed angry anymore, but there's a lot of tension going on between us right now. I just need some time to think and clear my head."

Outside the bedroom door, Lynnette turned back to look at Robert and acknowledged, "I love you with all my heart, but I won't let you stop me from living."

The next day, Robert was talking with James and Carla as they sat in the Sinclairs' living room. Robert leaned forward with his hands clasped together as he explained Lynnette's behavior.

"I can't reason with her. She says I'm treating her like a child. I've tried to explain to her that I just want us to spend more time together like we said we would when Josh and Randa got older. All she wants to do is hang out with Simone." Robert gritted his teeth. "I can't stand that woman. I try to get along with her for Lynn's sake, but she's a bad influence. Lynn just can't see it."

Carla had never seen her brother so chafed before. However, she refused to show any signs of sympathy for him. "Robert, why don't you stop whining and just let her enjoy herself? I mean, after all, hasn't she always devoted herself to you and the kids? Now she wants some time for herself. What's the harm in that?"

"Honey," James told his wife, "it sounds to me like all Rob's asking is that she not leave him out."

Carla waved her hand in the air. "You men spend most of your lives doing what you want to do, and when the women want to do something, you act like babies."

James protested, "You can't put all men in the same category any more than we can put all women in the same one. And especially not Rob. You know he's not like that."

"I know he's not. He just needs to give her some time."

"Hey, guys," Robert said, waving his hand in the air. "In

case you forgot, I'm still here. I didn't mean to start a debate. I just needed someone to talk to."

Carla displayed a little compassion this time when she spoke. "I'm sorry, Robert. Just try to be patient with her. This is just a phase she's going through. Once she gets it out of her system, she'll be back to her old self."

"Maybe you're right," Robert agreed. "But my patience has just about run out. I don't know how much more of this I can take."

Carla reminded her brother, "You know Simone is like a sister to Lynn. For a very long time, Simone and her mother were the only real family she had. Despite Simone's short-comings, which I'm sure Lynn sees but just ignores because she loves her, they're like family. You may not like it, but that's the way it is. Just keep talking to her, telling her how you feel, and trust her to do the right thing."

James encouraged his brother-in-law. "Rob, keep praying about it, and it'll work out."

"I hope you're right." Robert stood. "I better go." He gave Carla a hug. "Thanks, sis." Then he and James shook hands. "Thanks, James. You two pray for us, okay?"

"We will," Carla and James promised.

On the way home, Robert thought about what Carla and James had said. He did know how close Lynnette and Simone were. He did not want to break them up. Yet at the same time, he did not want his family broken apart, and he felt in his heart that Simone was doing just that. Perhaps not intentionally but doing it just the same.

When he arrived home Robert was not in the best of moods. He had a lot on his mind. Lynnette cheerfully greeted him at the door. "I need to go to town. Will you come with me?"

"What for?" he asked.

"I can't tell you. It's a surprise."

Robert rubbed the back of his neck. "I'm kind of tired. I wanted to lay down. Can it wait?"

"No. Please come," Lynnette begged.

"All right," Robert agreed. *Here you go again. Always giving in to her. She's getting worse instead of better.* "Let's go."

As Robert and Lynnette got to the huge shopping center parking lot, Robert eyed the rows and rows of shiny classic automobiles. It was a car show. Lynnette knew how much he loved them.

Robert grinned. "Wow! How did you find out about this?"

Lynnette smiled as she parked her SUV. As they climbed out, she said, "This morning when I was leaving the grocery store, I found a flyer on the windshield. Do you like them?"

"Of course, I do. Come on." Robert pulled Lynnette by her hand in his effort to take in the sights of each and every car. They came upon a brightly polished 1957 blue-and-white Chevy Corvette. "Look at this one. Isn't she beautiful?"

"Yes, she is," Lynnette concurred.

Robert held Lynnette's hand as he escorted her around for two hours until they had taken in the sights of every automobile.

"Hey," Lynnette said, "there's a park right down the street. Let's get something to eat. It's a beautiful day. We can eat at the park and then go walking." She stuck her foot out and looked down. "We've both got our tennis shoes on."

"After what you did to poor Carla the other day," Robert reminded Lynnette, "I don't know if I should go walking with you."

Lynnette playfully poked Robert in the stomach and teased, "Are you chicken?"

Robert laughed. "No, but you just gave me an idea of what we can get to eat."

At the park, they found a vacant picnic table and ate their chicken and biscuits from KFC.

"I appreciate what you did today," Robert said. "I had a ball."

"You're welcome. I'm glad you enjoyed it. I know we haven't been seeing things eye-to-eye lately. I'm sorry you've been feeling neglected. Sometimes it's hard for me to maintain a balance between the things I need to do and the things I want to do."

"I'm sorry if I've been giving you a hard time. I just want us to do things together while we still can. Maybe I've been somewhat overdemanding. I'll try to be more patient."

"Thank you. I appreciate that."

"Ready to walk?" Robert asked as he started gathering their trash.

Lynnette clapped her hands. "Yeah. Let's do this."

As they walked the trail, they talked as they took in the odor of freshly baked bread coming from the nearby Flowers Dakery. They walked the trail twice.

"Come on, slowpoke," Robert called after Lynnette.

"Slow down. I'm coming." She caught up.

"You okay?"

"I'm fine. I guess I put my foot in my mouth, huh?"

They put their arms around each other.

Robert answered, "I guess you did, but I still love you."

"I love you, too."

"You ready to go home?"

Lynnette threw back her head in laughter. "Yes, take me home."

As they walked to their vehicle, they talked and held

hands. It was such a beautiful day. For a few moments, they had shut out the rest of the world and only focused their attention on each other. The Lynnette Robert had seen that day was the one he loved and missed. Would she ever come back to stay?

Chapter 14

Robert wanted everything to be perfect when Lynnette got home. She said she needed him to be patient and understanding. She desperately needed his support during this difficult period in her life. He wanted to do something special for her. He wanted her to know that as much as he wanted to be a part of her life he also wanted her to have the freedom to enjoy some of it without him. Since Joshua and Miranda were at work, this was the perfect opportunity for Lynnette and him to have a nice, romantic dinner at home.

As he removed the last crab cake from the black iron skillet, he smiled. Lynnette loved his crab cakes. He had left work early so he could beat her home and have everything ready when she walked through the door. Perhaps he had been behaving selfishly. He had to put his feelings aside and think about what she needed.

When he saw her vehicle pulling into the driveway, he

rushed to the dining room to light the candles on the table. He heard Lynnette yelling from the kitchen.

Mmm. Something smells good. "Hel-lo-o-o. Rob-ert? Honey, where are you?"

Robert almost bumped into her as he rushed into the kitchen. "Here I am," he answered with a wide grin.

Lynnette smiled and kissed him. "Hey. What are you doing home before me?"

"Hey. I left work early."

"You did?"

"Yeah." Robert went to the refrigerator and opened the door.

"What for?" Lynnette noticed the bottle of wine in his hand. "What are you up to?"

He grabbed her hand. "Come on. I'll show you."

She followed him into the dining room. The table was arranged beautifully with candles, flowers, and two place settings of their finest china. She smiled. "Well, this is nice. Is this for me?"

Robert walked her to her seat and pulled out her chair. "Well, I thought I'd join you, but if you prefer to dine alone, I guess I can eat in the kitchen by myself."

Lynnette laughed. "Don't be silly. I'd love for you to eat with me."

Robert leaned down and kissed her cheek. "Thank you." Then he sat beside her.

She turned and looked at her husband. "So what's the occasion?"

Robert took her hand in his and looked into her face. "I just wanted to do something special for my girl. I know you're going through a lot right now, and I haven't made it any easier for you. Not with all my whining and complaining. I'll try to be more supportive. I love you."

Lynnette leaned over and kissed Robert. "Oh, honey, that's so sweet. I love you, too."

"There's more. After we eat, I have another surprise for you."

"Okay."

After Robert took the lead in offering a prayer of thanks, they ate and talked.

Lynnette licked her fingers. "Honey, these crab cakes are delicious. You should make them more often."

"If I make 'em too often, you'll get tired of 'em. I'll just save 'em for special occasions."

"Well, this was really nice. Thank you."

"You're welcome. Now for the biggie." Robert got up. "Stay here. I'll be right back."

Lynnette had to stop herself from squirming in her seat with anticipation. When Robert returned, he sat back down and placed a large white envelope on the table in front of her. It had pink and white curly ribbons tied around it, and on the outside in large bold letters was written *To My Darling Wife.*

Lynnette grabbed the envelope and removed the ribbons. Then she opened it wide and poured the contents out onto the table. She wanted to make sure nothing had stayed behind so she peeked inside to see if the envelope was empty. On the table in front of her was an assortment of brochures.

She smiled. "Are we going somewhere?"

"No," Robert answered. *"We're* not. *You* are. Remember years ago when we went to Pine Mountain and took the kids?"

Lynnette smiled again. "Yes. It was so beautiful there. Josh and Randa loved it. When Carla found out about the tumors and the surgery, she wanted you and me to go there with her and James to help take my mind off things."

"You didn't tell me."

"I know. I told her we couldn't go. I just wasn't in the mood."

"What about now?"

"You mean by myself?"

"Sure. Just for the weekend. Everything's arranged and paid for. You can leave Friday afternoon—that's two days away—and come back Sunday." Robert fumbled through the brochures and pulled one out. He handed it to Lynnette. "This is the bed-and-breakfast where you'll be staying. It's near Callaway Gardens in case you want to go there. There're all kinds of shops and restaurants nearby. The rest of the brochures are other places you may find interesting.

"You need this trip. You deserve it. I'd like to go with you, but you need some quiet time to think and just enjoy yourself. I know I haven't been very supportive, and I've only added to your stress, and I'm sorry. So go and have a good time. When you come back, you can tell me all about it."

Lynnette smiled. "I do want to go. Maybe you're right. Maybe it's just the thing I need. I know what I'm going through isn't easy on you either, and I know it's hard for you to send me on this trip without you." She held down her head and shook it slowly. She smiled again. "I can't believe I'm actually going." She put her hand on Robert's. "Will you be okay while I'm away?"

He smiled. "Don't worry about me. I'll be fine. You just go and have a good time and hurry back to me."

"Okay."

Lynnette was extremely appreciative of Robert's love and support. She realized that this trip must have been a difficult decision for him. It touched her heart deeply that he had taken the initiative and done something so special for her. She would try to clear her head while she was away. Perhaps when she returned, things would be better.

* * *

Saturday afternoon, Simone smiled as she maneuvered her candy-apple red Mustang into the parking lot of the bed-and-breakfast inn where Lynnette was staying. She was shocked but extremely excited when Lynnette had called and invited her to join her on her getaway weekend trip.

Before Lynnette told her, Simone had no earthly idea where Pine Mountain, Georgia, was. She'd never even heard of it, but she'd take a trip to the moon and back just to have some time alone with Lynnette so they could have fun like they used to.

Lynnette was in for a special treat. As soon as Simone had gotten off the telephone with her, she had gotten on the Internet and looked to see what nightclubs were nearby. She found several in Columbus, Georgia, which was only about thirty miles south of Pine Mountain. They were going to have a ball!

Lynnette and Simone greeted each other in the inn's sitting area. They chatted for a few minutes before Simone decided to spring the surprise on her.

She asked, "So what did you want to do this afternoon?"

Lynnette answered, "Well, I was thinking we could go to Callaway Gardens. It's so beautiful there. You'll love it."

"I've got a better idea," Simone proposed. "There's a night-club about thirty minutes south of here in Columbus that I want to take you to."

Lynnette promptly shook her head. "I'm not going to some nightclub."

"Well, why not? You need to get out and have some real fun once in a while. Stop being a stick in the mud. We're just gonna go listen to some music, do some dancing."

Lynnette shook her head again. "No, I can't. I'm a married woman with two teenagers at home."

"So does that mean that you're not entitled to have a little fun every once in a while? Lynn, you need to loosen up. Robert's got you wound so tight. I'm surprised he let you come this far by yourself."

Robert didn't have her wound. Lynnette was tired of Simone making those kinds of comments. She was her own person. She could go to a nightclub if she wanted. The fact was that she had no desire to go. But Simone was right. She should go out and have a little fun. Where was the harm in that?

Lynnette merrily responded, "I'll go."

Simone jumped up out of her seat. "You're serious?"

"Yeah."

Simone could not believe it. "You're not pulling my leg, are you?"

Lynnette stood. "No, I'm not pulling your leg. Come up to my room with me. I need to shower and change."

Simone squealed, "Oh, this is gonna be fun." She grabbed Lynnette and hugged her.

Lynnette never would have guessed that her friend would be this happy about them having an evening out on the town. They laughed and talked as they went upstairs.

Robert could barely keep up with Joshua and Miranda.

Miranda yelled over her shoulder. "Come on, Daddy. Let's ride Thunder River."

"I'm coming, but this is the last ride. Then we're leaving."

"Aw, Dad," Joshua teased. "You're not conking out on us, are you?"

Robert finally caught up. "I'm already conked. I don't have the energy you two have. I'm not as young as I used to be."

Miranda hooked her arm in her father's. "Daddy, you'll never be old to me."

"Thank you, honey, but try telling that to my poor aching feet."

Joshua and Miranda giggled. They approached Thunder River and entered the line. After thirty minutes, it was finally their turn to board. The three of them got on, and the ride slowly took off.

As they glided over the water and under the waterfalls, they laughed hysterically. When they got off the ride, Robert was plenty wet, whereas Joshua and Miranda appeared to have only been sprinkled with a few drops of water.

Miranda pointed to her father and laughed. "Daddy, you're all wet."

Robert laughed. "You two tricked me. I told you I didn't want to sit in that spot."

All three laughed as they exited the park.

On the way home, they stopped to eat at Outback Steakhouse. As they sat in a booth waiting on their food, Miranda exclaimed, "Daddy, I had a good time. I'm glad you came with us."

"I enjoyed it, too, even though I'm not completely dry yet," their father teased.

"Oh, Daddy, the best part is getting wet," Miranda advised.

Robert chuckled. "That's easy for you to say. You and Josh barely got a drop on you."

"Hey, Dad," Joshua said, "remember when Randa and I were little and you and Mom took us on vacation, and Randa just ran up and jumped in the swimming pool at the hotel?"

"Yeah, I remember that."

Joshua continued, laughing, "Mom was screaming and yelling, 'Robert, get her! Get her! Get her!' You dove in the pool with all your clothes on."

Robert and Miranda laughed at Joshua's imitation of Lynnette yelling for Robert to get Miranda out of the pool. Their food arrived. After each said a silent prayer of thanks, they talked and laughed while they ate.

When they got home, Joshua and Miranda were so tired they promptly informed their father that they were going to bed. Upstairs in the master suite, Robert looked around the room longing to see Lynnette there. He missed her. She'd only been gone since the day before, but it seemed like forever. It wasn't the first time she'd been away without him, but the circumstances were different this time. She was always going on buying trips for her store, but now she had needed to be away from him.

Robert finally decided to go to bed. After laying there wide awake for several minutes, he came to the realization that he was not going to be able to fall asleep any time soon. He got up and went downstairs to the den and tried to watch television. He was laying on the sofa when Miranda was headed toward the kitchen and heard the television.

She came up beside him. "Daddy, are you okay?"

Robert reached for Miranda's hand and grasped it in his. "I'm fine, honey. I'm just watching a little TV. I couldn't sleep."

"You miss Mama, don't you?"

"Can't fool you, can I?"

"She'll be home tomorrow."

"I know. I'm just lonely without her."

"You want me to stay and keep you company?"

"No, that's okay, honey. You go on back to bed. I'll be fine."

"Okay, but don't stay up too late."

Robert grinned. "Yes, ma'am."

Miranda leaned down and kissed her father's cheek. "Good night, Daddy. I love you."

"Good night, sweetheart. I love you, too."

Robert finally drifted off to sleep with thoughts of Lynnette prancing in his head.

Lynnette smiled as she glanced around the club from the table where she and Simone sat. She swayed to the music. "This is nice."

Simone was pleased that her friend had loosened up and was having a good time. "See. I told you it would be fun."

Lynnette acknowledged, "I'd forgotten how much I enjoy the music and the dancing." There was a crowd of people on the dance floor. Even though she wasn't one of them, she was content just being in her seat swaying to the music.

Simone declared, "All you needed was a little shove. Are you glad you came now?"

Lynnette's smile grew wider. "Yeah."

Just then, a couple of men came over to their table. Lynnette began to grow nervous. She had not anticipated this happening. While Simone became completely engrossed in conversation with the one who had come up to her, Lynnette turned away from the one attempting to converse with her. The next thing Lynnette knew, Simone was headed to the dance floor leaving her alone with him. Lynnette wanted to scream at Simone not to leave her. As soon as Simone was out of her seat, he was in it. Lynnette felt extremely uncomfortable.

The man asked her, "Do you wanna dance?"

Lynnette dared not look at him. She stuttered, "N-no. I'm married."

"Married people dance."

Her abrupt response was, "Not this one."

"Well, if I had a pretty li'l wife like you, I wouldn't let her out of the house. Where's your husband?"

His words annoyed Lynnette. She snapped, "It's none of your business where my husband is. Will you just leave me alone?"

"You're pretty, but you're kinda stuck-up, ain't cha? You're nothing like your friend out there." He nodded toward the dance floor where Simone was dancing. "She's been on the floor with just about every guy in here tonight. Can't I have just one dance? Your husband won't know if you don't tell him." He leaned forward, and caressed her hand.

Lynnette briskly jerked her hand away then jumped out of her seat and escaped to the ladies' room. She felt nauseated. She waited a few minutes before she came out. She looked in the direction of their table and saw Simone sitting there talking with a different guy. She had to get out of this place. She headed over to the table.

Simone looked up. "Where have you been?"

Lynnette ignored her question and firmly asserted, "I need to go."

"What d'you mean? We just got here."

Lynnette reiterated, "I said I need to go."

Simone's gentleman friend was staring at Lynnette as though she was crazy, but Lynnette didn't care.

Lynnette knew she shouldn't have gone to the club with Simone. Her friend seemed to have a magnetic force that pulled men toward her. Whenever she and Simone went somewhere, Lynnette noticed how men stared at Simone. She should have known that the two of them going to such a spot would send unwanted advances in her direction. How could she have been so gullible.

Simone asked, "Lynn, what's the matter? You said you were having a good time. It's still early."

Lynnette snapped, "How many more times do I have to tell you I need to go?"

"Okay, okay," Simone said. "I'm coming." She turned back to the man and grabbed a napkin. Then she took a pen from her purse, scribbled something on it, and slid it across the table toward him. "Here's my number. Call me."

On the drive back to the inn, Simone scolded Lynnette. "Why are you so upset? All the man did was ask you to dance."

Lynnette was enjoying herself until that man had come along. Now she felt guilty. She shouldn't have gone.

"Simone, I'm married. I love Robert. That guy was flirting with me, and I didn't like it. Maybe you like that kind of stuff, but I don't. I knew we should have gone to Callaway Gardens."

Simone laughed, "Oh, they don't have men at Callaway Gardens?"

Lynnette gave her friend a cold, hard stare. "That's not funny."

"Well, Lynn, you're an attractive woman. Are you gonna get upset every time another man looks at you? If you are, maybe you do need to stay at home."

"Simone, you just don't get it, do you? You're single now. I'm still married. I should have known that when a man sees a woman out tonight like we were he'll assume she's available no matter what her marital status. I'm not blaming you. Just don't ask me to go anywhere like that again."

Seeing how upset her friend was caused Simone to say, "Okay. I'm sorry."

They drove in silence the rest of the way to the inn.

Sunday morning, Lynnette stood gazing out of her bedroom window at the bed-and-breakfast inn. She would be leaving in a couple of hours. She'd had a wonderful time up until the night before. She was ready to go home. She missed her family. She was still glutted with guilt about what had happened at the club. After a few more minutes, she forced herself from the window and headed downstairs for breakfast.

On the hour-and-a-half drive home, she endeavored to listen to the radio and admire the beauty of the countryside. Yet, she found it difficult to concentrate and didn't hear the music or see the scenery. Finally, she reached their neighborhood and pulled into their driveway.

The house was unusually quiet for Sunday afternoon. Lynnette heard the television and went into the den where she found Robert on the sofa fast asleep. She tiptoed up behind him, leaned over, and kissed him. He opened his eyes and smiled when he saw her. He reached back to gently pull her around to sit on the sofa with him.

"Hey," Robert greeted her. "When did you get here?"

"I just got here," she answered. "Did you miss me?"

"Of course I did. How was your trip?"

"It was wonderful, but I missed you."

"Well, I would be highly offended if you didn't. Welcome home." Robert started to get up.

Lynnette gently pushed him back down. "Don't get up. You look so peaceful. Where are Josh and Randa? What did you guys do while I was gone?"

"They're at the mall. We went to Six Flags yesterday."

"Did you have fun?"

"Yeah, we did. Are you hungry?"

"No, I'll eat something later. Right now, I'd just like to sit here and talk to you."

Lynnette stood. She lifted Robert's feet, sat back on the sofa, and placed his feet on her lap.

Robert asked, "So how was the bed-and-breakfast?"

"It was wonderful. It was within walking distance of some of the shops. I got you something."

Robert raised up a bit. "Where is it?"

"It's in the car. I'll give it to you later."

"Did you get to go to Callaway Gardens?"

An uneasy sensation came over Lynnette. "No."

"Why not? You really wanted to go."

Lynnette felt anxiety taking over her entire body. She had to tell him. She couldn't live with herself if she didn't. "Honey, I have to tell you something. You're gonna be upset when I do, but I can't keep it from you."

Robert sat up and put his feet on the floor. He looked at Lynnette. "What is it?"

She couldn't look at him. She chose to stare at the floor instead. "I called Simone yesterday and asked her to come meet me at the inn."

Robert felt a huge rush of hostility well up inside of him, yet he struggled to remain composed. "This trip was supposed to be so you could have some time to yourself to think. Why did you do that?"

"I don't know. I thought it would give us a chance to spend some time together like we used to. I miss that, you know."

Robert shook his head. "No, I don't know. All I know is when I wanted to take you to Apple Mountain, you weren't in the mood. So I figured you needed some time to yourself. I give you that, and when you get away, you call Simone."

Robert could hold his frustration back no longer and bounded up from the chair. He turned to stare down at Lynnette. "I don't understand you. What did you and Simone do? Pine Mountain isn't the kind of town that's exactly up her alley."

Lynnette hesitated. If he was this upset about her calling Simone, he would be furious when she told him about the club.

When she didn't answer him, Robert asked again, "Well, what did the two of you do?"

Lynnette felt a gigantic lump in her throat. She might as well tell him. The sooner she got it out, the better. She hoped.

"We went to a club last night," she almost mumbled under her breath.

Robert did not want to believe what he was hearing. He sat back down beside Lynnette and stared at her. "Did you say you went to a club?"

Lynnette still could not bring herself to look at him. "Yes."

"So do you want to tell me about it?" Robert waited for an answer.

Lynnette was close to tears. "Well, at first, I was having a good time. Then these two men came over and started talking to us. Simone started dancing with the one who was talking to her. When the other one asked me if I wanted to dance, I told him I was married." She covered her face with her hands as she cried. "Oh, Robert, I'm sorry."

Robert felt no sympathy for Lynnette. She should have known better. "Lynn, what did you think would happen? Two women together in a club surrounded by a bunch of men. Did you think they were just gonna walk over you as though you were invisible? I can't believe you let Simone talk you into this."

This time, Lynnette looked at Robert, tears spilling down her face. "I said I'm sorry. I don't know what I was thinking. I just wanted to go somewhere and have a little fun."

"Well, you did. Are you happy now?" Robert left Lynnette sitting on the sofa.

Lynnette felt as though the world was coming to an end. How could she have been so insensitive? Robert had obviously planned her trip very carefully so that she could find some refreshment for her soul, and she had destroyed what he had tried to do for her. She realized she had hurt him terribly, and it was a heavy burden to bear.

Chapter 15

Monday afternoon Lynnette was getting dinner ready when she heard the doorbell. It was Simone.

Simone apologized, "I'm sorry for stopping by without calling first."

Lynnette was still feeling melancholy. "That's okay. Come on in."

Simone sensed that she was still upset about what had happened in Columbus but decided against mentioning it. "You look like you're fixing supper. I won't stay long."

"I'm finished. I just put some biscuits in the oven. Let's go to the den."

Simone followed Lynnette into the den, and they sat on the sofa. Lynnette's entire day had been awful. She kept calling to mind how upset Robert was with her. She hadn't felt like conversing with anyone. Even at the moment, she feared that if she said another word she would burst into tears.

Simone asked, "So how are you?"

"Okay," Lynnette replied. That one simple word was enough to open the floodgates. Her lips began to tremble as tears slid down her face.

Simone moved closer and grabbed Lynnette's hand. "Lynn, what's wrong?"

With her head bowed, Lynnette slowly unleashed her grief. "I told Robert about the club and what happened. He's furious."

Simone wasn't the least bit surprised that Robert was not pleased. She wished she'd warned Lynnette not to tell him. But knowing her friend as she did, even if she had, Lynnette probably would have told him anyway. "He'll get over it. Just give him some time."

Lynnette grabbed a tissue from the Kleenex box beside her and wiped her face. "I don't know. He's really upset."

"Lynn, you didn't do anything wrong. All you did was go to a club. Some guy asked you to dance. You said no, and we left. You came home and told Robert what happened. If you'd been doing something wrong, you would've kept it a secret from him, but you didn't."

"I know, but he doesn't see it that way."

"He'll come around," Simone assured her friend.

They talked for a few more minutes before going to the kitchen to check on Lynnette's biscuits. Simone soon had her smiling again.

Simone sat down at the table while Lynnette removed her biscuits from the oven and placed them on top of the stove.

"Ooh, girl," Simone declared, "your biscuits smell delicious. Do you remember when we couldn't cook a biscuit to save our lives?"

"Yeah. They were hard as rocks," Lynnette said, laughing. "I almost chipped a tooth once or twice."

"We sure had a lot of fun trying though."

"We sure did." Suddenly, Lynnette jumped up and went over to the refrigerator. She took out a large tub of margarine and grabbed a knife from the silverware drawer. Then she sliced open two biscuits and spread margarine in the center and placed each one on a separate paper towel. She returned to her seat and handed one to Simone and kept the other for herself.

Lynnette quickly held up her hand. "Wait a minute. Something's missing."

Simone grinned as she watched her friend go back to the refrigerator and take out a juicy red tomato. Lynnette rinsed the tomato under some running water, then peeled and cut it into thick slices, and placed them on a saucer. She sat back down. They each grabbed a tomato slice and placed in between their biscuit.

Simone added, "Don't forget the salt and pepper."

Simone grabbed the salt and pepper shakers from the table, sprinkled some on her tomato slice, and passed the shakers on to Lynnette. Lynnette did the same. They picked up the tomato biscuits and bit off huge juicy chunks as wide grins spread across their faces.

Simone announced, "Now *that's* good eating. I haven't eaten a tomato biscuit in years."

"It is good," Lynnette concurred. "I could make a meal just out of these. Want another one?"

"I better not. I've got to go." Simone finished her biscuit, folded her paper towel in half, and dabbed at the corners of her mouth with it.

Lynnette jumped up and grabbed a Tupperware container from the cabinet. She placed a biscuit in one section and handed it to Simone. "Here. Put a tomato slice in the other half and you can take it with you."

"Thanks." Simone put a slice of tomato in the container and pressed on the lid. She stood and walked to the door. "Call me, okay?"

The friends hugged.

"I will."

A few minutes after Simone left, Robert came home. He was still annoyed at Lynnette although he tried not to let it show. Every time he thought about some man drooling over her, it made his temperature rise. At dinner, he noticed what a good mood she seemed to be in. "You must have had a good day."

Lynnette smiled. "I did. Simone stopped by the house this afternoon." She let out a giggle.

Robert hated hearing Simone's name now more than ever. "What's so funny?"

"Simone and I ate tomato biscuits when she was here."

Robert gazed at his wife. *I've been trying for four months to make her happy, and all I had to do was give her a tomato biscuit?* "Well, if eating a tomato biscuit makes you this happy, I wish you'd eat one every day."

Lynnette dabbed at her mouth with her napkin before placing it on the table beside her plate. "It was just such a good feeling. We used to eat them all the time when we were younger. It reminded me of all the good times we had. I sure do miss the seventies. Don't you?" She wiped up some gravy with a morsel of biscuit and popped it into her mouth.

"Not really. I'm happy with my life."

"Those were the good ol' days. Life was good. I miss that era."

"That kind of thinking will only make you dissatisfied with what you have now. You should think more about the present."

"I do think about the present, but my past, as painful as some of it was, is a big part of who I am."

Robert wasn't pleased with what Lynnette was saying.

"You make it sound like you're not happy with your life now. Like you have regrets."

"Honey, that's not what I'm saying."

Robert stared at his wife. He was fed up. "Then what are you saying? I'm tired of breaking my neck around here to make you happy, when all I get in return is grief. You don't want to go away with me anywhere so I take the time to plan a trip for you. You go off, call up your girlfriend, and the two of you go out partying. It's obvious I'm not making you happy."

"I didn't say you don't make me happy. Of course you do. I was just trying to share my feelings with you. You don't have to feel threatened by everything I say and do."

"Lynn, what did you think about this past weekend while you were gone? When you weren't off gallivanting with Simone, did you stop to think about your family?"

"Yes, I thought about you and the kids. I thought about my life and how everything has changed in the past few months. Sometimes I'm laughing on the outside, but I'm crying on the inside. I don't know. Sometimes it's just hard to explain."

Robert didn't comment. He was fed up with her attitude. He did not know how much more of it he could take. He felt like he was going insane.

Lynnette's breathing was soft. She was sleeping like a baby. Robert wished he could do the same. It was two a.m. He got out of bed and went to his recliner and sat down. He was still pondering over his and Lynnette's conversation at dinner.

Lynnette called out his name, interrupting his thoughts. "Robert?"

"I'm over here," he answered.

She sat up and mumbled sleepily, "Honey, what are you doing out of bed? What's wrong?"

Robert got up. He felt like snapping at her but kept himself from doing so. Still, his tone was dogmatic. "Nothing's wrong. Everything's fine. Go back to sleep." He walked to his side of the bed and got in.

Lynnette laid back down and snuggled beside him. "Good night, honey."

"Good night." Robert pushed his negative thoughts aside and hoped he'd be able to get a peaceful night's sleep.

On Wednesday night, Rose had invited Lynnette, Robert, Carla, and James to her house for supper. After they had finished eating, Rose noticed Robert slipping out the front door. When she got an opportunity, she followed him. She stepped out onto the porch. The light was off, but she could see Robert on the swing in the glow that radiated through the living room window. She walked toward him. "Are you all right?"

Robert looked at Rose. "Yes, Ms. Rose. I'm fine."

"Do you mind some company?"

Robert slid over so Rose could join him. "No. Have a seat." He let out a light chuckle and added, "After all, it is your swing on your porch attached to your house."

Rose laughed. "You're awful." Then on a more serious note, she added, "You sure are quiet tonight. I'm not trying to be nosy, but is something wrong?"

"I've just got a lot on my mind. That's all."

"Are you still worried about Lynn?"

Robert sighed. "Yes. You know, she wouldn't come with me to Apple Mountain. When I wanted to take her a few months ago I thought she needed some time alone, so I arranged the trip to Pine Mountain to ease her stress, but when she gets there she calls up Simone, and they go out clubbing. She comes home still carrying on like she's dissatisfied with her life."

Rose had reckoned that the stress of what Lynnette was going through was also hitting Robert pretty hard. "She's going through a lot right now, and no matter what you do, no matter what you say, you can't make it better until she's ready to make it better. Right now, she feels lost and confused. I bet you're probably feeling a little lost and confused yourself, aren't you?"

"I am. I'm a little ashamed, too. I arranged the trip for her to have some time to relax and think, but deep down I was hoping that when the new Lynn left the old one would come back. It didn't turn out the way I hoped it would."

Rose patted Robert's hand. "I know you don't foresee it now, but things will get better. You'll see."

At that moment, Lynnette stepped out onto the porch. "Here you two are. Honey," she said to Robert, "we better be going. I've got an early appointment in the morning."

Robert leaned over, kissed Rose's cheek, and whispered "Thank you" in her ear. He stood. "Okay, I'm ready."

Rose stood. She and Lynnette hugged.

Rose declared, "I guess I better get back to my other guests. Bye, you two."

"Bye."

On the ride home, Lynnette noticed Robert was unusually quiet. "Why were you sitting out on the porch? I turned for a brief second and you were gone."

Robert mumbled, "I'm surprised you noticed."

"Now, Robert, what is that supposed to mean?"

"Around other people, you laugh and talk and have a good time. Around me, you're all gloomy."

"That's not true. Why do you always have to pick a fight?"

"I'm sorry if it seems that way. I'm not trying to pick a fight. It just seems to me that you enjoy being around other people more than you do me."

Lynnette folded her arms and stared at her husband. "Robert, what is wrong with you? I can't seem to do anything right where you're concerned. If I'm happy, I'm too happy. If I'm sad, I'm too sad."

As they approached their neighborhood, Robert slowly pulled the Suburban on the side of the road. He moved the gear to park and faced Lynnette. "Calm down," he told her.

"Don't tell me to calm down. You're the one who needs to calm down. Why are you constantly on my back about everything I do?"

"The trip to Pine Mountain was supposed to cheer you up. You came back home talking about good times from the past. I feel like you're miserable with me. I feel…"

Lynnette screamed, *"You* feel! Everything is about you. You think a weekend trip can erase a lifetime of pain?" She unlocked the door and jumped down onto the ground.

Robert sat there staring at her in disbelief. "Lynn, what are you doing?"

"I'm walking the rest of the way home." She slammed the door and started walking.

Robert got out of the truck and started after her. "I'm sorry. I didn't mean to upset you. You can't walk home. Get back in the truck." He touched Lynnette's arm as he attempted to stop her.

She snatched her arm away and kept walking. "Don't touch me," she snapped.

Robert continued following her. "Lynn, I said I'm sorry. Don't do this. Will you just get back in the truck? I'm sorry." He came around in front of her, walking backward as he pleaded, "Don't let our neighbors see us out here like this. Please get back in the truck."

Lynnette stopped in her tracks. Robert walked slowly to her and put his arms around her. "I'm sorry," he whispered.

She gently put her arms around Robert's waist and buried her head in his chest but didn't say a word.

He whispered in her ear, "Let's go home."

As they walked back to the truck with their arms around each other, neither said a word.

The next morning at breakfast, Robert and Lynnette attempted to act normal in the presence of Joshua and Miranda.

As soon as the kids left for school, Robert said, "You're still upset with me. I can tell."

Lynnette slowly shook her head. "No, I'm not. I can't believe I acted like that last night. I can't believe I actually got out of the truck and threatened to walk home."

The next thing they knew, they were both laughing hysterically.

Robert said, "That has to be the most embarrassing thing we've ever done."

"Tell me about it."

Their laughter subsided as quickly as it had begun.

Lynnette admitted, "I don't ever want to go through anything like that again. I'm really sorry I lost my temper like that."

A few minutes later, Robert was on his way. Lynnette went upstairs, showered, and got ready for her day.

At twelve o'clock, Lynnette met Simone for lunch at the Golden Corral in Douglasville. As they ate and chatted, Simone asked Lynnette how she was feeling.

Lynnette answered, "Okay, I guess. Sometimes I feel like I'm losing my mind. Last night, Robert and I were on our way home from Rose's, and I got mad at him about something he said. When he stopped the truck to talk to me, I just went crazy. I got out and threatened to walk the rest of the way home. This morning, we laughed about it, but it's kind of scary. I've never acted like that before."

"You're going through a lot right now. Robert knows that. This is a time in your life when you have to think about yourself and what you need. Don't you ever get tired of taking care of everybody else?"

Lynnette was feeling bad enough as it was without having to listen to Simone's shrewish comments. What she needed was to be lifted up. "Simone, don't start."

Simone ignored her. "Don't you ever just want to walk away and do something for yourself? You push yourself too much, you know that?"

Lynnette loved Robert and the kids. They were her life. The truth was she did want to do something for herself. Sometimes she wished she could be more like Simone. Just pick up and come and go as she pleased without having to answer to anybody. However, she realized the danger in such thinking. Yet it did nothing to obliterate her feelings for more independence.

Chapter 16

It was a Wednesday night in late April. All of the Montgomery clan, except for Lynnette, were sitting around the kitchen table. They had just finished saying the blessing when the telephone rang.

As Robert got up to answer the call, he commented to Joshua and Miranda, "Maybe it's your mom."

The two siblings attempted to eat as they eavesdropped on their father's conversation. He sounded annoyed.

"Lynn," Robert tried to whisper, "do you realize it's eight o'clock, and your family has been waiting more than an hour for you to get home so you can have supper with them? How come you didn't call earlier?"

On the other end of the line, Lynnette remarked, "Robert, Josh and Randa won't mind if I miss one meal with them. They're teenagers now."

"That's how it starts," Robert continued. "First, one meal.

Then two. Then three. They'll just keep adding up. What's so important that you're willing to sacrifice dinner with your family?"

"Simone and I—"

Before he could stop himself, Robert bellowed, "Simone! I should have known. Ever since she moved here, you've been spending all your time with her."

"We just want to catch this sale at the mall. The stores close at nine so I'll be home around ten."

"You can't do this over the weekend?"

"The sale ends today. Robert, let's not argue. Tell Josh and Randa I'll see them at ten. I've got to go."

Robert was annoyed. "I'll talk to you when you get home. Bye." He hung up before Lynnette could say anything else.

Lynnette pressed the end button on her cell phone and placed it back in the pouch inside her purse. She rested her elbow against the car window and rubbed her forehead with her fingers.

Simone looked at her from the driver's seat as she spoke. "What's the matter? Robert got his underwear in a wad again 'cause you're doing something without him?"

Lynnette didn't say anything.

"Lynn, come on. Don't worry about it," Simone said. "You're a grown woman. So what if your husband wants you to be home at a certain time. Once these men marry you, they think they become your master."

Lynnette didn't look at Simone but spoke softly, "Robert's not like that."

"Yeah, that's what you say. That's not what it sounded like a minute ago. Cheer up. Try not to think about Robert for a while. I'm sure your mind could use the rest."

Lynnette couldn't take her mind off Robert. He was her

husband, and she loved him. Why did he have to get so upset when she wanted to do something on her own?

Robert returned to his seat. "That was your mom. She won't be able to have supper with us tonight. She'll see us about ten."

Joshua and Miranda looked at each other.

"Daddy, are you okay?" Miranda inquired.

"I'm fine, honey," Robert said, picking up his fork. "Let's just eat."

After supper, the threesome tidied up the kitchen. When Lynnette arrived home around eleven, she looked in on Miranda first. Miranda was standing beside her bed, which was covered with clothes still on the hangers.

"Hey, sweet pea," Lynnette greeted her daughter as she placed one arm around her. "Sorry I'm late. What are you doing?" She glanced down at the clothes on the bed.

"Trying to find an outfit to wear to school tomorrow. Which one do you like?"

Lynnette was pleased that her teenage daughter was still interested in her opinion. She reached down and picked up a pair of alabaster pants with ankle slits and a persimmon-colored stretch shirt. "I love these. When did you get them?"

"Last weekend when Sharon and I went shopping."

Lynnette nodded her head in approval. "Nice. I like your style. I'm sorry I missed dinner. Are you upset?"

"No, but I think Daddy is. After he talked to you, he didn't have too much to say during dinner."

"I'll talk to him. How was school?"

"Fine. How was your day?"

"It was okay. Well, let me go look in on Josh. I'll see you in the morning. Good night." Lynnette kissed her daughter's cheek.

After Lynnette spent a few minutes with Joshua, she found

Robert in the den. As he sat at the desk reviewing some blue-prints, Lynnette walked over to a nearby chair and sat down.

"I know you're upset that I got home late," she uttered. "Simone and I were hungry after shopping so we stopped at a Thai restaurant."

Robert didn't look up but kept his eyes glued to the blue-prints. "Why would I be upset? Just because of your thought-less disregard for your family and their feelings? Because you would rather spend all your time away from your family? Never mind us. You just go ahead and enjoy yourself. Maybe we'll still be around when you finish."

Lynnette acknowledged, "I guess I deserved that."

"I guess you did." Robert looked at her. "You know, it's one thing to push me away, but I won't stand for you doing it to Josh and Randa."

"Robert, you're acting like I've abandoned my family. There are just some things I need to do now for me."

"At what cost are you willing to do them? At all costs? One day Josh and Randa are going to venture out on their own. Right now, you still have a little time left with them. You need to make the most of it. And as for me, I married you for better or worse. You know I take our vows seriously, but don't expect me to sit around here and let you treat me like a doormat."

Lynnette stared at her husband in disbelief. "Are you saying you'll leave if I don't do everything your way?"

"I don't want everything my way. Marriage is give and take. That applies to both of us. I love you. I'd go to the moon and back for you. I've tried to be understanding of your situa-tion, and I've tried to be supportive.

"You're so wrapped up in what you're going through that you don't seem to care about anyone else. I don't know who you are anymore. You want your independence, and you're pushing your family away. Maybe we need some time away from each other. Maybe I should go to a hotel or see if I can stay with James and Carla for a while."

Lynnette was shocked at what Robert was suggesting. Their marriage had never been to the point of their separating. "I admit I've made some bad decisions lately, but nothing that warrants that."

"In your opinion."

"Well, what you're saying is your opinion."

"What I'm saying is factual. Let me ask you a question. One night when you were telling me about your feelings for your mother, you asked me how would I feel if the shoe were on the other foot. Now I want to ask you that same question. How would you feel if I were putting my desires ahead of my family's emotional needs?"

With those words, the realization of what she had been putting Robert through hit Lynnette like a brick. "You're absolutely right. I wouldn't like it at all. I've been unfair."

"I'm not asking you not to have interests outside of the family. I'm just asking you to keep room in your life for us, too. You're a great mother and wife, and you deserve some time for yourself. It wouldn't be reasonable of me to try to deny you that."

Lynnette hung her head. "I know you're not like that. I've been acting so crazy lately."

Robert got up and walked over to her. He got down on his knees in front of her and lifted her chin. "It's not just you. We both have our moments."

As they hugged, Lynnette wished she could rewind their lives to before things had gotten so chaotic and complicated. She wished she could go back to the woman she was, but things were different. Robert didn't understand. Sometimes she didn't even understand it herself.

* * *

"You're kind of quiet today," Carla commented to her sister-in-law as they ate lunch at LaFiesta. "What's the matter?"

"It's Robert," Lynnette responded. "He got upset with me a couple of days ago because I missed supper and went shopping with Simone. He even suggested that maybe we need some time apart. I can't get him to understand that I'm at a point where I need to explore life in ways that I haven't before. I didn't have a real family when I was growing up so I made him and the kids my whole world. I still want to spend time with them, but I also need some time for myself.

"I know I've been acting crazy lately. I told him that, but the thing is, I'm still craving some independence. Don't misunderstand me, Carla." Lynnette smiled as she confessed, "I love Robert. I love him with all my heart. I want us to spend time together, but I also want a life outside of him and the kids. Do you understand what I'm saying?"

Carla nodded as she placed her glass on the table. "I think so. Robert loves you. He's just feeling a little left out of your life right now. It's hard to balance all our responsibilities at times. Sometimes in the process, people get their feelings hurt."

Lynnette agreed as she nodded. "That's true. Do you and James ever experience problems finding time to be together?"

"Sure we do, but your situation is different from ours. You have two children—and two teenagers at that. This can be a difficult time for them as well as you and Robert, and jealousy is probably a factor in all of this."

Lynnette thought for a moment. "You know, Robert and I have really been at odds with each other lately. Whenever I want to spend time with Simone, he gets all crazy." She rolled her eyes heavenward.

Against her better judgment, Carla decided to question her sister-in-law about Simone, the source of Robert's provocation.

"Didn't she and her mother more or less take you in as part of the family when you were younger?"

"Yes. I didn't actually live with them, but I spent a lot of time at their house. Simone's like a sister. She and Robert don't get along that well though. She can be overbearing at times, but she's got my best interests at heart."

"Are you sure about that?" Carla questioned before she was able to stop herself. She had been determined she would not get involved. She did not want Lynnette to think she was taking sides with Robert against her.

Lynnette was stunned at Carla's judgmental question. She looked at her sister-in-law. "What do you mean?"

Carla attempted to choose her words carefully. "Well, I just meant that sometimes when we care about someone, we fail to see the negative effect they're having on us."

Lynnette's mouth fell open. "Has Robert been talking to you about Simone?"

Carla purposely failed to answer Lynnette's question. "He's really concerned about you. Just be careful about who you associate with. You know, people's habits, bad or good, can rub off on us."

Lynnette was perturbed at both Robert and Carla. Her voice was stern when she spoke. "I appreciate your concern, Carla, but I didn't know you were in the habit of judging people you hardly know."

Carla felt awful. She wished she had not opened her mouth. "Lynn, I'm sorry. I didn't mean to upset you. It's just that I care about you. That's the only reason I said anything."

Lynnette's voice softened somewhat. "I know you care about me. I'm sorry, too."

They talked some more while they ate. However, Lynnette was still fuming at Robert. She just knew he had been bad-mouthing Simone.

Finally, the waitress approached their table with their bills.

"Well," Lynnette said, "I guess we better get going. I have a couple of appointments this afternoon."

The two women stood.

"Yeah. I've got some appointments, too," Carla stated.

Lynnette and Carla paid their bills and left.

Lynnette asked, "What time are Robert and I supposed to meet you and James tonight? If I miss another Friday night out, he'll pitch a fit."

They reached their vehicles, parked beside each other, and stopped behind Lynnette's Land Rover.

"James and I were thinking of letting you guys have tonight to yourselves. You need some time together, just the two of you. Maybe we can get together next Friday."

"That's sweet. Are you sure you don't mind?"

"Sure, we're sure."

Lynnette and Carla hugged.

"Still friends?" Carla asked.

Lynnette smiled. "Of course."

"Have a good afternoon. Love you," Carla said.

"Thanks. You, too. Love you back."

Yes, everything was okay between her and Carla, but Lynnette was still upset with Robert. Carla would never have said those things had Robert not been putting Simone down to her.

Lynnette was quiet on the ride to Douglasville's Red Lobster as Robert attempted to make light conversation.

"That was really nice of James and Carla to let us have tonight to ourselves," Robert commented.

"Yes, it was," was Lynnette's simple reply.

Silence filled the air as Robert drove and Lynnette stared out her window. She was trying hard not to bring up her conversation with Carla, but it was all she could think about.

Suddenly, she asked, "What have you been telling James and Carla about Simone?" Lynnette turned to stare at Robert.

Robert was caught off guard and stalled in an effort to come up with an answer to her question that wouldn't have them arguing again. He stole a quick glance at Lynnette. "What? Why are you asking me that?"

"Today at lunch, Carla and I had an interesting conversation about Simone. Carla was telling me how people's bad habits can rub off on us. I know you've been talking about Simone to her and James so you may as well admit it."

Robert didn't say anything. He still had not thought of a good answer.

He was not thinking fast enough for Lynnette. She asked again, "Have you been telling them negative things about Simone?"

Robert finally admitted, "Okay. Yeah, I did. I needed somebody to speak with, and I talked to them. I couldn't have a conversation with you. Every time I try to talk to you about certain things, we end up arguing."

"Robert, you know how much Simone means to me. How could you do that?"

"I'm sorry. Don't I mean anything to you? You act like the sun rises and sets on Simone."

"Robert, you know that's not true. You know I love you. Why do we have to keep arguing about this? Can't you give me a break?"

"I'm sorry. You're the one who brought it up. I don't want to argue. I just want us to enjoy our night out together. I'm sorry I bad-mouthed Simone to James and Carla. From now on, I'll try not to say anything negative about her."

Lynnette was still annoyed but managed to find some humor in Robert's last statement. "Yeah, right."

Robert looked at her. "Well, if I say anything, it'll be to you, nobody else."

Lynnette shook her head in disbelief and turned back to look out her window so Robert couldn't see her grin. *Either I'm going to be gray headed or bald dealing with Simone and Robert.*

During dinner, Lynnette was aware of Robert gazing at her. She asked, "What's wrong?"

"Are you still angry with me?"

Lynnette popped a piece of lobster into her mouth. "No. Why?"

"Well, I know you think I've been giving you a hard time lately, and James and Carla cancelled our plans tonight for us. I just don't want you to be angry that it's just you and me here."

Lynnette touched her husband's hand. "I'd never get angry at you for wanting to be with me. I love you, and I want to be with you. In the future, I'll try to be more considerate of you and your feelings when deciding how much of my time to spend away from you. Now, can we talk about something else?"

"Sure. Just let me go to the restroom first. I'll be right back."

When Robert returned, he saw a woman standing at their table talking to Lynnette. *Simone!* He couldn't seem to get this woman out of his hair. She was like the plague.

Lynnette knew Robert was chafed upon seeing Simone, but she appeared cheerful. "Honey," she said, "look who's here."

Robert and Simone shook hands. He attempted to be civil. "Hi, Simone. How are you?"

"I'm fine, Robert. How are you?"

"Good." Robert sat down while the ladies talked.

Finally, Simone said, "Well, I'll let you two get back to your dinner. Lynn, let me know if you change your mind. Robert, it was good seeing you again."

Robert nodded.

When Simone was gone, Robert asked, "What did she mean let her know if you change your mind?"

Lynnette didn't want her and Robert arguing again. She could kill Simone for making that statement in his presence. Simone knew how Robert was. "Nothing."

Robert wasn't buying it. "No, it's not nothing. It's something. What is it?" he insisted.

Lynnette dreaded telling him, but she decided to go ahead and get it out of the way. He wasn't going to stop harassing her about it until she did. "She's having a few of her friends at her house tomorrow. She invited me," Lynnette mumbled.

Robert let out a heavy sigh. "She acts like you don't have a family at home. Just because she doesn't have a life doesn't mean you don't have one."

Lynnette stared disapprovingly at her husband. "Robert, don't be like that. I think she's lonely now that she and Marshall are divorced and Samantha's away at college."

"Lonely. I can relate to that. That's exactly how I feel when you're off gallivanting with her."

"Robert," Lynnette pleaded, "please stop."

Robert thought about their argument on the way to the restaurant. It seemed that most of their squabbles lately were about Simone. The woman made his blood boil. "I'm sorry. I just don't like you hanging around her. I don't like the effect she has on you."

Lynnette leaned forward a little and attempted to whisper. "Robert, I am my own person. What I do, I do because of me and not anyone else. Can we please change the subject and enjoy the rest of our meal?"

As they finished eating, Lynnette thought, *I'm so tired of all this arguing. I love him, but he has just about gotten on my last nerve.*

Chapter 17

Saturday the weather was beautiful and just right for gardening as Rose and Miranda planted flowers in Rose's flower bed on the side of the house.

"Are you tired yet?" Rose inquired of her young assistant as they knelt on knee cushions digging in the moist soil.

Miranda wiped the beads of sweat from her forehead with the back of her gloved hand. "No, ma'am. Just hot."

Rose agreed. "Me, too. We've only got a few more. I've got us a nice, cold pitcher of lemonade in the refrigerator. Let's finish up, and then we'll get us a glass. Okay with you?"

"Yes, ma'am."

They set out the four remaining plants and went inside to wash up.

Rose removed two chilled glasses from the freezer and filled them with the cold, lemony liquid. She joined Miranda at the kitchen table. "You're probably going to be too tired for your lesson this afternoon. I shouldn't have worked you so hard."

Miranda took a sip of lemonade, allowing it to trickle down her warm throat. She smiled. "I'm fine. I had fun. I can still play the piano."

"You're so full of energy, aren't you? I remember when I was your age. Now I do good to make it from one room to the next."

"Don't say that, Ms. Johnson. You still seem to have a lot of energy to me. Mama's always talking about how spunky you are." Miranda paused. "Mama really likes you. I do, too. I hope you don't mind me saying this, but it's just like having a grandmother."

Rose was flattered at Miranda's sentiment but felt a lump in her throat the size of a cantaloupe.

Miranda continued, "Josh and I never knew any of our grandparents except for Granny Lil. She was Daddy's mama. She died a few years ago. I sure do miss her. She always kept peanut butter and apple jelly in her pantry just for me and Josh. Every time we went to her house, we'd make peanut butter and jelly sandwiches."

As Rose listened to Miranda rave about her grandmother, a huge piece of her heart ached as she contemplated the pain Miranda's family must have endured in their time of sorrow. "Your Granny Lil sounds like she was a special person."

Miranda smiled and took another sip of lemonade. "She was." After pausing, she asked, "Ms. Johnson, are your parents still living?"

"No, sweetie. They passed away many, many years ago."

Miranda nodded. "Oh. I'm sorry."

"Thank you." Rose was getting an uncomfortable feeling in the pit of her stomach so she tried to change the subject. "So how is school?"

"Okay, I guess."

"Are you sure? You don't sound very enthusiastic."

"Well, I'm not doing too good in history."

"What do you think the problem is?"

Miranda held down her head, covered her mouth and snickered, "It's boring. Who wants to hear about a bunch of stuff that happened hundreds of years ago?"

"Have you tried making it interesting?"

Miranda's eyes grew large. "How do I do that?"

"Well, when the teacher goes over the lesson or you're reading it, have you ever tried picturing the scenes in your head?"

Miranda giggled again. "No, but I have tried picturing myself somewhere else, like the mall or the movies."

Rose let out a giggle of her own before she realized it was coming.

"But I see your point," Miranda went on. "When I read a book I like, I form mental pictures of the scenes. So maybe if I do history the same way, it'll be more interesting."

Rose smiled. "Exactly."

Miranda stood with her glass in her hand and picked up Rose's empty glass from the table. "Would you like some more lemonade?"

"No, thank you, dear."

Miranda rinsed the glasses and placed them in the dishwasher. As she dried her hands on a paper towel, she informed Rose, "I'm going home to bathe and change. I'll be back at five for my lesson unless you're too tired."

Rose stood. "Oh no. I'm fine. Five is good." She held out her arms. "Give me my hug before you go."

Miranda giggled as she backed away from Rose. "I'm sweaty, and I smell."

Rose laughed. "I don't care. So am I. Now get over here."

Miranda laughed as she fell into Rose's outstretched arms. "I love you, Ms. Johnson."

"I love you, too, Randa." Miranda's words brought tears to Rose's eyes. It was the best thing she'd heard in a while.

"Mom's gonna flip when she sees the fish we caught," Joshua boasted to his father on the ride home.

"She sure is," Robert agreed. "We're gonna have to clean 'em though. You know she hates to do that."

"Do you think we can have a fish fry tonight and invite Jeremy?" Joshua liked to include his friend in some of their family activities since Jeremy's father was deceased.

"Maybe. Let's check with your mom."

"Dad." Joshua looked at his father with a serious expression on his face. "Is Mom okay?"

"She's fine." Robert felt guilty for not being totally honest with his son. The only other thing he could think of to say was, "Why?"

"Well, I know something's been bothering her these last few months, and she's not home as much as she used to be. The night she skipped dinner, you seemed upset."

Robert attempted to reassure his son. "Don't worry. Mom's fine. She's just going through some things right now. Turning forty was a little hard for her. She just needs to have a little time for herself. We have to be patient and understanding and show her that we love her."

Joshua nodded in agreement.

Robert pulled into the garage. Joshua put up their fishing poles and assisted his father in getting the cooler of fish into the kitchen.

"Robert. Josh. What are you doing? I just finished mopping

in here," Lynnette said, frowning. "You're tracking up the floor. Did you wipe your feet?"

Robert and Joshua placed the cooler on the counter. "We're sorry, Mom," Joshua apologized. "Come look at the fish we caught."

Lynnette walked over reluctantly and took a look. "They're beautiful. When are you going to cook them?"

Robert answered, "Josh wants to have a fish fry tonight and invite Jeremy."

"That's fine," Lynnette stated. "You'll have to do it without me though. I'm going out."

Joshua's excitement soon turned to disappointment. "Oh."

"Honey, I'm sorry. I already made plans. You and your dad always clean these anyway." Lynnette motioned toward the cooler of fish. "You both know how to cook them. You can still have your fish fry."

"I guess so," Joshua said. He looked at Robert. "Dad?"

"Sure. We can do that."

"See you, sweetie." Lynnette kissed Joshua's forehead and scurried upstairs.

As she rummaged through her closet, Robert approached her. "What are you doing?"

Without taking her eyes away from the array of clothes, Lynnette's reply was, "Looking for something to wear."

"You know what I mean. Is doing your own thing so important that you can't give your son a little of your time?"

"Robert, are you going to start that again? I have plans. Besides, how was I supposed to know that Josh would want to have a fish fry?"

"You knew we went fishing. You always cook some of the fish after we catch them."

Lynnette pulled a pair of khaki pants and a yellow long-sleeve cotton blouse from the closet and laid them on the bed. Then she went into the bathroom and started running her bath water. She stepped back into the bedroom and started looking through her jewelry armoire. "Why does everything around here always have to be so routine? Sometimes I want to do something different."

Robert stood with his arms folded. "You're being selfish."

Lynnette turned to stare at him in disbelief. "I'm being selfish? You know, all you do is complain that I'm neglecting you. Like now. You're not upset that I won't be here for a fish fry for Josh. You're upset because I'm going out without you."

"That's ridiculous."

"Oh, is it?"

Robert refused to answer and asserted instead, "So I guess you decided to go to Simone's after all."

"Robert, do we have to have this discussion every time I go out with Simone?"

"Lynn, Simone's a single woman now. You're still married with a family. You need to get your priorities in order."

"My priorities are in order. Why don't you find a hobby or spend some time with some of your own friends? We just went out last night. Do we have to be in each other's face all the time?"

Robert was shocked and deeply hurt at Lynnette's choice of words. He was not pleased that she considered them to be in each other's face when they spent time together. She certainly didn't seem to mind being in Simone's face all the time. "I'm not saying you have to spend all your time with me."

"Well, that's how you're acting."

"Your seventeen-year-old son wants to spend a night at home with his family, which is rare since he's usually busy doing something else. You're going to want this time back one day, and he won't be interested."

They heard the telephone ring. Neither bothered to answer it and continued talking.

"Robert, I'm delighted Josh wants to be home for a change, but am I not allowed some time to do some of the things I want to do? How many times do we have to talk about this?"

Just then, Joshua could be heard from the hallway. "Mom! Telephone. It's Sister Dotson."

Lynnette called out, "Honey, I can't talk to her right now. Take a message, please."

Robert was not pleased that Lynnette would not even stop what she was doing to take a few minutes of her time to talk to Josephine. She and Henry were the ones Lynnette had turned to for prayer and guidance when she'd first found out about the surgery. In his mind, Lynnette was shutting out everyone who meant something to her other than Simone. He was about to tell her so.

Lynnette closed the armoire and stood in front of Robert. "Is that too much to ask? I've always been here for you and the children. I will always be here, but you have to give me the freedom to live my life without you as well as with you. That's all I'm asking. Do you understand? It doesn't mean I love you less or that I don't want to spend time with you. We're one, you and I." Lynnette pointed to Robert, then herself. "But I am also an individual. Do you understand what I'm saying?"

Robert looked forlorn. *Please help me to be patient with her.* He unfolded his arms and wrapped them around Lynnette. "I do. It's just that sometimes I feel like I'm losing you. I don't want us to grow apart. We used to be so close."

"We still are. Spending time apart doesn't mean we aren't. I love you, and nothing's going to change that."

Robert didn't think that his and Lynnette's marriage had ever been tested to the degree that it was now. He felt them being drawn apart, and he was beginning to think Simone was doing it purposefully.

As Miranda finished the last note on the piano, Rose exclaimed, "That was wonderful, Randa. You're coming along beautifully."

Miranda, proud of her accomplishment, smiled. "Thank you. I can't wait until I'm good enough to play for my family. They'll be surprised."

"Well, they certainly are in for a treat." Rose stood. "Are you hungry? I can fix us something to eat."

Miranda got up from the piano bench. "I'm starved, but let's go out to eat. My treat."

Rose's face lit up. "Okay, but I can't let you pay for me."

Miranda hugged Rose. "But I want to. You do so much for me. You're giving me free piano lessons. I want to show my appreciation. Please."

Rose thought for a few seconds. "Well-l-l, okay. Let me get my purse."

"Okay. I'll drive. You're not scared to ride with me, are you?"

"Heavens no." Rose smiled. "I trust you. I'll be right back."

They ate dinner at Ruby Tuesday and talked nonstop.

"You are so mature for your age," Rose commended Miranda. "I find that an admirable quality in a young person such as yourself."

Miranda half-smiled. "Well, I'm glad somebody likes it. All my friends say I'm too serious. They think I don't know how to have fun."

"Why do they think that?"

"Josh tells me I don't smile enough. I guess he's right to a certain extent. I'm afraid if I let my guard down, someone will try to take advantage of me, and I'm afraid of getting hurt."

Rose nodded as she bit into a cheesy potato strip. "I see your point. Nobody wants to be hurt, but it happens sometimes regardless of what we do to try to prevent it. But if we go around all the time suspecting that people are going to hurt us, we'll miss out on a lot of wonderful friendships."

Rose thought about her own situation. She felt guilty giving Miranda advice that she wasn't applying herself. She had secrets. Things she needed to share with Lynnette and her family. She hadn't told them yet because she was afraid of being rejected.

"That makes sense," Miranda agreed.

They talked some more while they finished eating. On the way to the car, Miranda tucked her arm in Rose's and asked, "Do you want to go roller-skating?"

Rose threw back her head as she burst into laughter. "Ooh, child, no. I don't wanna bust my bottom."

"Aw, Ms. Johnson, come on. It'll be fun."

"Randa, honey, I'm sixty-seven years old. I've never been in a pair of skates in my entire life."

"So. You're never too old to learn. I'll teach you. You're teaching me to play the piano. I'll teach you to skate. I'll hold your hands the whole while if you want me to."

Rose pondered the idea. "I must be crazy. I don't believe I'm letting you talk me into this."

Chapter 18

Saturday night was a busy one for skating. The rink was packed to capacity. Modern-day tunes played as the skaters whirled around the rink. Miranda held on to Rose's hands as she glided Rose slowly over the floor.

Rose laughed as everyone else zipped past them. "Don't let go!" she yelled over the noise of the crowd and the music. "If I fall in front of all these people, I will die from embarrassment."

Miranda shouted, "I won't let go. I've got you. Just move slowly."

"This is kind of fun. I just wish I knew what I was doing."

"You'll get the hang of it. You just have to get used to it. There you go."

Rose was proud of the progress she was making. "Hey, I think I'm catching on."

Miranda smiled. "Do you want me to let go?"

Rose's eyes grew big as saucers. "Oh no. I'm not catching on that good."

Miranda laughed. "Okay. I won't let go. You're doing great."

Miranda and Rose skated for more than an hour before they decided to call it quits. On the way back to Rose's house, Rose was so excited she couldn't sit still. "I can't wait to tell Greg and Sheree I went roller-skating. They're gonna die. Thanks to you, I don't have any bruises or broken bones," Rose said, laughing. "That was fun. I had a wonderful time, Randa."

Miranda glanced quickly at Rose and smiled. "I told you it would be fun."

Rose was touched by Miranda's genuine desire to be with her. Most teenagers would have wanted to spend Saturday night with their peers. "I hope I didn't spoil any plans you had with your friends tonight."

"You didn't," Miranda assured her. "Every now and then, we do our own thing."

Miranda pulled into Rose's driveway. She started to unfasten her seat belt. "I'll walk you to the door."

"No, you stay here. It's getting late. I'm fine."

"Yes, ma'am. I'll wait until you get inside."

"Okay." Rose leaned over and kissed Miranda's cheek. "Thank you for taking time out of your schedule for an old lady."

"You're welcome. And you're not old. You're just very mature for your age."

Rose laughed. "You're sweet. Bye. Drive safely."

"Bye."

When she arrived home, Miranda found her mother in the den reading. "Hey, Mama. Waiting up for me?" She sat on the opposite end of the window seat.

Lynnette smiled. "Hey, sweet pea. Yeah. You know I can't sleep until I know everyone's home safe and sound. Did you and Ms. Rose have a good time?"

"Yes. Mama, you should have been there. We went out to eat, and then I took her roller-skating."

Lynnette opened her mouth in disbelief. "You're kidding. Ms. Rose went roller-skating? Did she like it?"

"She had a ball. She'd never been before so I held her hands the whole time. She is so much fun to be around."

"You really like her, don't you?"

"Yes, ma'am. I more than like her. I love her. It's like having a grandmother but a friend, too."

"That's nice. She adores you, too."

"Where are Josh and Daddy?"

"Probably asleep. We better get to bed, too. We've got to get up early in the morning."

Since Robert had been complaining about her neglecting her spiritual needs, Lynnette had decided she would attend worship services the next day with her family. She got up and placed her Bible on the desk. As she and Miranda headed upstairs, they put their arms around each other.

"Mama?"

"Hmm?"

"I just thought of something."

"What's that?"

"You've never been roller-skating. Maybe next time you can come, and I can teach you, too."

Lynnette giggled and eyed Miranda pathetically. "You wanna see your mama in a body cast?"

Miranda laughed. "No-o-o."

"I didn't think so."

They said good-night. As the two parted ways, Lynnette could not help but think how wonderful it was to have Rose in their lives.

It was almost two o'clock in the morning. Rose had so much on her mind she couldn't sleep. She lifted herself slowly out of bed, ambled over to the closet, and turned on the light. She stepped on her tiptoes, reached onto the shelf, and clutched a shoebox. Then she walked back to her bed and dumped out the contents. She picked up the folded, faded birth certificate. Her fingers gingerly unfolded it. She looked it over, reading it word for word as though it was her first time doing so. She refolded it and placed it back in the box. Next she picked up a photograph. She gazed lovingly at the young man and woman and the little girl.

Tears began to well up in her eyes. Within a matter of seconds, they were flowing down her face. How could she have done something so terrible? If she could only turn back the hands of time. She would do things differently. She wouldn't make the same mistake twice.

Rose had so much fun roller-skating with Miranda, her granddaughter. Miranda had told her that being with her was like being with her grandmother. Rose loved being with her grandchildren.

Despite what Rose had done to her, Lynnette was a loving wife and mother. She had a good husband in Robert, and they had raised two wonderful children. Rose felt a huge lump in her throat at the mere thought.

Sunday morning service began promptly at ten o'clock. The entire congregation raised their voices high, singing praise to God. *Look at creation and who do you see? God who wants you to live eternally. Free from all death, sorrow, crying, and pain. If you obey Him, life everlasting you'll gain.*

The words and melody were stirring. They touched Lynnette so deeply that she felt a gigantic lump well up in her throat. She thought briefly about the physical, mental, and emotional pain through which she was going. Tears began to rise to the surface. She forced her tears back inside and lifted her voice high throughout the remainder of the song.

After the opening prayer, everyone said "Amen" and took their seats. A visiting minister was delivering the sermon, entitled "Life: A Precious Gift From God." As the message was imparted, Lynnette admired the gentle face of the older man providing fatherly counsel to the congregation.

At the end of the rousing service, the congregation started to mingle. Lynnette and her family only stayed for a few minutes since they were picking Rose up to eat dinner with them. Lynnette did not understand why Rose would not attend service with them. The few times Lynnette had invited her, she always came up with a reason she couldn't go.

Back at the Montgomery house, everyone was laughing as they sat around the table on the deck.

Rose was saying, "So I told Thurgood, you've brought me hundreds of miles from home, and you're telling me I've got to sleep in this car on my honeymoon. It's a good thing I love you, Thurgood Johnson 'cause if I didn't you'd be snuggling up with that steering wheel tonight."

Miranda asked, "You mean you really had to spend your honeymoon in the car?"

"The first night we did. It turned out that my Thurgood had failed to make our hotel reservations, and we couldn't find a room anywhere. There weren't any vacancies until the next day."

"Weren't you scared to sleep in the car all night?" Lynnette asked.

"Oh no. I was too mad to be scared."

Everyone laughed.

"Mama. Daddy, tell us again about when you got married," Miranda implored.

"Well," Lynnette began, "we both got sick on our honeymoon from some sort of food poisoning, and we were sick the whole time."

Robert added, "And it rained the whole while."

"Well, honey, it didn't rain the entire time. The sun shone a little."

"Yeah, the day we left."

They started laughing again.

"So how did you two lovebirds meet?" Rose asked.

"Well," Lynnette started, "I lived in Chicago, and Robert and his mother were visiting. I was in college and working at a department store. He came in one day, saw me, and in order to talk to me—" she elbowed Rose then she continued "—pretended he was interested in purchasing a pin for his mother."

They laughed.

Robert intervened, "I wasn't pretending." He chuckled. "I really was looking for a pin for Mama." Then he turned to his wife. "Don't get me started on you now."

Lynnette blushed. "What do you mean?"

"You know exactly what I mean." To Miranda and Rose, Robert gave his version of what took place. "She liked me from the first time she saw me. She couldn't keep her eyes off me. Yeah, she was trying to act all shy, but she didn't fool me."

Lynnette laughed. "Robert, you should be ashamed of yourself. Never before have I heard the truth stretched so far out of proportion."

They could hardly sit up straight for laughing.

After they finished eating, Rose helped Lynnette clean up the kitchen. When they were done, they retired to the living room.

"Randa told me about you skating last night. Sounds like you two had a wonderful time."

Rose sat back on the comfortable floral sofa. "We certainly did. I felt like I was a teenager again. She is an amazing young woman and very mature."

Lynnette was proud of her daughter. "She is. She loves you. She talks about you all the time. It's always Ms. Johnson this and Ms. Johnson that. I tell her, 'child, if I hear another word about Ms. Johnson, I'm gonna send you to live with her.' " They laughed.

"Well, the feeling is mutual. I love her, too." After the way Rose's emotions had overcome her that morning, she felt the need to change the subject. "When are we going to some more flea markets and yard sales? The table we did looks great. I love it."

"Maybe we can go one day next week. I'll check my schedule and let you know."

Rose felt scared and nervous. Although she had just changed the subject, she decided she had to know how Lynnette felt about her birth mother so she said, "You have a wonderful family, Lynn. You all seem so happy."

Lynnette smiled. "Thank you. We are happy. God has blessed us, but like any family, we have our moments."

Rose grinned. "But at least you have one another." There was a pause. *Go ahead and ask her. How else are you going to find out?* "Lynn, may I ask you something? It's kind of personal."

Lynnette turned to face Rose. "Sure. Ask away. If it's too personal though, I may have to plead the fifth."

Lynnette laughed. Rose managed to let out a light chuckle.

Rose couldn't believe she was doing this, but she had to know how Lynnette felt before she gave her the news. "Well, I've never heard you talk about your parents."

The smile from earlier left Lynnette's face. "I don't talk about them much. That's kind of a tough topic. My father died when I was four, and my mother abandoned me shortly there-after." She shocked herself at how blunt she was.

Lynnette's words pierced Rose like a knife. "I'm sorry."

"Thank you, but it's okay."

"Perhaps your mother will get in touch with you someday."

"What for? She hasn't bothered to get in touch with me after all these years, so why now? Besides, I have no desire to see her. What kind of woman would walk out on her only child, and one only four years old at that? It wouldn't bother me if I never saw her face again, not that I remember what it looks like. No loving mother would have done what she did."

Lynnette stopped talking when she became aware of the look of astonishment on Rose's face. She realized Rose had never seen her in this state before. "Ms. Rose, I'm so sorry. I shouldn't have said those things to you. Let's talk about something else."

Rose managed to gently pat Lynnette's hand. "It's okay, dear. I'm sorry I caused you to discuss something so painful."

"I'm fine." Lynnette jumped up and grabbed Rose's hand. "Come on. I want to show you something."

Rose followed her into the den. She was curious. "What is it?"

Lynnette sat Rose down on the love seat. "You'll see." She went to the window seat, opened one of the doors on the front, and pulled out two photo albums. She sat down beside Rose. "I feel as though you're a member of our family. I want you to see some of our family photos. Some of Josh and Randa's baby pictures are in these."

Lynnette opened one of the albums and began to gloat over her offspring. "See," she said, pointing, "here's one of Randa on her first day home from the hospital. Look at those big, beautiful eyes."

Rose gazed at the photograph with adoration. "Oh, she's adorable." Rose pointed to another picture. "This has to be Josh."

"Yes, it is. Look at those chubby cheeks."

"Oh, he's simply breathtaking."

Rose was moved. She had not been present during her grandchildren's births, but what Lynnette had just shown her was special indeed.

When Lynnette flipped the page, Rose felt her head spin. At the sight of a dark-haired little girl, Rose fell back against the seat with her hand to her chest.

Lynnette shut the album quickly and placed it on the end table. Touching Rose's shoulder, she demanded, "Ms. Rose, are you okay? What's the matter?"

Rose's breathing was erratic. "Nothing, dear. I'm fine."

"You are not fine. Are you having chest pains? You look flustered."

"No, I'm fine. Can you get me a glass of water?"

"Of course. Don't get up," Lynnette yelled over her shoulder.

Rose looked at the album on the table as though it would attack her. She wanted to pick it up and look at the picture again, but her body was paralyzed with apprehension.

Lynnette interrupted her thoughts. "Here you go, Ms. Rose."

Rose slowly sipped the cool liquid. "Thank you, dear."

"I'm worried about you. I should take you to the emergency room."

"No, I'm fine. I'm just tired. I think I'll go home and lie down."

Lynnette leaped up. "You're not driving. I'll go get Robert.

I'll drive you home in your car, and he can trail us. Stay here. I'll be right back."

"Thank you, Lynn. You're so sweet."

"You're welcome. Wait here." Lynnette went to get Robert.

Rose kept thinking about the picture. She had to tell Lynnette the truth even though it meant taking a risk on losing everything she had found.

Chapter 19

Lynnette was passive as Robert drove them back home.

"She'll be okay," Robert reassured her.

Lynnette propped her elbow on the doorframe and rubbed her fingers across her forehead. "She should have let me stay with her. She needs someone to look after her. She wouldn't even give me Greg's number so I can call him. She's so stubborn."

"Honey, I'm sure if she felt like she needed someone to look after her, she would have allowed you to stay."

"Take me back."

"What?"

"Take me back to Ms. Rose's. I'm going to spend the night with her and take care of her whether she likes it or not. Randa will know what I need. Have her get some things together for me and bring them back."

Robert turned the vehicle around, and a few minutes later, they were back in Rose's driveway.

Lynnette told him, "You can go ahead and leave. At least that way, she'll have to let me in when she sees you've gone." She and Robert kissed quickly.

Robert said, "Call if you need anything."

"I will." Lynnette hopped out and strolled up to Rose's front door.

When Rose opened the door, she was astounded to see Lynnette standing there. "Lynn, what are you doing back? I thought you'd gone."

"I did, but I came back to spend the night. I don't want you by yourself."

Rose started to object, but Lynnette dismissed her with a wave of her hand and stepped inside. "You may as well let me in because Robert's gone, and I don't have a way home."

Rose stepped aside and allowed her to enter. "Yes, ma'am." There was no arguing with Lynnette. She was so obstinate. Rose knew exactly where she'd gotten it: her father.

"How are you feeling?" Lynnette questioned Rose.

"I'm fine."

"Are you hurting anywhere?"

"No. I was just going to run some water for a bath."

Lynnette escorted Rose to her bedroom. "Well, you can get your things while I start your water."

While Rose bathed, Lynnette pulled back her bedcovers and fluffed her pillows. Then she went into the den and took a book from the bookcase and started reading. She was deeply engrossed in some writings of Emily Dickinson when Rose joined her.

Lynnette looked up. "How are you?"

Rose smiled and sat down on a chair opposite Lynnette. "I'm fine." She cracked a smile. "Quit fussing over me."

Lynnette closed the book. "I can't help it. I'm worried about you. You scared me this afternoon."

"I know, but I'm fine." Rose motioned toward the book, which Lynnette still held in her hands. "What were you reading?"

"Some of Emily Dickinson's poetry."

"Ah. Do you like her?"

"I love her. When I was in school, we read a lot of her poems. I used to write poetry myself when I was younger. I even won a few contests."

"That's wonderful. Do you still write?"

Lynnette put the book back on the shelf. "Oh no. That was all back in the day." She sat back down.

"Why not?" Rose inquired.

Lynnette shrugged. "I don't know. I haven't written anything in years. I don't even know if it's still in me."

"Well, you never know 'til you try."

The doorbell rang. Lynnette started toward the foyer. "That's probably Randa with my things."

When Lynnette returned, Miranda was with her. Miranda ran to Rose and grasped her hands. "Ms. Johnson, Daddy said you were sick. How are you?"

"I'm fine, dear. Stop worrying. Y'all are making a fuss for nothing. If I wasn't enjoying your mother's company so much, I'd make her get her li'l self in the car with you when you leave."

"Well," Miranda replied, "we love you, and we don't want anything to happen to you."

"I know. I love you all, too."

"Randa," Lynnette said, "I know you're concerned about Ms. Johnson, but you've got school tomorrow so you need to be going. Call me when you get home."

"Yes, ma'am." Miranda leaned down and threw her arms around Rose who returned the sentiment.

"Come on," Lynnette said, hurrying her daughter. "I'll walk you to your car."

When Lynnette came back, Rose informed her that she was going to bed. "Make yourself at home. You can sleep in whichever room you want. Good night. I'll see you in the morning."

The two women embraced.

"Good night, Ms. Rose."

Lynnette stayed up a few more minutes. *Lord, please watch over Ms. Rose. Take care of her. She means a lot to me. She's like the mother I never had.*

Rose stared groggily at the clock on her bedside table. The huge red numbers indicated that it was 3:17. She went to the kitchen and poured herself a glass of cold water. As she headed back to her bedroom, she heard cries coming from another room. She slowly walked toward the direction of the moaning.

"Ma-ma-a-a-a, don't leave. Please don't leave me. Why, Mama?" It was Lynnette.

Rose went into the guest room where Lynnette tossed and turned in her sleep as she cried out in grief. She rushed over, sat down on the bed, and called out her name as she gently shook her. Upon hearing her name, Lynnette woke up. When she caught sight of Rose, she immediately sat up and swung her arms around Rose's neck.

Rose held on to Lynnette tightly as she rocked her back and forth. "It's okay, dear. Rose is here. You're not alone. You don't have to be afraid."

Rose's utterances soon soothed away Lynnette's fears. Rose stayed with her until she was certain she had fallen asleep. Then back in her own bed, Rose agonized over the pain her action of so long ago had caused a little girl and now a grown-up woman.

Her mind wandered to the day she had given birth to Lynnette. Her labor pains had been excruciating, but when she had seen the beautiful little creature she had helped to create, her heart had seemed to melt. Every minute of the pain had been well worth bringing her tiny bundle of joy into the world.

As Rose laid there, she asked herself the same question she had asked a million times: *How could I have walked out on my child?*

The next morning, Rose woke up to the marvelous aroma of breakfast cooking. When she went into the kitchen, Lynnette was scurrying about.

Rose started to pull out a chair to sit down. "Mmmm, something sure smells good."

Lynnette turned around frantically. "Ms. Rose, good morning. What are you doing up so early? I was going to serve you breakfast in bed."

Rose smiled. "Good morning. It's seven o'clock. This is late-rising for me. I'm usually up at six. Anyway, I'd much rather eat breakfast here with you. How are you this morning?"

Lynnette grabbed the toast from the toaster. She looked a little embarrassed. "Oh, you mean last night. I'm fine. I'm sorry about that."

Rose looked at Lynnette sympathetically. "Don't apologize for things beyond your control."

Lynnette smiled. "I'll try to remember that. Okay, here you go." She placed a plate full of food in front of Rose.

"Thank you. I'll wait for you. That way, we can say the blessing together."

Lynnette fixed her plate. Rose asked her to bless the meal. They held hands and bowed their heads.

They chatted as they ate breakfast. Then Lynnette cleaned up the kitchen. An hour later, they were both in jeans and T-shirts.

"Where are you off to?" Lynnette inquired of Rose when she saw Rose heading for the back door.

"I'm just going outside to work in my flower beds. I like to get started before it gets too hot."

"That's a good idea. I'll help." Lynnette followed Rose outside.

"Look," Rose said, kneeling and pointing to a colorful array of impatiens. "Randa helped me put these out Saturday. Aren't they beautiful?"

Lynnette admired the flowers as she knelt a few feet from Rose and started to pull up weeds. "Yes, they are. I can't believe you were able to get Randa to plant flowers and play the piano. She's always been such a tomboy. Usually all she wants to do is play ball with Josh and his friends. She and Josh have always been close, but it seems the older they get, the more they argue. I think sometimes she feels that his friends are her rivals and she has to compete with them for his attention."

Rose dropped a handful of weeds into the wheelbarrow. "Jealousy can sometimes get the best of us. It makes us do and say things we later regret. It can even cause us to push away the ones we love the most without meaning to."

Lynnette nodded in agreement and wondered if Rose was referring to her.

They worked in the flower beds for a couple of hours as they chitchatted. They were almost done when Lynnette felt the muscles in her legs straining and stood to stretch. As she stood, she felt a sharp pain in her abdomen. She grunted.

"Dear, are you all right?" Rose asked.

"Yes," Lynnette lied. "My legs are just a little sore."

"Oh, dear!" Rose exclaimed. "Look at your clothes. I've

got you out here helping me and now your clothes are all dirty. Did Randa bring you any extras?"

"Just underwear, but that's okay. I'm fine."

"You know, you and I are about the same size and height. I may have something you can wear. Let me get this last little bunch of weeds here, and we can get cleaned up."

"All right. I *have* worked up a sweat. A shower and some clean clothes would be nice."

Rose pulled up the last bunch of weeds, stood, and tossed them into the wheelbarrow. "There. All done."

Lynnette grabbed the wheelbarrow by the handles. "I'll get rid of this."

"Thank you, dear."

"You're welcome. Why don't you go on in? I'll be right there."

Rose headed inside as Lynnette proceeded to push the wheelbarrow toward the large plastic trash can near the edge of the yard.

Lynnette grasped her stomach with one hand and used the trash can to support herself with the other as she leaned over until the pain subsided.

When she got inside, Rose greeted her with a clean pair of jeans and a shirt. "Here you go."

"Thank you. As soon as I shower and change, I'll fix us some lunch."

"You don't have to do that."

Lynnette looked at Rose. "Ms. Rose, I'm not going to argue with you now. Stop being so hardheaded. I'll fix lunch."

Rose smiled. "Yes, ma'am. Whatever you say."

They both laughed as they went their separate ways to get cleaned up.

Thirty minutes later, they were done.

Rose surveyed Lynnette with approval. "Those look good on you."

"Thank you. I appreciate your letting me borrow them. So what do you want for lunch?" Lynnette asked as she rummaged through the refrigerator.

"There's some sandwich meat in there. Let's just make us some sandwiches."

Lynnette started pulling items from the refrigerator. "That sounds good. You have a seat, and I'll make them."

"I can make my—"

"Ms. Rose…"

"I know," Rose said as she sat down. "You're the boss today."

"Absolutely."

While Lynnette made their sandwiches, Rose talked.

"I hate that you're missing a whole day's work because of me, but I have to admit I'm enjoying you being here."

"I'm enjoying it, too. I'm just glad you're okay. You should probably let your doctor check you out though."

"I'm fine."

Lynnette set Rose's plate on the table in front of her. "Well, you can never be too sure." She sat across from Rose. "Would you do the honor of saying the blessing?"

Rose didn't do much praying. For reasons only she knew, she didn't feel worthy. She usually passed the privilege on to someone else, but she supposed she could handle a simple blessing. Afterward, they talked as they ate. Rose felt so good having Lynnette by her side. Would Lynnette still want to be there once she learned the truth?

Chapter 20

Jeffrey Osborne's soft, mellow voice emanated from the stereo as he sang "We Both Deserve Each Other's Love." Robert and Lynnette held each other as they danced.

Robert whispered in her ear, "When was the last time we danced together?"

Lynnette didn't say anything. Robert stopped dancing and placed his right index finger on her chin and lifted her head so that she was looking up into his face. "Lynn?"

"What is it? Why'd you stop?"

"You're here, but you're not here."

"I'm sorry, honey. Did you say something?"

"Never mind. What's the matter?"

"I was just thinking about Ms. Rose."

Robert sighed, but spoke softly. "She looked fine when I picked you up this afternoon. Besides, she said she's all right."

"I know. I'm just worried. You should have seen her in here yesterday. I thought she was having a heart attack."

"Lynn, I like Rose, and I know you have strong feelings for her. This may sound selfish, but right now I want us to forget about everybody else and concentrate on us. Do you think we can do that?"

Lynnette blushed. "Yeah. We can do that. What was it you were saying?"

They resumed their dancing.

"I was just wondering when was the last time you and I danced together."

"Oh, that's easy. At our wedding reception."

They both burst out laughing.

"That long?" Robert asked.

"I'm afraid so, darling."

"That's pathetic."

Lynnette laughed. "You're making it sound like one of the seven deadly sins."

"It's not that. It's just that we used to dance a lot when we were younger. We both enjoy it. We should do it more often. We should go out one night to Atlanta to one of the nice hotels or restaurants where they have dancing. We need to keep our marriage interesting. When people have been together as long as we have, they need to keep things from going stale."

Lynnette nodded. "True."

Just then, the telephone rang. Robert continued swaying to the music. "Let the machine get it."

After the fourth ring, the answering machine answered the call. After the tone, Simone's cheery voice could be heard. An annoyed look came over Robert's face. "Can't she let us enjoy some time together?"

"Just let me see what she wants. I'll tell her I can't talk long."

The song ended, but Robert refused to let go of Lynnette. "Why don't you just let her finish leaving her message and call her back later?"

Lynnette pulled herself from Robert's embrace and walked in the direction of the telephone. "Because I want to talk to her. I won't be long." She lifted the phone off the receiver.

"Yeah, right," Robert mumbled and walked away. As he left the den, he could hear Lynnette laughing as she conversed with his rival. He went downstairs to the exercise room and attempted to work out. Just hearing Simone's name made him tense. All Lynnette wanted to do was spend time with her. She enjoyed Simone's company more than his.

Robert worked out for an hour before going back upstairs. He couldn't believe it. They were still talking. He peered at Lynnette, but she pretended not to see him. Irritated, he went upstairs and got into bed.

At breakfast the next morning, Robert was jovial with Joshua and Miranda but appeared cold and reserved toward Lynnette. After the children left for school, Lynnette remained at the table as she finished her breakfast.

As Robert rinsed his dishes, she declared, "Robert, I know you're upset that I talked to Simone so long last night, and I'm sorry. Please forgive me."

Robert did not respond. He placed his dishes in the dishwasher.

"Robert," Lynnette pleaded, "please say something."

He didn't bother to turn around. "What do you want me to say?"

"I don't know. You're angry? You're upset? You forgive me?"

Robert shut the door of the dishwasher and turned around slowly. He leaned against the counter with his arms folded across his chest as he stared at her. "Okay, I forgive you. Are you satisfied? I have to tell you that I don't know how much more of this I can take. I feel like I'm on a roller coaster. One minute, we're up and things are fine. The next minute, we're in a slump. You make me feel as though I'm wrong for wanting to spend time with you. You make me feel like I'm no longer interesting to you. That you're bored with me.

"My parents were two of the most happily married people I ever knew. They enjoyed being together, and then one day my dad was gone. You have a husband who wants to be with you. You're not a single woman like Simone. You have to set some boundaries. She can come and go as she pleases because she's not committed to anyone. One day, you may want my time, and I may not be here."

"Robert," Lynnette implored, "why are you being so difficult? Why does it always have to be your way or the highway? I still make time for you and the kids. You're being selfish. You don't want me to have a life outside of you. Before I met you, I was an individual. I am still an individual."

"I'm not being difficult, and it's not my way or the highway. No matter what I do, no matter what I say, your mind is already made up to do exactly what you want. What I say to you goes in one ear clear out the other." Robert grabbed his lunch box off the counter. "I've got to go." Then he was out the door.

Later that afternoon on her way home from a full day of appointments, Lynnette stopped by to check on Rose and show her the final layout for the children's home.

As the two women sat in Rose's living room, Lynnette eyed Rose suspiciously. "How have you been today?"

Rose smiled and swatted Lynnette's knee. "I'm fine. Quit fussing over me."

Lynnette returned her smile. "Okay. I'll take your word for

it." She nodded toward the design in Rose's hands. "Are you pleased with the layout?"

"Yes, indeed. I'm so excited."

"Me, too. Three more months, and it'll be under way. As soon as we get back from vacation. When are Greg and Sheree coming?"

"November or December. I'll be going up there in August for the wedding. They seem to be excited about moving here."

Lynnette smiled. "I think they'll like it here. Compared to where they're from though, it may seem small at first. I know it did to me. If anyone had ever told me I'd move from the big, windy city of Chicago to a small town in Georgia, I would have told them they were off their rocker."

The women chuckled.

"You really like it, huh?"

"Yes. I feel as though I've lived here all my life. Life was good up until a few months ago. So much has changed. I've changed. I'm about to drive poor Robert crazy. We keep having all this conflict about me wanting some independence.

"I guess I'm just starting to feel old, and it's making me want to explore new things. Josh will be graduating high school next month. Randa will be graduating next year. The next thing I know, they'll be leaving home for good. They don't need me as much as they used to."

"It's hard to let go, isn't it?"

"Yes, but I think it's going to be harder for Robert. All he talks about is the fact that one day they'll be gone. He's not like most men. Of course, that's what I've always liked about him. There's a very sensitive side to him." Lynnette smiled. "My big teddy bear. He makes me so angry sometimes, but I love him."

Rose smiled. "He loves you, too. There's no doubt about that."

"I know." Lynnette stood. "I better be going."

Rose got up. "I wish you could stay longer, but I know you have to get home to your family."

They hugged and said good-bye.

Rose was worried about Robert and Lynnette. They had a strong bond with each other, but could their marriage survive this test of their love?

During Bible study, Lynnette noticed that Robert was not his usual talkative self. He seemed to be in a daze. She elbowed him slightly and asked, "Are you okay?"

He didn't say anything. When Brother Dotson called on him to read a scripture, it was as though Robert hadn't heard him. Lynnette elbowed him again. This time, he looked up and Brother Dotson repeated, "Brother Montgomery, will you read John 3:16, please?"

Robert answered, "Sure." He flipped to the scripture in his Bible and began reading.

When he was done, Brother Dotson said, "Thank you. Would anyone like to comment on the scripture Brother Montgomery just read?" Hands were raised, and Brother Dotson called on a young sister to comment.

Lynnette looked at Robert and asked in the lowest whisper possible. "What is wrong with you?"

Still, he would not answer. When Bible study concluded, Robert immediately went outside and left Lynnette to mingle on her own. After a brief moment, she decided to leave, too.

On the ride home, he was quiet as well.

Lynnette eyed him in the driver's seat as she attempted to make conversation. "Ms. Rose likes the layout. I took it to her today."

Robert didn't feel like talking but replied, "That's good. Is she okay?" His voice was flat.

"Yes, she says she's fine."

"You sound like you don't believe her."

"I'm still a little worried about her. That's all."

Robert said nothing further.

Lynnette stated, "You were quiet tonight during Bible study. You didn't participate except for the one time Brother Dotson asked you to read a scripture. That's not like you. You always have something to contribute to the study."

Robert became annoyed at Lynnette's persistence. "I'm tired. I didn't feel like participating. Is that okay with you?" he snapped.

"Why are you being so hostile?" Lynnette looked at him.

He kept his eyes on the road and didn't say anything.

"Robert, I'm so tired of us arguing. We didn't used to do this. Why can't we go back to the way we were?"

"I guess because who we were is not who we are anymore. You've changed."

Lynnette became slightly offended. "What is that supposed to mean? I've changed. You make it sound so horrible."

Robert was tired of talking. All they ever did was talk, but things weren't getting any better. Lynnette always insisted on pushing him to talk even though she never wanted to hear what he had to say. Nevertheless, he said, "There was a time when we worked together trying to make a happy life for our family. But now, we're constantly at odds with each other. I'm not saying it's all your fault. Sometimes I get upset with you when I try to reason with you and you won't listen."

"I do listen, but sometimes you make me feel as though you're trying to control every aspect of my life. You don't understand what I'm going through mentally, emotionally, and physically. You will never understand. I've got all these thoughts racing through my head.

"Life just seems so different now. There's another side of me that's dying to come out. I don't see it as a bad side, but you do. The problem is you don't like it because you're not used to it, and perhaps you feel threatened in some way."

"Maybe I do feel threatened. I feel like I'm losing you. This is supposed to be one of the happiest times of our lives. We've raised two wonderful children. This is an opportunity for you and me to get to know each other all over again." Robert's heart turned sentimental. "I'll never forget how sweet and innocent you looked the first time I saw you in that department store in Chicago." He smiled at the thought and shook his head.

He went on. "Now you're this strong, independent, opinionated woman." He held up his hand before Lynnette could protest. "I'm not complaining. I'm proud of the person you've become. Maybe I am a little selfish and jealous when it comes to you, but it's only because I love you, and I never want to lose you."

Hearing Robert bare so much of his sentimental feelings for her really touched Lynnette. She turned slightly to face him. "You're not going to lose me. You know, when we met I was a confused young woman who didn't know what it was like to be really loved. When you showed a genuine interest in me, it felt so good to have someone truly care for me. It was your love that helped me to become the person I am today. Of course, right now we're not exactly seeing eye-to-eye so you may not see that as a good thing."

They both chuckled.

At least we're laughing again, Robert thought. It sure felt good, but how long would it last?

* * *

On Friday night, the Montgomerys, the Sinclairs, and Beverly were gathered at Rose's house for supper. While everyone else was inside, Robert and Lynnette sat outside on the swing in Rose's backyard.

"Hey!" Carla yelled to her brother and sister-in-law as she approached them. "Are you two lovebirds going to sit out here all night smooching, or do you plan to join the rest of us inside?"

Robert and Lynnette laughed.

"We're coming, sis." Robert stood, pulling Lynnette up with him by her hand.

Carla walked ahead of them as the couple followed still holding hands. Robert gave Lynnette a quick peck on her cheek as they entered the house.

Rose grabbed Lynnette by her hand and led them into the dining room where everyone else was already seated. "Here they are," Rose announced.

"Nice of you two to join us," James commented.

Robert and Lynnette blushed as Robert pulled out her chair. "Here you go, honey."

Lynnette turned slightly to look up at her husband as she sat down. She smiled. "Thank you, sweetie."

"Oh, how sweet," Beverly observed.

Everyone looked at the happy couple and smiled.

Rose took her seat. "Robert, will you please do us the honor of saying the blessing?"

"Yes, ma'am."

Everyone held hands as Robert expressed their gratitude for their spiritual and physical blessings.

"Amen," they all said.

As they passed around platters of hot, steaming food, they chatted away.

"Ooh, Ms. Rose," Carla declared as she took a bite of turnip greens. "These greens are delicious. This is Sunday dinner on a Friday night. Do you cook like this all the time?"

"Thank you, Carla. Not all the time. I love cooking, but I usually don't cook like this unless I know I'm having company. I'll be doing a lot more of it though when Greg and Sheree move here. He eats like a horse."

Laughter filled the room.

James asked, "Well, who can blame him?" He bit off a piece of corn bread. "This is delicious."

"Thank you, James." Rose was delighted that they were all pleased. They were a happy group of family and friends, and Rose felt just like family. But then, of course, why shouldn't she?

Four weeks later, Rose experienced more joy as she sat on the bleachers of the high school football stadium with Lynnette and the rest of the family at Joshua's graduation. Afterward, everyone met in the ballroom of Carrollton's Maple Street Mansion Restaurant for his surprise graduation party.

Rose smiled as Joshua thanked the two most important people in his life for making his graduation possible.

Joshua was saying, "My mom and dad always told my sister and me that getting a high school education was very important in life. They said it would help us to achieve whatever we want." He chuckled, "Sometimes they had to really ride my back to get me to study."

Laughter echoed from the crowd as Joshua continued. "I remember the nights I'd go to bed angry with them, thinking they were putting too much pressure on me to get good grades. I see now that they only wanted the best for me."

He held his diploma high in the air for all to see. "So, Mom, Dad. As far as I'm concerned, this diploma should have your names on it, too, because I never could have earned it without you. Thanks. I love you."

Everyone clapped as Joshua left center stage, went to his parents, and gave them both huge hugs.

Lynnette and Robert were grateful that their son had made it to graduation. Completing high school was a big accomplishment in a teenager's life. One down. One to go.

Chapter 21

"Lynn," Rose called out, "I think some of these impatiens will look lovely underneath this crepe myrtle tree. What do you think?"

Lynnette placed a tangerine-colored flower in a hole and covered it with soil. "They sure will. How many do you need?"

"Can you spare ten?"

"Sure. There are twelve left. I'll put two over here, and then I'll help you put the others over there. I'll bring them to you."

As Rose got up and walked toward Lynnette, she teasingly chastised her. "I'll get them. What have I told you about treating me like an invalid?"

Lynnette laughed. "I'm sorry, Ms. Rose. I keep forgetting how stub—I mean, independent—you are."

Rose grabbed the tray of flowers and playfully swatted Lynnette on her backside. "Okay, missy." Lynnette giggled.

After they had put the last flower in the ground, the two

women stood back side by side with their arms around each other's waist and admired their work.

"Just wait until they grow some more," Rose pointed out. "They'll be thick with color. They'll be so pretty."

"I can't wait. Thanks for your help. I've been wanting to liven up this spot. I think that did the trick. I'll be glad when Robert and the kids get home tomorrow so they can see them."

"Where's the reunion?"

"Birmingham. It's on Robert's mother's side."

As they walked inside, Lynnette and Rose chatted.

"Did Carla and James go, too?" Rose asked.

"Yes."

"I can't believe you didn't want to go."

"I don't feel up to being around a lot of people this weekend. That's why I invited you to spend the night. I just want some one-on-one conversation with one special person." Lynnette put her arm around Rose and squeezed her.

"You're sweet."

"Well, let's hit the showers. Then I'll call in our pizza order."

After the pizza arrived, they sat on the floor in the den in their bathrobes eating pizza and talking.

Rose wiped the corners of her mouth with her napkin. "Are you excited about your vacation in a couple of weeks?"

"Yes," Lynnette answered. "I just wish the kids were coming."

Rose nodded. "I know you do."

Lynnette smiled. "They grew up so fast." She started reminiscing. "I've been thinking about some of the things they used to do when they were little. When Josh was seven or eight, he'd take his bath the night before and then sleep in the clothes that he was going to wear to school the next day. He told me he was just trying to save himself some time in the mornings by already being dressed for school when he got out of bed."

They laughed.

"And Randa. She hated to clean her room so bad she wouldn't let her friends play with her toys so she wouldn't have to help them clean up before they went home."

They laughed again.

Lynnette continued, "Robert got Josh interested in building at an early age. The only problem was Josh was more into taking things apart than putting them together. We were always finding something he'd taken apart and just shoved somewhere. He was the curious type. He wanted to see how things worked. Kids are funny. They can make you laugh, and they can make you cry."

"Well, you and Robert have certainly done a wonderful job with Josh and Randa. It looks like you'll have Josh home for a little while. He tells me he's going to attend the university here."

"Yes. He doesn't really seem to be in a big hurry to move away from home." Lynnette batted her eyes. "Now Randa, on the other hand, is probably going to bust down the door trying to get out of here."

Their laughter rang out in the air again.

"I don't know, Lynn. She and Josh are close. As long as he's at home, she'll probably want to stay, too."

Lynnette smiled at the thought of her twosome. "They are close. The problem is that Robert and Josh spoiled Randa when she was little. She doesn't like it if she can't have their undivided attention. She used to mimic everything they did, which is probably why she's such a tomboy now. I remember one time when she was little and had to wear a dress. Whew! She was highly upset with me."

They chuckled.

"You stay here and relax," Lynnette politely commanded as she grabbed the large pizza box, paper cups, plates, and napkins. "I'll get rid of these."

When Lynnette returned, she heard music as she walked in on Rose dancing to the O'Jays's "Love Train."

"Go, Ms. Rose!" Lynnette shouted as she clapped.

Rose smiled and motioned for Lynnette to join her. Lynnette joined in, and she and Rose did the bump.

The next day, they slept late since Rose had again declined Lynnette's invitation to Sunday morning worship service. Lynnette just could not understand why Rose always turned down her invitations but didn't attempt to discuss it with her.

Later in the day, the women went to Rose's house and prepared a quick dinner to eat on the patio. When they had finished eating, they played various card and board games while they chatted.

"Uno!" Lynnette shouted gleefully.

"You're good at this game," Rose commended her.

"I should be. After all the practice I've had with Robert and the kids. When Josh and Randa were younger, they couldn't get enough of this game." Lynnette threw down her last card. "That's it. Game over."

"Oh, well. You beat me two out of three. I'll get you next time," Rose teasingly warned Lynnette. "Are you thirsty?"

"I sure am."

"Come on. Let's go inside for a few minutes and get something to drink and cool off."

Lynnette followed Rose. While Rose went to the kitchen, Lynnette made her way to the living room. When Rose returned with two ice-cold glasses of tea, she found Lynnette standing beside the piano. Rose handed Lynnette her glass.

"Thank you."

"You're welcome."

They went over to the couch and sat down.

"Ms. Rose, I was admiring your piano, and it just occurred to me that I've never heard you play. Would you play something for me?"

Rose smiled. She was delighted that Lynnette wanted to hear her play. "Sure. Any requests?" Rose put her glass on a coaster and went over to the bench and sat down.

"Oh, I don't know. Anything. Something pretty."

Lynnette put down her glass and focused her full attention on Rose. Once Rose started playing, it didn't take long for Lynnette to recognize the tune. Her face lit up. She loved Stevie Wonder's "You Are the Sunshine of My Life." She sat there mesmerized by the melody and the astonishing way Rose made it flow throughout the room.

When the music concluded, Lynnette applauded and praised Rose. "Ms. Rose, that was beautiful. You certainly are gifted."

"Thank you." Rose slid over on the seat to make room for Lynnette and motioned for her to join her. "Come on," she beckoned.

Lynnette shrank back. "Oh no. I can't play. I don't know how."

"I'll teach you."

"I'm too old to be trying to learn now."

"You're never too old to learn new things. It keeps your mind alert. Now quit saying no and come over here."

Lynnette was still having mixed emotions.

Rose held out her hand again. "Come on."

Lynnette willingly obeyed this time. Something in Rose's tone made her feel as though she could accomplish anything. She joined Rose on the bench. For the next thirty minutes, Rose assisted Lynnette in making sweet sounds stream throughout the air.

At the moment, with Rose was where Lynnette wanted to be. Here with the woman who understood her so completely. The woman who made her bubble up on the inside and helped to fill her heart with joy and laughter.

"Did you and Rose enjoy your time together?" Robert asked Lynnette as he laid on the sofa in the den with his head on her lap.

"Yes." Lynnette was all smiles. "She taught me to play the piano," she said, giggling. "Well, I still don't know how to play, but I know more than I did to start with."

"That's good. So I guess now we're going to have two pianists in the house."

"I wouldn't say that. I enjoyed it, but I don't know if it's something I want to further pursue."

"Why not? I bet you're good even though it was your first time. You've always been good at everything you do. Look at how you built your business from the ground up."

"That's different. Besides, I couldn't have done it without you."

"Sure I provided the building, but you built up your clientele. You have clients all over the world."

"So do you. We both have successful businesses because we support each other."

"I know. I just want you to be happy. You sound like you had fun today."

"I am happy. I have you and Josh and Randa. I don't need to play the piano to be happy. I did enjoy it, but it was all in fun."

"Okay. Whatever you want to do." Robert decided to change the subject. "Everybody was asking about you today."

"What did you tell them?"

Robert decided to have some fun with his wife. He needed

to see her laugh. "Just that you had to stay within close proximity of a bathroom because you had taken a laxative."

"What? No, you didn't!" Lynnette almost dumped Robert onto the floor when she jumped up from the sofa. "You told them what? Robert, how could you?" At that moment, she realized that Robert was rolling around hysterical with laughter. She playfully tapped him and started laughing. "You're awful."

Robert shouted, "Gotcha!"

He was laughing so hard that he thought he would explode. She seemed to have mellowed out a lot. He was glad.

"Mama." Miranda peeked into the dimly lit den where her mother was sitting. "What are you doing?"

The pain had awakened her from her sleep again. Lynnette looked at her daughter. "Hey, sweet pea." She held out her hand for Miranda to join her on the window seat. "I'm just thinking."

Miranda sat down. "Is something bothering you?"

Lynnette smiled. "Remember what I used to tell you and Josh when you complained that I worried too much?"

Miranda returned the smile. "Yes, ma'am." She moved her head and shoulders from side to side and imitated her mother. "I'm your mama, and it's my job to worry."

Lynnette laughed. "Aren't you exaggerating a little? I didn't say it quite like that. Anyway, your dad and I want the best for you and Josh. We want you to do good things with your lives and always be there for each other, no matter what."

Miranda smiled. "We will, Mama. And we know you and Daddy only want the best for us."

Lynnette was proud of her children. She asked, "So, you really had a good time at the reunion, huh?"

"Yes. There were so many people there. I saw relatives I forgot I had. Mama?"

"Yes."

As much as Miranda hated to keep bringing it up, she couldn't drop the subject altogether. She knew how important family was to her mother. "Do you think you'll ever find your mother?"

Lynnette took her daughter's hand. "I don't know, baby. It doesn't matter now. I've got all the family I need."

"Do you want to find her?"

"No, I don't think so. Not anymore."

"Why not? You deserve a chance. If it were me, I'd want to."

Lynnette slowly shook her head. "You don't know that. If you were really in that situation, you might feel differently."

"I just can't imagine not knowing your parents. I can't imagine my life without you and Daddy. I don't even want to think about it." Miranda threw her arms around her mother. "I love you, Mama."

"I love you, too, baby."

It felt so good to hold and love her daughter. Lynnette felt as though she would never know what it was like to hold and love her own mother. How sad that they would never share what she and Miranda did.

Chapter 22

As Robert and Lynnette stood in the lingering line at Walt Disney's Space Mountain, Lynnette grew extremely tense as she beheld the flutter of lights in the darkness from the roller coaster they would soon be boarding. "I can't believe I'm doing this," she mumbled under her breath.

Robert squeezed her hand and tried to reassure her. "It's just a roller coaster. We ride them all the time at Six Flags."

"This one's different though. It's inside this huge building in the dark. I wonder what genius came up with this bright idea. I've got to be stone crazy for even considering doing this."

"Look. We don't have to ride if you don't want to. Let's just get out of line." Robert started to step away, taking Lynnette with him.

"I don't want to get out of line," she protested. "I want to ride." She pulled Robert back beside her.

"You just said you didn't want to ride."

"No, I didn't," she whispered. "I said I can't believe I'm doing it."

Robert grinned to himself. Just then, the roller coaster stopped, and it was their turn to get on. After everyone was securely strapped in their seats, the coaster slowly took off. As it gained momentum, it zoomed up, down, and over the track in the darkness. Lynnette jeered as the wind swept over her face. The sensation was exhilarating.

When the coaster finally came to a stop, Lynnette exclaimed, "Wow! That was great! Let's do it again!"

After they rode Space Mountain a second time, they did some souvenir shopping and walked around the park, taking in the marvelous sights and sounds of the Magic Kingdom. Lynnette couldn't believe she was actually there.

When they got to Mickey's Toontown Fair, Lynnette cried out, "I've got to see Mickey Mouse."

Even though all the other adults had children with them, Lynnette didn't let that stop her. She hadn't waited this long to get to Disney World only to come and not see him. After their group toured Mickey's Country House, the park staff took pictures of each family with the Disney character. As Robert and Lynnette posed with the famous mouse character between them, Lynnette kissed Mickey on the cheek as their picture was taken.

They spent the remainder of the day on as many rides as possible, taking pictures, shopping, and just walking around holding hands. After dusk, they enjoyed the Fourth of July Fantasy in the Sky fireworks display. The sky sparkled in various colors high above Cinderella's castle. The sight was simply breathtaking. Afterward, they stopped at the Camera Center and picked up their photos with Mickey.

On the boat ride back to the main entrance of the park, the

moon glistened on the surface of the waters below. It had been a day full of splendor and excitement. Robert felt a sense of contentment at seeing his wife so cheerful.

As they stood side by side near the boat's rails, they peered out over the waters and up at the beautiful night sky. What a beautiful sight to behold. But more wonderful than that was Robert's having Lynnette there beside him. And to think, she'd almost changed her mind about coming. Robert tightened his hold around her waist.

"Is this beautiful or what?" Lynnette interrupted Robert's thoughts.

"You sure are," he whispered.

Lynnette looked at him, smiled, and jabbed him playfully in his side. "I'm not talking about me, silly. I'm talking about the moon, the stars, the water, the sky."

Robert laughed and pulled her closer. "I know what you meant. Yes, it's all beautiful, and so are you. Now aren't you glad you came?"

Lynnette nodded. "Yes. I felt so alive today. I love you."

"And I love you."

Robert had not seen Lynnette this happy in a long while. He wished her smile would never fade.

Robert and Lynnette spent their last day at Kennedy Space Center. On their drive back to the hotel, Robert was talkative. Lynnette was not contributing much to the conversation.

"You sure are quiet," Robert observed. "Got a lot on your mind?"

"I've had such a wonderful time this week, I hate for it to end."

"Yeah, I know. Me, too, but there'll be other times."

"I know. It's just been so nice to clear my mind of all the things that have been stressing me out. I know I can't run away from my problems. It's just that tomorrow, we go home, and it's back to reality."

"Well, we've got the children's home project to work on when we get back. Maybe that'll help keep your mind occupied."

"Maybe you're right. I've enjoyed this time away, but I miss the kids and Ms. Rose."

The next day, Joshua and Miranda ran outside as the Suburban pulled into the driveway.

"Mama! Daddy!" Miranda cried out. "Welcome home. How was your trip?"

As soon as their parents were out of the truck, Miranda grabbed them and gave them big hugs. Joshua followed suit.

"Hey, you two!" Lynnette exclaimed. "We had a great time, but I sure did miss my babies."

Joshua took Lynnette's suitcase as she kissed him on the cheek. He playfully scrunched up his face. "Mom, I'm not a baby," he respectfully reminded her.

"What is this?" Lynnette teased. "You never complained about it before. We were only gone a week."

As they went inside, Miranda questioned her father. "Daddy, how was Disney World?"

"It was great. I almost had to drag your mother away." Robert leaned down and whispered, "Just between you and me, I think she's in love with Mickey Mouse."

Lynnette playfully poked Robert.

They were exhausted. After a quick supper of grilled cheese sandwiches and fries, Robert and Lynnette cozied up on the sofa and watched a Jerry Lewis movie. As she rested her head on his lap, they laughed at the humorous parts and chatted briefly during commercials.

Halfway through the movie, Robert realized his wife

had fallen asleep. He sat in silence, except for frequent chuckles at Jerry's antics. They had had a lot of fun in Orlando, but he had really been looking forward to coming back home. He looked down into Lynnette's sleeping face and smiled.

Chapter 23

"I wish you were coming with me," Rose lamented as she placed the stack of neatly folded blouses in her suitcase.

Lynnette glanced at Rose from the wicker rocking chair where she was sitting. "I wish I could, too, but since Robert and I just went on vacation last month, I need to stay here." When she noticed Rose about to shut her suitcase, Lynnette added, "Don't you think you need to take a coat?"

Rose chuckled. "Heavens, no. It's August. This time of year, Pennnylvania's hot like it is here. I'll probably take a sweater or a light jacket though. Is that okay, Mama?"

Lynnette smiled. "I suppose so."

"I feel bad about taking you away from Robert on a Friday night." Rose stepped into the bathroom.

"Now, Ms. Rose, you know you're family to us. Anyway, Robert's going to a ball game with a buddy of his. This may sound crazy, but I'm glad he's showing an interest in something else besides me. I mean, I love him, and I'm glad he loves me, but sometimes I just need some time to do what I want to do. When your husband was alive, didn't you ever feel that way?"

Lynnette's question caught Rose by surprise. She grew nervous. She yelled from the bathroom. "You mean Thurgood?"

Lynnette chuckled. "Of course, I mean Thurgood, Ms. Rose. Who else would I be talking about?"

Rose came out of the bathroom with her arms full of toiletry items and dumped them on her bed. "Yes, I did. It's important that a husband and wife spend time together, but it's just as important that they have it away from each other. We're individuals. Sometimes we want to do things together, and other times we want to be alone or with other people. There's nothing wrong with that as long as we keep our priorities in order."

Lynnette nodded in agreement. "Sometimes I don't understand why I think so differently from the way I used to. When Josh and Randa were younger, all Robert and I talked about was what we were going to do together once they got older. I never thought about what I as an individual wanted to do. I still want to do some of the things we talked about, but I also want to do things separate from him. Why is that?" Lynnette looked at Rose, longing for the answer to her question.

Rose sat on the bed and looked solemnly into Lynnette's face. "All I can tell you, dear, is that as we get older our circumstances change. Along with that, our thinking changes. You did find out, too, several months ago that you may need surgery. That alone brought on emotional, physical, and mental changes, but remember it doesn't all have to be bad. It's what you make out of it."

"You're right," Lynnette agreed. "For the first time in a long while, I'm beginning to feel an inner calm of peace and happiness. Sometimes I think the only thing left in the world that would make my life complete is if I had a mother in my life who had loved me enough to stay with me."

Rose knew she was about to roam into a place she had no desire to go, but she couldn't keep herself from asking, "If your mother walked into your life right now, Lynn, what would you say? What would be your reaction?"

Lynnette crossed one leg over the other. "I don't know. She walked out on me. I have a lot of bitter feelings inside that have been there for years. I don't think they'll ever go away."

They were both quiet for a few seconds before either said anything. "I'm sorry, Ms. Rose." Lynnette attempted a smile. "Leave it to me to turn a normal conversation into a sob story." She jumped up, grabbed Rose's hand, and pulled her up. "Come on. We've got to get to the airport early in the morning. Let's go for a walk before it gets too late, and I'll help you finish packing when we get back."

Rose followed Lynnette. How she longed to confess the truth to her right then and there. A part of her wanted to so badly, but another part simply wanted to let their relationship remain as it was. Two women, two friends who truly loved each other.

Lynnette was experiencing anxiety. At the airport when she and Rose had said their good-byes, she had never seen Rose so emotional. She had wrapped her arms around Lynnette and clung to her tightly as she cried a river of tears and told Lynnette how much she loved her.

Lynnette felt the same way about Rose. During the last several months, the two had developed a bond. Lynnette missed her already. She'd be back home in a little over a week though. Lynnette had made Rose promise to call to let her know that she had arrived safely.

Lynnette forced her mind to focus on other matters. When she pulled into the driveway, Robert and Joshua were playing a game of one-on-one. "Hey," she greeted them.

"Hey, babe." Robert gave her a quick kiss on her cheek.

"Hi, Mom." Taking advantage of his father's brief moment of distraction, Joshua dribbled the ball past Robert and slam-dunked it into the hoop.

"You two having fun? Who's winning?"

"Me, of course," Joshua replied with a big, wide grin.

Robert suddenly turned around. "Hey! That's not fair. I was distracted."

"Sorry, Dad. You snooze, you lose."

"Okay, you two. Behave," Lynnette admonished.

As she turned to go inside, Robert had Joshua in a playful headlock. She smiled and shook her head.

Several minutes later, Lynnette and Miranda were on their way to the mall. As they rode down Interstate 20, Lynnette put her hand on Miranda's knee, looked at her, and smiled. "So my little girl and I finally get to spend some time together."

Miranda blushed. "Mama-a-a. I'm not a little girl. I'm almost seventeen."

Lynnette playfully tapped Miranda's knee. "What happened to you and Josh while your dad and I were away? Did you suddenly become adults and forget to tell me? I know you're not babies anymore, but you'll always be my little girl even when you're old and gray." She added, "And wearing false teeth."

Miranda giggled.

"So how are things at work?"

Miranda looked straight head. "Okay."

The Mom radar went up quickly. Something was wrong. Lynnette took a quick glance at her daughter. "What's the matter?"

"Nothing. Just some of the girls don't like it because I won't hang out with them after work. You should hear the way they talk. It's sickening the language they use and the things they talk about. They don't have any morals. Most of them are my age. They say I think I'm better than them."

"What did you tell them?"

"I explained that I have to follow the Bible's standards regarding that kind of behavior, but Mama, sometimes I think about going along just to get them off my back."

"You're doing the right thing by not giving in. Sometimes it's not easy coping with peer pressure. Everyone wants to feel accepted, young people especially, but if someone is trying to entice us into wrongdoing, we have to be strong." Lynnette thought about her relationship with Simone. Sometimes she did allow Simone to influence her thinking in negative ways. She realized she needed to heed her own advice.

Miranda wanted to know, "Did you have to deal with peer pressure when you were my age?"

"Yes, but the peer pressure back then was quite different from what you young ones face today. Today, there's sexual immorality, violence, drinking, drugs, and the list goes on and on. I'm not saying those things didn't exist in my day. They did, but they weren't as widespread. When I was in school, I got in trouble for talking and chewing gum."

"That's nothing compared with what the kids at school do today."

"Times have definitely changed."

"Sometimes it's so hard to do the right thing."

"Well, your dad and I are always here to help. You can talk to us at any time. Okay?"

Miranda smiled. "Okay." She felt a sense of relief. A lot of young people didn't have parents who cared as much as hers. She was thankful for her mother and father.

Robert and Lynnette were behind schedule getting ready for their night out at the movies, and Lynnette began to get concerned.

"The movie starts at seven, and Rose hasn't touched base. She said she'd call."

Robert got up from his chair. "Doesn't she have your cell phone number?"

"Yes, but she won't call me on it. You know how she is. If she can't get me at home, she feels like she's bothering me. Can we wait a few more minutes?"

Robert stood in the door of the bathroom. "Do you have Greg's number?"

"No. She didn't offer to give it to me, and I didn't want to seem pushy and ask for it."

Robert thought he was out of Lynnette's reach when he turned to walk away, chuckled, and mumbled, "That never stopped you before."

Lynnette caught him before he could get away and thumped him playfully on his back with her hand towel. "I heard that."

He chuckled again. "I'll be downstairs."

When Lynnette heard the telephone ring a few minutes later, she almost stubbed her toe as she ran and fell across the bed to answer it. She swiftly answered on the second ring. "Hello," she said, gasping, almost out of breath.

"Lynn?" The voice on the other end sounded concerned. "Are you okay?"

"Ms. Rose. Yes, I'm fine. I almost fell trying to get to the phone. How was your flight?"

"Nice and smooth."

"That's good." Lynnette managed to pull herself up and sit on the edge of the bed. "How's the weather?"

"Hot. I told you I didn't need a coat. Greg and Sheree are having an outdoor ceremony. I told them if it's this hot next Saturday, I'm wearing shorts to their wedding."

Lynnette threw her head back and laughed as she formed a mental picture of the scene in her head.

"Anyway," Rose went on, "I won't keep you. I know you and Robert are probably going out."

Lynnette smiled. "We're going to see a movie."

"Well, tell him and my two babies I miss them. I miss you, too, already."

"I'll tell them. I miss you, too. I'll see you at the airport next Sunday."

"Okay, dear. I love you."

Lynnette felt her heart flutter at the words. "I love you, too."

They said their good-byes.

Lynnette was still on the bed contemplating the conversation she and Rose had just had when Robert interrupted her happy thoughts. He stood in the doorway. "Was that Rose?"

She stood and walked over to him. "Yes."

"How is she?"

"She's fine. She had a good trip."

"Good." Robert took her hand. "Can we go now?"

"Sure."

As the two of them walked downstairs, Robert inquired, "Why are you smiling like a Cheshire cat?"

"I'm just happy, that's all."

Indeed, she was. Lynnette felt like shouting it to the world.

Chapter 24

The week was dragging by at a snail's pace. Rose had been away four days. Lynnette missed her something awful. She and Beverly had come into the store an hour early so Beverly could brief her regarding some of their future jobs. Lynnette attempted to keep her mind focused as Beverly brought her up to date.

Beverly informed Lynnette, "Mr. and Mrs. Mitchell like your idea of installing built-in bookcases in their home office."

"That's good. I thought they'd like them better than the standard freestanding shelves. What about the Nesbitts? Did they decide whether they want to bump out the front of the house to extend the kitchen?"

"Yeah. They like that concept. They say they really need the extra space because their kitchen is so small. You know, they have three children. Mrs. Nesbitt jokes that if they all need something from the kitchen at the same time, they have to ask another family member to get it or take a number and wait in line."

Lynnette let out a quiescent laugh.

Beverly sensed that something was up. "You're not feeling good today, are you?"

"Not really. Rose is out of town. She went to Pennsylvania to her son's wedding. I miss her. She's become such a huge part of my life. I've gotten so used to seeing her and talking to her." Lynnette attempted to perk up. "But don't worry about me. I'll be okay."

"I know you will. You're a strong person, Lynn. So how's the children's home coming?"

"Great. Robert and his crew are working hard. This is going to be so good for the community. They think it'll be ready to open in January if all goes well."

"That's good. I admire what she and her family are doing. It takes a strong love of children to take on such a huge responsibility as the one they're about to. She's a wonderful human being. If her son and daughter-in-law are anything like her, they'll do a terrific job."

Lynnette smiled. "I agree."

Beverly stood. "Well, it's almost nine o'clock. I better go open up for business."

"Thanks, Beverly. You do a pretty terrific job yourself. I don't know what I'd do without you."

Beverly smiled. "Thanks. It's nice to be appreciated."

While Beverly went to open the store, Lynnette sat at her desk wondering what Rose was doing at this very moment. She shook her head in order to bring herself out of her daze. She picked up the telephone and proceeded to make some business calls.

Later that day, Lynnette stopped by the Nesbitts to go over the final plans for their renovation. She showed Mrs. Nesbitt the floor plan as they sipped coffee in the living room.

Lynnette pointed to seven windows on the plan one at a time. "All of the windows on the front of the house will have eyebrow arches. Since you're going with the yellow vinyl siding and green asphalt shingle roofing, white vinyl trim on the windows will really look good."

Mrs. Nesbitt looked on with interest. Her expression indicated she was well pleased. "Oh, Lynn, I love it."

Lynnette smiled. "Good. Now about your front door. You know, Mrs. Nesbitt, the door really is the focal point of your home. It's inviting and draws the eye's attention. Instead of the traditional plain metal door, I would like to suggest that you and Mr. Nesbitt go with wood, like pine, or oak, or red mahogany with glass. What do you think?"

"It sounds beautiful."

"Well, it's only a suggestion. Since Mr. Nesbitt couldn't be here today, I know you have to run it by him. Beverly did a checklist of everything I'm going over with you today so you can discuss it with him and check off what you want." Lynnette reached into her briefcase and pulled out a sheet of paper and handed it to the woman. "Here it is."

"Thank you. Let me ask you this, Lynn. What about shutters? Don't you think they'll add to the appearance of the house?"

"Well, in some cases, they do. But frankly, Mrs. Nesbitt, I don't think you'll need shutters with the eyebrow arch windows. The windows are so uniquely designed that shutters would probably dominate them and just take over their appearance. Of course, the ultimate decision is yours and your husband's. You're my clients, and I want you to be happy. If you need help in making a decision, I can bring you some pictures of some of our other projects."

"Oh, Lynn, that would be wonderful. You are so sweet. We really appreciate all you've done."

Lynnette stood. "Well, you're certainly welcome. I aim to please. I better be going."

Mrs. Nesbitt stood, too, and held up her hand. "Oh, wait. Before you go, I've got something for you. I'll be right back."

When she returned, she had a huge wrapped bouquet of pink and red roses. She handed them to Lynnette. "These are for you. I just cut them this morning."

"Oh, Mrs. Nesbitt, they're beautiful. How sweet." Lynnette was so touched she felt she would cry. She hugged the woman. "Thank you."

"You're welcome. I just wanted to show you how much I appreciate all you've done."

"Well, I'll put them in the store window for everyone to see."

Lynnette felt a sense of pride on her way back to the store. She loved making people's dreams come to life with her work.

Friday night, Miranda invited a few friends for a sleepover. There were five girls, including Miranda. They sat around the kitchen table eating pizza, talking, and giggling. The Montgomery home hadn't been this lively in a long time. It was music to Lynnette's ears. When Joshua and Miranda were younger, they had sleepovers all the time. Now that they were older, the house had become much quieter, which was just a constant reminder that one day the nest would be empty.

As Lynnette relaxed in the den at her favorite spot, she listened to the excited teenagers and thought about how Robert assumed that she wasn't troubled about how the two of them would handle their children's eventual departure. It was something she contemplated on a regular basis.

Lately, Robert had really been striving to adapt to her new personality. He had even become more flexible when she wanted to venture from their regular routine. That night, he and James had taken Joshua and Jeremy out to eat and bowling. She had started reading a good book the week before. She only had a few more chapters to go and hoped to finish it that night.

Lynnette redirected her attention to her book. The teenagers strolled into the den talking and giggling. Miranda's friends quieted down long enough to speak to Lynnette. "Hi, Mrs. Montgomery," the girls chimed all at once.

Lynnette looked up from her book and smiled. "Hello, ladies. How are you?"

"Fine," they answered.

"Mom," Miranda said, "do you mind if we turn on the radio?"

"Of course not, honey. I was going upstairs anyway."

Miranda selected an R & B station. Lynnette knew the girls would be all over the floor dancing in a matter of seconds so she stood to leave.

Miranda begged, "Mama, don't leave."

"I'm going upstairs to finish my book."

Miranda gently tugged on her mother's arm. "Don't go yet." She started moving to the music. "Dance with us."

"No, I don't think so," Lynnette declined, shaking her head.

"Aw, come on, Mrs. Montgomery," Miranda's friend Sharon urged.

Miranda continued to pull her mother toward her. "Mama, please. Do the electric slide with us."

"Randa," Lynnette reminded her daughter, "you know I can't keep up. I mess up every time I try to do it."

"We'll help you," Sharon volunteered.

"Yeah," the other three girls chimed in.

Lynnette placed her book on the desk and grinned as she wiggled her way toward the teenagers. "Okay, you talked me into it."

Lynnette attempted to stay in step with Miranda and her friends. *Hey,* she thought, *I'm getting good at this.*

The girls cheered Lynnette on. Before long, she was in direct movement with them. When the song ended, they applauded her.

Lynnette was proud that she had finally mastered the dance. The smile on her face was evidence of it. She bowed several times saying, "Thank you very much."

The girls gathered around Lynnette, and she hugged them one by one. Then she grabbed her book and waved. "Good night, ladies. Thank you for a wonderful evening."

"Good night, Mama," Miranda said.

The girls waved and said, "Good night, Mrs. Montgomery."

As Lynnette walked away, she heard one of Miranda's friends comment, "Randa, your mom is so cool. My mom never would've done that."

Another one added, "Mine either. That was fun."

Lynnette laughed as she went upstairs. She hadn't had this much fun since she and Robert went to Disney World. The song still playing in her head, she hummed and danced all the way up the stairs.

Lynnette hummed as she drove along Camp Creek Parkway toward the airport. She could hardly wait to see Rose. The week had seemed more like two. They had so much catching up to do. She was still rocking and reeling from her dancing with Miranda and her friends Friday night.

Her heart fluttered as she eased her SUV into the airport traffic. She pulled up into the parking deck and found a space quickly. When she got out, she almost ran to the airport. She made her way to the baggage claim area and checked the schedule. She was pleased to see that Rose's flight was right on time. She waited eagerly, hoping to catch a glimpse of her.

As soon as their eyes met in the crowded Hartsfield airport, Lynnette and Rose hurried toward each other. They hugged one another for what seemed like several minutes. When they finally let go, Rose retrieved her luggage.

Lynnette gently removed the suitcase from Rose's hand and said, "I want you to tell me all about your trip on the way home."

During the ride, Rose filled Lynnette in on the wedding.

"Oh," Lynnette exclaimed, "it sounds beautiful and so romantic. I can't wait to see the pictures."

Rose turned sideways a bit and looked at Lynnette. "You look different," she acknowledged. "You sound different, too. What have you been up to?"

Lynnette smiled. "I feel great. I feel so alive and free. Like a huge load has been lifted off my shoulders."

Rose was happy for Lynnette. "Well, what brought about all this?"

"Well, it's not any one particular thing. I think it's a combination of stuff. For one, I've had to readjust my thinking, and I just feel better. Randa had a sleepover Friday, and I let her and her friends talk me into dancing with them. It was so much fun. It reminded me of when I was a teenager. I feel like I can conquer the world and nothing can bring me down."

Rose smiled at the new woman beside her. She was ecstatic that Lynnette had had such an awakening.

Chapter 25

Summer was over. Autumn was Lynnette's favorite season.

Robert woke up and looked at the digital clock on the bedside table. It was 3:33 in the morning. What was that noise? It sounded like it was coming from downstairs. Where was Lynnette? He got up and put on his robe. As he went downstairs, the noise got louder and louder. It sounded like the vacuum cleaner. He found Lynnette vacuuming the den. He had to call her name several times before she heard him. She shut off the power.

"What are you doing vacuuming at three-thirty in the morning?" Robert asked her.

"I'm not sleepy."

"You need to try to get some sleep. Come to bed."

"I'm not sleepy," Lynnette repeated. "You go on. I've got some clothes in the washer."

"Okay, but don't stay up all night. You need to come to bed if you're going to work in the morning."

"I know."

Robert went back to bed. Lynnette finished her tasks and finally went to sleep around five o'clock. When she attempted to get up at seven-thirty, she felt horrible. She was nauseated and had to run to the bathroom to throw up.

Robert sat on the side of the bed as she laid there. "I'll stay home and take you to the doctor."

"No, that's okay. I'll be fine. Will you call Beverly and tell her I won't be in the store today and ask her to cancel my appointments? Her number is in my address book by the phone in the den."

"Yeah, I'll call her." Robert went downstairs and called Beverly. When he returned to the bedroom, he found Lynnette standing in the doorway of the bathroom doubled over as though in pain. He rushed to her. "Honey, what's wrong?"

Lynnette's speech was broken. "The pain…in my stomach…is horrible. I think I need…to go to the…emergency room."

Robert assisted her to the bed and she sat down. He felt her forehead. "You're burning up." He dashed to the medicine cabinet and pulled out a bottle of Tylenol. He poured two tablets in his hand, grabbed a plastic cup, and filled it with water. Then he rushed back to Lynnette's side and offered her the pills. "Take these."

Lynnette put the pills in her mouth and washed them down with the water.

Robert told her, "I'll help you get dressed." He hurried to her closet and pulled out a pair of blue jeans and a sweater.

After she was dressed, Robert helped her downstairs and out to the Suburban.

They arrived at the hospital approximately fifteen minutes later. Robert helped Lynnette to a seat and went to sign her in. Afterward, he rushed back to her side and held her tight. "How are you?"

Lynnette attempted to speak through her pain. "I've never...hurt like this before."

She was called back to an exam room. Robert held her. After a few minutes, the emergency room doctor came in and introduced himself as Dr. Peters. He pointed to a chart on the wall and asked, "On a scale of one to ten, what would you say the pain in your abdomen is?"

Lynnette looked at the chart and answered, "Eight."

"Have you been experiencing any nausea or vomiting?"

"Yes. Both."

"Any headaches, muscle cramps?"

"No."

"What about diarrhea?"

"No."

Dr. Peters advised, "All right, Mrs. Montgomery, we're going to take you to the lab for testing. One of our technicians will be in to get you in a moment. Until then, just try to relax. Okay?"

"Okay," Lynnette answered.

Robert said, "Thank you, Dr. Peters."

The doctor smiled. "You're welcome. Mrs. Montgomery, I'll be back after your test is done."

"All right."

Dr. Peters left the room.

Lynnette and Robert sat in silence. Sometimes fear scared people beyond words. Finally, the technician arrived and took Lynnette away.

Robert waited in the exam room while Lynnette was taken

back to the lab. Afterward, she was brought back to her room where they waited until Dr. Peters returned.

This time, the doctor pulled up a stool and sat down. Lynnette could tell it was not good news. He began, "Mrs. Montgomery, did you know that you have fibroid tumors on your uterus?"

Lynnette nodded. "Yes, Dr. Mandell told me in January."

"Did he recommend surgery—a hysterectomy?"

"Yes, but I told him I didn't want it."

Dr. Peters said, "Your ultrasound indicates that in addition to the fibroid tumors on the inside of your uterus, you have tumors growing out of it on stemlike structures. Sometimes these stems twist and cause pain, nausea, or fever. That's why you're experiencing the symptoms you have."

Lynnette could not believe her ears. She dropped her head.

Robert asked, "So what needs to be done?"

Dr. Peters answered matter-of-factly, "Surgery."

Lynnette spoke up. "You mean a hysterectomy?"

"Yes," the doctor answered.

Lynnette turned her head away and stared at the wall as tears welled up in her eyes.

"Mrs. Montgomery," Dr. Peters said, "I need to call Dr. Mandell. He may want to keep you overnight for observation."

Lynnette frowned. She did not want to stay in the hospital.

"I'll let you know what he says after I talk to him." Dr. Peters went to call Dr. Mandell.

Lynnette complained, "Robert, I want to go home. I don't want to stay here."

"Relax," Robert told her. "You might not have to stay."

Robert was right. She didn't know, but she felt confident that she would have to stay.

Lynnette complained, "I wish I hadn't even come here. I should have just stayed home until the pain stopped."

Robert said, "You don't know that it would've gotten better. We did the right thing. Look at it this way. By coming, you got a second opinion about the surgery. That should make you feel a little better."

Lynnette guessed Robert was right again; however, she still wanted to go home.

When Dr. Peters came back, Lynnette could tell she was not going to like what he was about to say.

He said, "Dr. Mandell wants to keep you overnight for observation."

Lynnette protested, "I'm better. Can't I go home?"

The doctor's tone was gentle. "Mrs. Montgomery, you're having severe pain in your abdomen, and you're running a fever. I'm not trying to scare you, but I want to be upfront and honest with you. This is serious. We don't want to take any chances. Perhaps we're being overly cautious, but you're our patient, and we want to do what's best for you."

Lynnette sighed.

Dr. Peters advised her, "Just try to relax, and we'll have you in a room in a few minutes."

Lynnette didn't say anything.

Robert said, "Thank you."

"You're welcome." The doctor left the room.

Robert sat beside Lynnette and put his arm around her. He had never been as frightened as he was at this moment. He said a silent prayer.

As soon as she had found out about Lynnette, Rose was by her side. Both she and Robert spent the night at the hospital. Rose had tried to get him to go home and get some rest, but he refused to leave Lynnette's side. And so did she.

As Rose sat in a chair in a corner, she was moved by the

love in this family. She was so happy to be in their lives. Still, she had an empty feeling deep down inside. *They don't know who I am. I have to tell them. We've lost so much of our time together already.* Her thoughts were interrupted when Dr. Mandell entered the room.

Dr. Mandell had an odd look on his face. "Dr. Peters told you about the fibroids. You need to have a hysterectomy. I can perform it while you're here in the hospital. Or you can go home today, call my office and make an appointment to see me tomorrow, at which time I'll examine you further and we can talk more about the surgery."

Lynnette's mind was racing. *What do I do, Lord? At this point, I don't think I have much choice but to have the surgery.*

A voice inside her head said, *You've done all you can do. You put the surgery off for as long as you could. You did good to make it this far. Trust God and do what you have to do. Remember, He'll be with you. If you make it through, this will all be behind you. But just in case you don't, He'll take care of your family.*

Lynnette looked at Dr. Mandell as she spoke. "I want to go home. I need to be with my family before I do anything. I'll call your office and set up an appointment to see you tomorrow. Then I'll come in and talk to you about the surgery."

Dr. Mandell's heart went out to Lynnette and her family. He wanted to assure them that everything would be okay, but he couldn't make them any promises. After all, he was just another human being, not God.

"All right," Dr. Mandell said. "Things are looking better than they were yesterday so I'm dismissing you." He pulled out his prescription pad and scribbled on it as he spoke. "This prescription will shrink the fibroids. Remember it only works as long as you're taking it. It's a temporary treatment until you have the surgery. It will reduce the amount of estrogen in your body. Estrogen causes the tumors to grow. Get this filled on your way home and start taking it immediately."

After Lynnette checked out of the hospital, she and Robert hugged Rose and thanked her for being by their side. Rose stood in the parking lot beside her car as she watched them drive away. A lone tear began to roll down her cheek. *I've got to tell them. They may hate me later, but I have to tell them the truth.*

Chapter 26

The countryside was draped in a vast array of rustic colors. There was a slight chill in the October air. Renovation of the children's home was right on schedule. It appeared that the grand opening would be in early January as predicted. Rose was excited. Except for a slight head cold and her decision to finally tell Lynnette her true identity, she was on top of the world.

A few days earlier, she had gotten the wedding pictures Greg and Sheree had promised to send her. She had put off telling both Lynnette and Greg the truth for as long as she could. There would be no more secrets.

She had called Greg the day she got the pictures. Naturally, he was shocked. She attempted to answer his questions and give him all the details. It pained him to learn that he had a sister he didn't know about and had never gotten the chance to know. He couldn't believe that his mother had kept such a deep, personal secret hidden all these years, but he had taken it better than Rose expected.

Now it was time for her to tell Lynnette. How would she react? Rose was already very well aware of the feelings of hatred and resentment Lynnette had toward her birth mother; however, as much as it pained her, she had to tell Lynnette the truth. She deserved that much. She had already been robbed of her entire childhood. Not only that, Lynnette was having her surgery next month. Robert wanted her to have it right away, but Lynnette wouldn't go for it. Robert backed down after Dr. Mandell told them that she could wait. Rose was fearful that something would go wrong and Lynnette wouldn't make it. She had to come clean.

It was Saturday. Lynnette had been out of the hospital a week and a half. Since Rose's cold had her feeling poorly, Lynnette had done some shopping for her and was coming over. Rose would show her Greg and Sheree's pictures and then have a serious talk with her.

Upon her arrival, Lynnette put away the groceries and warmed some soup for Rose. Later, they sat in the living room looking at the pictures as Lynnette oohed and aahed. When they'd seen the last picture, Rose shivered slightly. She didn't know if it was more from the chill in the air or her nervousness.

Rose looked at Lynnette sitting beside her. Her face was solemn as she spoke. "Lynn, I need to talk to you. There's something…"

Lynnette noticed Rose shiver again and interrupted. "Ms. Rose, you keep shivering. It's a little chilly in here. Are you cold? I can get you a blanket."

Rose thought a blanket might help so she agreed. "Yes, if you don't mind. I washed my throw the other day, and instead of putting it back across my chair, I folded it and put it on the closet shelf in my bedroom. Can you get it for me, please? You know which one—the beige one with the flowers."

"Yes, ma'am. I'll be right back."

Lynnette walked as fast as she could up the stairs. As she walked past Rose's bed, she reached down to straighten out a corner of the comforter. She stole a quick glance at some pictures on a corner tier shelf. Pictures of Rose, her family and friends. She smiled at the warmth she felt in her heart just from being around Rose.

Lynnette opened the door to the walk-in closet, felt for the wall light switch, and flipped the switch on. She stepped inside. Then she reached up and pulled Rose's throw from the shelf. A shoebox plopped to the floor. The lid popped off, and some of the contents fell out. As Lynnette stooped down to return the items to the box, something captured her attention. She knelt down and picked up a picture of a little girl who looked like her sitting in a rocking chair with a man and woman sitting on the floor on either side of her.

Lynnette's heart began to pound heavily. The picture was a black-and-white similar to the one of her as a little girl that she had at home in their family album. She pulled the picture closer to get a better look. The woman resembled a younger version of Rose. Who was the man? A voice inside her head screamed. *No! It can't be. Mama? Daddy?* She noticed a folded piece of paper on the floor. She grabbed it and pulled it apart. It was a birth certificate. The child's name was Kathryn Lynnette Alexander. The mother's maiden name said Roselyn Marie Jiles. The father was Daniel Lewis Alexander. It was exactly like the copy she had at home. The pounding in Lynnette's heart was more rigid.

Since Lynnette had not returned, Rose assumed she might

be having trouble locating the throw. She walked to the bottom of the stairs and yelled, "Lynn, do you see it!"

Lynnette hastily began throwing the items back into the box. Her voice shook when she shouted back, "Ye-yes, I have it! Ju-just a minute!" She returned the box to the shelf, switched off the light, and closed the closet door. She ran back down the stairs to the living room.

Lynnette rubbed her forehead with the back of her hand. Rose became alarmed when she saw Lynnette's expression. "Dear, what's wrong? Are you all right?"

Lynnette quickly draped the throw around Rose's shoulders. "I-I'm not feeling well. I have to go."

Rose held out her hand to stop Lynnette as she protested, "You can't drive like that. Let me take you."

Before Rose could do anything or say another word, Lynnette was gone. On the ride home, she could barely see through her tears to drive. This woman who had come into their lives was her mother. *How could I have been so stupid? She betrayed me. She betrayed my whole family. This can't be happening. Oh, God, please help me. I can't take this.*

Robert was in the kitchen when Lynnette burst through the door. "What's wrong? Rose called and said you ran out because you weren't feeling well."

Lynnette huffed and puffed as she attempted to catch her breath. "Josh. Randa. Where…are they? Are they…here?"

"No, they're at work. Sit down." Robert helped her to the table and a chair. "What's the matter?" He sat beside her.

Lynnette started to cry so hysterically she could barely speak. "Ms. Rose. She's my…mother."

Robert's eyes grew huge. "What?"

"She's…my mother."

"What do you mean she's your mother?"

Lynnette continued gasping through her tears. "When I…was at her…house…just now…I saw…a picture…and a…birth…certificate. Mine."

Robert gently rubbed his wife's back. "Honey, try to calm down. You must be mistaken. She can't be."

"I'm…not mistaken. Remember the picture of me…the one where I'm…sitting on the rocking chair?"

Robert nodded. "Yeah."

"She's got one like it. Only…there's a man…and woman in it. Her…and my father."

Robert took Lynnette's hands in his. "Okay, honey, try to calm down. Did you talk to her about this?"

Lynnette opened her eyes wide and shook her head. "No-o-o. I left."

"You've got to talk to her."

She snatched her hands out of Robert's, jumped to her feet, and started pacing. "I can't talk to her. I don't want to talk to her. What am I supposed to say? She walked out on me."

Robert jumped up and took his wife into his arms. Lynnette buried her head in his chest and started to moan. He took her gently by her wrist, put his other arm behind her back, and started to escort her out of the kitchen. "Come on. You're too upset to talk about this now. Let me help you upstairs. You can lay down while I run you a tub of hot water." She moaned all the way up the stairs.

In the bedroom, Lynnette sat on the side of the bed crying out in agony while Robert drew her bath. As he approached her, it occurred to him that he had never seen her in so much emotional pain. Not even when she'd found out about the surgery. This was not his wife. He didn't know who this woman was. She just sat there moaning, tears streaming down her face. He took her hand. "Come on. Your water's ready."

All Lynnette could do was lie there in the tub of hot, sudsy water. She felt as though her whole world was coming apart. She would be having the surgery soon, and now this. And with the way her life was going, the tumors would probably be cancerous. How could Rose do this to her? How could she walk out on her and then show up years later under false pretenses? Pretending she wanted to help children and using Lynnette and Robert. But the absolute worst part was lying to Lynnette about her true identity. Lynnette felt completely and utterly betrayed.

After about an hour, Robert helped her out of the tub and into her pajamas. Then he walked her over to the recliner where she sat curled up in a ball.

"Josh and Randa are home," he informed her as he placed a blanket over her to keep her warm. "I haven't said anything about what happened. I just told them you aren't feeling well."

When Lynnette didn't respond, Robert added, "Is that okay? You don't want to tell them yet, do you?"

She continued staring straight ahead. When she spoke, it was soft and slow. "That's fine. No, I don't want them to know yet."

Robert came to stand in front of her and got down on his knees. He removed her hands from underneath the blanket and held them. "Honey, I know you're upset, and I know you're hurting. Rose's abandoning you was wrong, but it took a lot of strength and courage for her to find you after all these years. She obviously loves you or she wouldn't have come here."

Lynnette snatched her hands away from Robert and stared at him as though he had gone insane. "How can you say that? Strength and courage? Where was her strength and courage when she left me? And as for love. If she had loved me, she never would have left in the first place. And after all this time, she has the nerve to waltz into my life and wreak more havoc."

Lynnette closed her eyes as she clenched her fists and hung

her head. She continued angrily, "I was doing just fine without her. The least she could have done was been upfront and honest with me."

"She was probably scared of what your reaction would be. How do you know that she didn't try to tell you and never could get the words out?"

Lynnette glared at Robert again. "Why are you taking her side? And why are you trying to make excuses for her? You're making it seem as if I'm the bad guy here."

"I'm not taking her side, and I'm not trying to make excuses for her. I just want you to be fair and reasonable."

"Fair? Reasonable? Was what she did to me fair and reasonable?"

"No. I'm not saying it was, but you have to be the better person and do the right thing."

Lynnette looked at Robert with tears in her eyes. "Why, Robert? Why does it have to be me? She didn't do the right thing."

"Because you know in your heart that it's the right thing to do. When Jesus taught us in the Lord's Prayer how to pray, didn't he say that if we want God to forgive us that we have to forgive others?"

"Yes, but it's not that easy."

"I know. You're upset and you're hurting. I can't feel your pain the way you do, but I'm hurting for you still because when you hurt I hurt. If I could take your pain away and go through it for you, I would. You love Rose."

Lynnette cut in abruptly. "That was before I found out who she really is."

"So you don't love her now?" Robert looked deep into the depths of his wife's eyes, waiting for an answer.

"I love the person I thought she was. I don't know if I can

love the person she is. All my life I've tried to do the right thing, and all I ever got was dumped on. She left me when I was four, and I was shifted around from house to house, never feeling like I belonged anywhere."

At the mere thought of mentioning another painful experience, Lynnette choked on her own tears. "The next thing I know, I find out I may need surgery, and now this. How much more do I have to take?"

Robert continued to speak consolingly to his wife. "Your life with your mother was taken away from you when you were very young. You have been living with the pain of it for a long time. Now is the opportunity for the two of you to share the rest of your lives together. Think about it. You can't get back what you lost, but here's your chance for some closure. Now you know where your mother is, and it's up to you what you're going to do about it. I know it's hard, but you have to deal with it.

"Out of all the years I've known you, you've never given up on anything or anybody. You're a very strong woman, and if I didn't have you in my life, I don't know where I'd be. Talk to Rose. You don't have to do it tonight or even tomorrow, but you need to do it soon because if you don't, it's going to keep eating away at you. Give yourself a few days, if that's what you need, to clear your head. Then talk to her and get your emotions out in the open. All those hurt feelings you've been dealing with all these years, let her know in a mild manner how you feel."

Lynnette knew Robert was right, but she wasn't yet ready to face Rose. She didn't think she could ever face her again.

Sunday was rainy, and the temperature outside was around fifty degrees. Lynnette was home alone. Robert had wanted to stay with her, but she had finally convinced him that there was no reason for him and the children to miss out on their spiritual food because she was depressed. She knew she needed to be with her fleshly and spiritual family in order to gain the needed strength and encouragement to go on, but for the moment, she had no desire for fellowship.

She sat in a ball, wrapped in a blanket on the den window seat, staring out the window. As she watched the droplets of rain splatter against the window, she thought about how the weather and her mood were a perfect match.

Her own mother had deserted her—went off and started another family without her. Now here she was building a home for other people's children. She hadn't even raised her own child—at least not Lynnette. Was this home supposed to somehow compensate for what Rose had done to her?

Lynnette sat in the same spot all morning, thinking and praying. She reopened her Bible to the fifty-fifth chapter of the book of Psalms. She mumbled under her breath as she read verse twenty-two. Then she leaned her head back and closed her eyes. This was what she had to do. Cast her burden upon the Lord.

She still had not been able to bring herself to talk to Rose, not even when Rose had called first thing that morning to check on her. Robert had told her that Lynnette still was not feeling well and wasn't up to talking.

Lynnette had not slept a wink the night before. She felt her eyelids getting heavy. The rain sounded so soothing. It was like an instant tranquilizer.

The next thing she knew, Robert was shaking her gently. "Lynn. Honey, let me help you upstairs so you can lay down."

Lynnette was so exhausted she didn't argue with him. She got up, and they proceeded upstairs. She was quiet. Robert tried to make conversation along the way. "Josh and Randa are downstairs fixing dinner."

She attempted a smile. "That's nice."

"Well, we cheated a little," Robert said, chuckling. "We stopped at KFC and got some chicken, but we're gonna cook some vegetables and bread to go with it."

Robert pulled back the covers on the unmade bed and helped his wife slide in. He pulled the covers up over her and got down on his knees beside the bed and held her hands.

"Honey, I know you may not want to hear this," he began, "but Rose is very worried about you."

When Lynnette didn't respond, Robert continued, "Remember what we talked about last night? You have to talk to her sooner or later."

Robert was really looking after her and trying to give her the love and encouragement she needed in this dreadful hour. Everything he said made sense, but she was hurting so much. "I know. Honey, I'm tired. Right now, I just want to go to sleep. Okay?"

"Sure. I'll wake you when dinner's ready." Robert leaned over and kissed her cheek.

As he headed back downstairs, he wondered if his wife would ever make it through this.

As Rose was hanging up her sweater in the closet, something on the floor caught her eye. She reached down and picked it up. When she saw what it was, her heart sank. It was the last picture that she, Daniel, and Lynnette had taken together as a family. Had Lynnette seen it the day before? She must have. Right after she had gotten Rose's throw, she appeared upset about something. The birth certificate. Had she seen it, too? Rose looked up at the box on the shelf. The lid was crooked.

This was horrible. Rose started putting together the events of the day before and Lynnette's sudden indifference toward her. No wonder she had rushed out the way she had and had been avoiding her. Rose had not wanted her to find out this way. *I should have told her the truth from the start. Any chance I had of being her mother now is gone.*

Chapter 27

Miranda answered the telephone. "Daddy, it's for you. It's Ms. Johnson." She held the phone out to her father.

"Hello," Robert spoke into the phone.

Rose's voice was quiet. She spoke slowly. "Robert, this is Rose. Lynn knows, doesn't she?"

Robert watched his two children scurrying about the kitchen. He wasn't going to tell Rose anything. He faked ignorance. "Knows what?" he whispered.

"I think you know what I'm talking about. I'm sorry to put you on the spot. I know Josh and Randa are there, and you can't talk. Robert, I want you to know that I never meant to hurt Lynn or any of you. I love you all dearly, and I'd never do anything to intentionally hurt you."

Robert continued to speak in a whisper. "You need to talk to Lynn. She had a rough night. She's sleeping now."

"She won't talk to me."

"She will. Just give her time."

"I'm really sorry, Robert."

"I know. I'll tell her you called. Bye."

"Bye."

Rose's heart ached at the thought of the pain Lynnette was in, all because of her. Lynnette would probably never speak to her again.

Carla poked her head through Robert and Lynnette's bedroom door before entering. When she saw Lynnette resting on the recliner, she tapped lightly on the door. "Hey, girl."

Lynnette looked at Carla and faked a smile. "Hey. Pull up a chair."

Carla grabbed a provincial chair from a corner and sat beside Lynnette. "James and I stopped by to see how you guys are. Robert said you're not feeling well. The tumors causing you pain again?"

Lynnette shook her head. "No."

Carla touched her sister-in-law's forehead with the back of her hand. "You're not running a fever. What's the matter? Are you catching a cold?"

"No. Robert didn't tell you?"

Carla shook her head. "He just said you weren't feeling well. Lynn, you're scaring me. I've never seen you like this. What's wrong?"

Lynnette didn't know how to go about telling Carla, so she just blurted it out nonchalantly. "It's Rose. I found out yesterday she's my mother."

Carla's eyes were like saucers. "What? You're kidding. She can't be. How do you know?"

Lynnette leaned back farther in her chair and closed her eyes as she relived the painful moment. "I was at her house yesterday. I was getting her throw from her closet when this box fell off the shelf. When I reached down to get it, I saw a picture of her, my father, and me together when I was little. The picture is similar to the copy I have of me in a rocking chair. I saw my birth certificate, too."

Carla was still in shock. "But you don't look anything like her. How did she get away with it?"

"It's obvious from the picture I saw that I favor my father. Her real name is Roselyn Marie Jiles Johnson. She just shortened Roselyn to Rose, or maybe Rose is the name she's always gone by." Frustrated, Lynnette added, "How would I know? I never knew her."

"I am so sorry. What explanation did she give you?"

Lynnette opened her eyes. "None. I didn't give her a chance. I ran out."

"Aren't you going to talk to her?"

"I don't know. Right now, I just need some time to think."

"Lynn, I know how close your family and Rose have become. I've seen you two together. It's obvious you love each other. You've always seemed like mother and daughter to me. Whenever you were together, your whole face just lit up the sky. I know I have no right to tell you this because I grew up with both my parents so I don't know what it's like to be in your shoes, but give her a chance to explain things to you."

"It's all so frustrating. The person I love is not at all the person I thought she was. Rose came here negotiating a business deal with us, knowing who I was. I feel like such a fool. Maybe that was her plan all along: to come here under false pretenses so she could win me over, thinking that would change how I really feel about her."

"How do you really feel about her?"

"A huge part of me still loathes the woman who walked out

on me, but the other part loves the woman I've come to know over these last several months. It's strange. Whenever she and I were together, I was so happy and always thought about how I wished she was my mother or that my mother had been like her. I certainly didn't want it to turn out this way. Not for her to be the person who actually walked out on me.

"And on top of it all, she went and started another family without me. What was wrong with me that she left me? What made Greg so special that she stayed with him?" Lynnette's lips trembled as she spoke. "She was showing me his wedding pictures yesterday, and I was all smiling and carrying on, all the while not even knowing I was looking at my half-brother and sister-in-law. It's not fair. I should have been at his wedding. My family should have been there. She robbed me of that, too. All this while, I've had a brother who I didn't even know about. Josh and Randa had an uncle they didn't know existed. Robert, a brother-in-law. All that time wasted. I feel cheated. My kids were cheated. My whole family was cheated."

Carla whispered, "Do Josh and Randa know yet?"

Lynnette shook her head. "No. Robert and I don't want them to know yet. I'm worried about how they'll take it."

"Kids are resilient. They usually bounce back pretty fast, but perhaps it is best to wait until after you talk to Rose."

Lynnette and Carla talked a few more minutes before Carla and James left. Then Lynnette took a hot bath and went downstairs to her favorite spot on the den's window seat. She was in deep thought when Miranda came in with two mugs of steaming hot cocoa.

"Thanks, sweetie. Have a seat." No matter how miserable she felt, she was determined to make time for her family. Lynnette made room for Miranda and took a sip of the hot chocolaty liquid. "I really appreciate how you and Josh always

pitch in and help out around here. Thanks for helping your
dad with dinner today. It was good. The potatoes you made
were delicious. The onions, bell peppers, and cheese topped
them off. Where'd you get the recipe?"

Miranda beamed with pride. "I didn't use a recipe. I
made it up."

"Wow. It was really good. Do we have a chef on our
hands? Move over Emeril Lagasse. Make room for Miranda
Montgomery."

They were both laughing. As a matter of fact, it was the
first time since the day before that Lynnette had done so.

"It's good to see you laughing, Mama," Miranda observed.
"I've always loved your laugh. Josh and I heard Daddy talking
to Ms. Johnson on the phone today. Are you and she upset
with each other about something?"

"We had a misunderstanding. It's personal, but we'll
work it out."

"I hope so."

They talked a few more minutes before Miranda stood
and took her mother's empty mug. "Well, good night. I'm
going to bed."

Lynnette was shocked. The grandfather clock indicated it
was still early. "It's not even nine o'clock."

"I know, but I'm tired. I'm about to drop."

"Okay. Go on and get your beauty rest," Lynnette encouraged her daughter.

Miranda leaned down and kissed her mother's cheek.
"Good night."

"Good night, sweetie."

The next morning, Lynnette was still in a dismal mood. She
decided to stay home and called Beverly. She didn't feel like

talking about what had occurred between her and Rose, so she simply stated that she wasn't feeling well. During the latter part of the morning, the telephone rang as she was headed upstairs. When she heard Rose's feeble voice on the answering machine, Lynnette's heart began to pound in her chest.

"Lynn, this is Rose. I'm sorry to bother you at home. I'm worried about you. I called the store. Beverly said you didn't go in today. I know it's because of me. I know you're hurt and angry with me, but I'd like to talk to you. Please call me. Bye."

Maybe a walk would help Lynnette clear her head. The weather was warmer, in the low sixties, even though it was October, and the sun was shining. She grabbed a light jacket and headed south up the street. As she walked through the neighborhood, she admired the spacious two- and three-story homes. The area was beautiful. Not because of its wealth but because of its natural surroundings. The trees were majestic. Regal magnolias, maples, and oaks stood high against the open sky.

As Lynnette continued her walk, she wondered if she could have a change of heart. Could she let go of the feelings of enmity she had built up over the years?

She and her mother had not gotten the chance to form a lifelong bond like so many other mothers and daughters. When Lynnette had gone from childhood to puberty, where was her mother? When she had gone on her first date, where was her mother? What about her wedding day? When her children were born? Even several months ago when she had found out about the tumors and the surgery, it would have been so nice to have had her mother by her side to help her through it.

With that thought in mind, Lynnette quickly realized that her mother had been by her side during that troublesome moment. Only she hadn't known it at the time. Rose had helped her through with words of reassurance, her friendship, and most of all, her genuine love and concern. They had not shared their past, but perhaps they could share their present and future lives with each other. *I just don't know.* Could she let go of a hurtful past and get on with a promising future that included her mother?

As Lynnette made her way back toward their house, she noticed one of their neighbors outside playing with her young children on a swing set. She waved. They waved back. They were laughing with such joy and excitement. She and Robert used to play with Joshua and Miranda like that. She didn't know if she had ever done anything of the sort with her parents. If she had, she certainly didn't remember it. She had no memory of a bond with them.

Lynnette felt herself about to break down. She didn't want anyone to see her and managed to keep the tears at bay until she reached the garage. She fell back against the passenger side of the Land Rover and slid slowly down to the ground as she burst into tears.

Oh, God, please help me. I can't take this. I can take a lot of things, but not this.

Lynnette sat there crying until she thought she could cry no more. She was feeling sorry for herself again. What was it Rose had told her? The worst kind of pity is self-pity. Yes, Rose was full of words of wisdom. Too bad she hadn't thought of any for herself when she walked out on her child.

God is my salvation. He is my strength and my song. I will trust Him and not be afraid.

Lynnette stood straight, wiping her face with her hands. She knew what she had to do.

Rose hadn't heard anyone drive up. When she asked who it was at the door, she was shocked, excited, and nervous to discover that it was Lynnette. Rose wanted to throw her arms around her but didn't for fear that she would be rejected. She led the way to the living room and offered Lynnette something to drink. Lynnette declined. Rose sat on the sofa, and Lynnette chose a chair on the opposite side of the room.

It was obvious to both of them how uncomfortable the other was as they sat in brief seconds of silence. From the first day they'd met, they had never felt this way with each other— until that moment.

Lynnette was disappointed with her inability to speak. She had finally gotten up the nerve to confront Rose, and the words would not come. She wanted to lash out at her, but despite what Rose had done to her, she knew that was not the Christian way.

Rose looked pitifully at Lynnette. "Lynn, I am so sorry. I never meant to hurt you. I love you."

Lynnette looked at Rose as a lone tear began to run down her face. "Why didn't you tell me the truth?"

"I should have. I wanted to. Every time I tried, I talked myself out of it. I was scared, and I didn't want to hurt you."

Lynnette glared at Rose. "Didn't want to hurt me?" she repeated. "Did you think it would hurt any less the way I found out?"

"No. I was going to tell you Saturday when you were here. I was about to tell you when you went to get my throw."

At that point, Lynnette recalled that Rose had said something about needing to talk to her. That didn't matter though. She should have told her long before then.

"You should have told me when you first came to me. You deceived me into believing you were someone else. You even deceived my family and friends. I have two children at home who never knew their grandparents except for Robert's mother, and all the while they could have been getting to know you as their grandmother. They were thinking you were just some incredibly nice lady who had come into their lives.

"All my life, I've been trying to figure out what I did so wrong that would make my own mother leave me. How could a mother abandon her own flesh and blood? And then you went off and started a whole other family with someone else. The only difference is you stayed with them. All I want to know is why. Why did you leave me?" Lynnette had almost succeeded at holding back a floodgate of tears. Now they were streaming down her face.

Rose wanted to run to her, throw her arms around her, and comfort her. Instead, she attempted to offer an explanation. "It happened not long after your father was killed in an automobile accident. You were only four. We were a happy family. When we lost your father, I could no longer function mentally or physically."

Rose shook her head in shame. "I was not a strong person back then. I couldn't deal with your father's death. I wanted to take you with me, but if I couldn't take care of myself, I knew I couldn't take care of you. So I left you with a neighbor one day while I went to seek help for myself, and I never came back. Years later, I met Thurgood. We got married, and Greg was born a few years later."

Lynnette's brain was trying to soak in all that Rose had just told her. "Did Thurgood know about me? What about Greg? Does he know?"

"After Thurgood and I had been married for a while, I told him. I was plagued with feelings of guilt for leaving you. We hired a private investigator who found you about four years ago. We relocated here three years ago but never approached you. Thurgood begged me to contact you, but I was scared.

Then a little more than two years ago, he died. My next biggest regret after leaving you is that he never got to meet you. He wanted so much for us to be reunited."

Lynnette was stunned that Rose had known of her whereabouts for such a long period. "So," she stated, "you lied when you approached me and Robert about the children's home. All this was some hoax to get close to me." The more she thought about Rose's deception, the angrier she became.

Rose shook her head. "Oh no, it wasn't a hoax. I admit I did want to get to know you, but the idea for the children's home was sincere. All those years, I lived with the guilt of what I'd done to you. I resolved in my heart to help other children and families in need. Thurgood knew that was a dream of mine. I didn't know about the house until after he died.

"Then one day, I got the idea to approach you and Robert about fixing it up, but I also hired you for your talent. It's true that I had seen your and Robert's work in *Southern Homes* magazine. That was after I found out where you were. This was a serious project to me, and I didn't want just anybody doing it.

"As for Greg, he didn't know about you until last week. In August, when I was preparing to leave for the wedding, I wanted you to come with me so badly. I wanted you to be at your brother's wedding. That's when I made up my mind that when I returned, I would tell you.

"I wanted to tell Greg when I was there, but I felt that was too much to put on him during one of the happiest times of his life. I waited two months, but it seemed more like two years. When the pictures came last week, I picked up the phone and called him."

Lynnette wiped away her tears as she sniffed. "What did he say?"

"He was shocked, of course. And disappointed that he

didn't know of your existence and hadn't gotten to know you. He couldn't believe I had kept it a secret all these years, but his main concern was you. He said you have a right to know and that I needed to tell you right away. I assured him that was my intention. Do Josh and Randa know yet?"

"No."

"Would you like for me to tell them?"

Lynnette shook her head. "No. I think it'll be better coming from Robert and me."

"Lynn, leaving you was the worst mistake of my life. Do you remember asking me if there was anything that I wish I'd done differently? Now I can tell you the answer to that question is that I wish I had stayed with you or taken you with me and been the mother to you I should have been.

"I know you hate me, and I can't say that I blame you. In your shoes, I think I'd feel the same way. I hate myself for the pain I've caused you all these years. If I had to, I'd give my life for you. I know you think it's not fair of me to ask you this, but I have to. Do you think you can ever find it in your heart to forgive me for what I did to you?"

Lynnette had not expected Rose to ask for her forgiveness. She thought back to her and Robert's conversation. It would take time for the healing to begin, and who knew how long before the wounds closed, if they ever did? Finally, she answered, "It will take time, but all I can tell you is I'll try."

"That's all I ask. That you try."

Lynnette looked at her wristwatch and stood. "It's almost three. I should be going." She proceeded toward the door.

As Rose followed, a thought occurred to her. "I have something for you. Can you wait just one minute?"

Lynnette felt as though she would lose her mind if she didn't leave, but she answered, "Yes."

Rose walked away. When she returned, she held a photo in her hand and handed it to Lynnette. "Here. This belongs to you. I'll have a copy made for me later." It was the picture Lynnette had seen just two days before in Rose's closet.

All she could say was, "Thank you." When Lynnette opened the door and stepped onto the porch into the pleasant afternoon air, Rose shamelessly asked, "Would it be too much to ask for a hug?"

Lynnette wanted to be happy about this turn of events, but indifference had taken over her. She hesitated. Then she turned around and took two steps toward Rose. Her movement was slow, but the embrace was quick. Not at all like previous times when she couldn't bear to let Rose go. She wanted it to be like it used to be, but this newfound knowledge of truth had brought with it an oddness, and she was still feeling a little uncomfortable. She could tell from the look on Rose's face that she was disappointed at the lack of warmth in her embrace.

"Good-bye, Lynn," Rose whispered.

"Bye," Lynnette echoed in her own whisper; then she started down the sidewalk to her vehicle.

What Rose couldn't see or hear as she stood there watching Lynnette's back as she walked away were the words Lynnette mouthed: "Bye, Mama."

Chapter 28

Robert found Lynnette on her window seat. "Hey."

She looked up at him and attempted to smile. "Hey."

He joined her on the seat. There was a brief moment of silence.

Then Lynnette said, "I talked to Rose today."

Robert was pleased. "That's good. How did it go?"

"She told me why she left."

Lynnette tried not to cry as she relayed to Robert everything Rose had told her.

"I want to go on hating her for what she did to me, but in my heart, I know I can't. I can't hate her because…I love her so much. But now, she's not just Rose Johnson anymore." Lynnette's next words brought the tears she was so desperately trying to conceal. "She's my mama. Even though she took away a huge part of my life, a part that I will never be able to redeem, she's still my mama."

Robert didn't say anything. He knew Lynnette needed to talk. He moved closer and put his arms around her as he listened intently while she poured out her feelings.

"I went over there angry with her. I'm still angry, but instead of it being a loathsome kind of anger, it's more a disappointing kind like what we go through here at home with each other and the kids when we mess up. I'm angry that she wasn't honest with me, but there's another part of me that's somewhat relieved she didn't just come out and tell me.

"The pain probably would have been too much for me to bear. I had such detestable feelings for her that if she had told me who she really was, I probably wouldn't have given her the time of day. Then I wouldn't have gotten to know her for the person she is now. Does that sound crazy?"

"Not at all. Sounds like normal human feelings to me. You've been through a lot. Your suffering all started back then with that one act, and you've been trying to deal with it all these years. You dealt with it the only way you could, but now it's time to move on. Do you think you can do that?"

"I don't know. I want to. I'm so tired of all this hatred I feel. I wish it would go away. I wish I could just pretend it never happened. Right now, I feel like my heart has been ripped apart. When I was young, I dreamed of the day my mother and I would be reunited, but when it never happened I lost all hope.

"I remember being at school and hearing the other girls talk about what they did with their mothers. All I could do was sit there and listen. I wouldn't let them see that their happy stories were tearing me apart, but when I was by myself I'd cry until I couldn't cry anymore. I needed her, Robert, and she wasn't there for me." Lynnette moaned. "I needed her-r-r-r-r-r-r-r."

Robert took Lynnette in his arms and held her tight as he

whispered words of comfort to her. "It's okay, sweetheart. She's here for you now. She loves you. She wasn't the mother to you then that she should have been. Let her be the mother to you that she can be now. God will supply you with the strength you need to let the healing begin. Just rely on Him. He'll help you through."

Robert held Lynnette for several minutes and let her cry. Finally, she spoke again. "We have to tell Josh and Randa."

"Do you want the two of us to talk to them tonight when they get home from work?"

Lynnette looked up into the face of the one who'd been there for her through thick and thin, her protector, and answered, "Yes, but there is one thing that would make me feel a whole lot better first."

Robert knew what it was. They closed their eyes and bowed their heads as he offered a prayer to God, asking Him to help them to choose the right words to impart this extremely emotional news to their children.

In the den, Robert and Lynnette sat across from their children.

Lynnette began, "Let me just say first that no one is about to give you any bad news that anyone is sick or hurt. What we have to tell you is about Ms. Rose." She couldn't go on. *Just say it.* "I recently found out that she's my mother." It was finally out.

Shocked expressions appeared on the faces of Joshua and Miranda.

"Mama," Miranda spoke slowly, "you can't be serious. That's not true."

This was a mistake, Lynnette thought. *We should have waited.*

Robert said, "It's true, honey. Ms. Johnson is your grandmother."

Joshua was finally able to speak. "Wow. Ms. Johnson's our grandmother? Mom, when did you find this out?"

"Saturday," Lynnette answered.

"Did she tell you?" Joshua wanted to know.

"Not exactly. I found out by accident."

Joshua asked, "But how did she find you after all these years?"

Lynnette answered, "She hired a private investigator."

Miranda argued, "Ms. Johnson is not my grandmother. She's not the kind of person who would do what your mother did. Mama, you know her. She would never do that."

"Honey," Lynnette said to her daughter, "remember the day you and I were on our way to Ms. Rose's house? You hadn't met her yet. We were talking on the way there. You were asking me questions about my mother. You told me that maybe she left me because she couldn't handle it when my father died. Then you said you knew that wasn't an excuse, but perhaps it was the reason?"

Miranda looked disappointed. "I remember, but all I was doing was trying to make you feel better."

Lynnette acknowledged, "I know, but when you made that statement, you had no idea that what you were saying was actually true. Sometimes people do things for reasons we don't know or understand. That's what happened with my mother."

Miranda was upset. "It doesn't matter to me what her reasons were. If she really is your mother, she shouldn't have left you." She stormed out of the room.

When Joshua noticed his mother about to get up to go after Miranda, he said, "Mom, let me talk to her."

Lynnette nodded and leaned back against the chair. She slipped her hand into the pocket of her sweater and pulled out a picture. She handed it to Joshua. "Josh, let her see this. It's a picture of me with my parents, your grandparents."

Joshua looked at the picture and went upstairs.

Robert told Lynnette, "She'll listen to Josh. If anybody can get through to Randa, it's Josh."

Lynnette didn't say anything. She simply laid her head on Robert's shoulder.

Upstairs in her room, Joshua approached Miranda as she sat at her desk pretending to do homework. He pulled up a chair and sat beside her. "This is a shock, Randa, to all of us, but now that the truth is out, we have to move on."

"That's easy for you to say," Miranda shot back. "You think it's cool. Our grandmother has been under our nose all this time, and we didn't even know it. How can you just act like everything's okay?"

"Everything's not okay, but think about it. We never had a chance to know any of our grandparents except for Grandma Lil. As for Mom's mother, we didn't know if she was alive or dead, and from the looks of things we would never find out. Now we have a chance to get to know her even better. We've already come to know and love her as a friend. Now we can know and love her as our grandmother."

"I do love her. We all do, especially Mama. But what she did was awful."

"Look." Joshua put the photograph on the desk in front of Miranda.

She picked it up. "It's Mama...and Ms. John—" Miranda couldn't finish because of the shock of what she saw before her. These were their grandparents. Their mother's parents. "Where'd you get this?"

"From Mom. You left before she could show it to you."

"Mama looks just like her daddy," Miranda acknowledged.

"Yeah, I know."

"Look at them. They look so happy."

There was a knock on the door. "Come in," Miranda said.

Robert and Lynnette entered the room. "Everything okay?" their father inquired.

Miranda answered, "Yes, Daddy. I'm okay."

"Good. Mom and I are going to bed. We'll see you two in the morning. Don't stay up too late."

"We won't," Joshua assured them. "We're gonna talk for a few more minutes."

As Robert and Lynnette walked away, they could hear the soft murmur of Joshua and Miranda talking.

The following week, Lynnette was in her office when Beverly peeked her head in and told her that Rose was in the store to see her. There were some moments when Lynnette would avoid Rose except for when it was absolutely necessary to bring her up-to-date on the progress of the children's home. She was having high and low moments. One minute she was ecstatic that her mother was in her life, but the next minute she was dealing with feelings of betrayal. It was a constant battle, back and forth, from sheer euphoria to wretched despair.

Not wanting to put poor Beverly in the middle of their dilemma, Lynnette reluctantly went out to greet Rose.

Rose greeted her with a cheerful smile. "Hi. How are you?"

Lynnette attempted to return the smile. "Hi. Okay. What about you?"

"I'm fine. I came to see if I can take you to lunch. How does Chinese sound?"

"Sounds good, but I'll have to pass today."

Rose sensed that Lynnette was keeping something from her. "Is everything okay?"

"Everything's fine," Lynnette lied. "I'll probably just order in and try to catch up on some work while I eat."

Rose attempted to smile. "Well, okay. Maybe another time."

Lynnette smiled. "Sure."

Rose kissed Lynnette on her cheek and left.

As Beverly returned to the front from the supply room, she noticed Lynnette just standing there staring after Rose. She dropped the box of envelopes onto the counter, walked around behind the counter, and looked at Lynnette as she stood there. "Are you two going to be okay?"

Lynnette dropped her hands to her sides and spun around as she walked over to Beverly. "I don't know. I hope so. I can't seem to stop thinking about the past and all the pain involved."

Beverly looked at her friend and coworker sympathetically. "You know, I think it's like my mama always told me. If it didn't happen overnight, it's not going to get better overnight. You have to give yourself time. There's another saying, you know, that I'm sure you're familiar with." She looked at Lynnette without going any further.

"Time heals all wounds?" Lynnette asked.

"Yes. It doesn't mean you won't still have some scars, but the pain will get less and less. But I know you know that."

"Yeah. I'm trying, Beverly. It's so hard sometimes. I want to just forget about what happened in the past and let it go, but it's a real struggle."

Beverly gently patted Lynnette's hand on the counter. "You can do it though because your faith is strong."

Lynnette smiled. She walked behind the counter and hugged Beverly. "Thanks, Beverly. I needed that."

At that moment, they heard the door chime and in rushed Simone. "Hey, what are you two up to?"

Lynnette swirled around with one of her big, wide grins on

her face. "Hey, you." The two women wrapped their arms around each other.

Simone greeted Beverly, "Hi, Beverly. You doing okay?"

"Hi, Simone. I'm fine. What about yourself?"

"I'm good. Just came to take my friend here out to eat." Simone asked Lynnette, "What about it?"

"Well, I had planned to order in and work through lunch."

"Work through lunch? That's no fun. You need to at least get an hour away from this store. You're going to stress yourself out. Come on. What d'you say?"

Beverly gave Lynnette a sweep of her fingers toward the door indicating that she should go. "Go on. You do need to get out of here."

Lynnette grinned in appreciation. "Okay. Let me get my purse."

Beverly and Simone chatted while Lynnette went to get her purse. When she returned the two friends laughed as they left the store.

Rose had just left Kmart. As she pulled back onto the main highway and began to pass Pizza Hut, she caught a glimpse of Lynnette and Simone going into the restaurant.

When she saw the two women together, an intense feeling that she had not experienced in a long time swept through her body like flames of fire. Jealousy! *Didn't Lynn tell me not too long ago that she was ordering lunch in?*

Rose knew Lynnette had been avoiding her as of late, but she had no idea things would come to this. Not to the point where Lynnette would be lying and making excuses not to be with her. *How dare she!* Rose was very well aware that what she had done to Lynnette many years ago was wrong, but was she going to have to pay for it for the rest of her life?

She would not be made a fool of, and she would not force

her company on someone who didn't want it. She would let Lynnette know in no uncertain terms that she didn't appreciate her dishonesty. She was not going to let Lynnette put her off. This time she would confront her face-to-face.

Later that afternoon as Rose drove to the Montgomery house, she began to have second thoughts about her quest. Who was she to criticize?

Before she realized it, she was in the Montgomerys' driveway. She was glad to see that Lynnette's vehicle was not in the garage. She had to get out of there before Lynnette got home and saw her.

Just as Rose was about to back out of the driveway, Lynnette drove up. She pulled into the garage, got out of her vehicle, and went to the driver's side of Rose's car. She lightly tapped on the window. Rose slowly rolled the window down halfway.

"Hi. Were you waiting for me?"

Rose cleared her throat. "A-Ah, n-no," she stuttered. "I was just leaving."

"Is something wrong?"

"N-no."

"Would you like to come in?"

"No, I don't want to impose."

"You won't be imposing." Lynnette opened the door. "Come on," she insisted. Rose rolled up the window and complied.

Once inside, Lynnette stirred the chili she had left cooking in the Crock-Pot. While she mixed together the ingredients for some corn bread, Rose grated some cheese.

The air was quiet until Rose spoke out softly. "I have a confession to make."

Lynnette arched her eyebrows as she looked at Rose. "Really?"

Rose looked away, as though embarrassed. "Yes."

"What is it?" Lynnette put the corn bread in the oven.

"I saw you and Simone today going into Pizza Hut. I got angry—jealous—because you wouldn't go to lunch with me, but you went with her. I came over here this afternoon to express my displeasure, but on the way here I realized that I have no right to do that. You don't owe me anything. I owe you. I owe you so much. I'll never be able to give you back what I took from you.

"I love you. I love you with all my heart. If I could turn back the hands of time, I'd do things differently. I would take you with me or stay with you and try to be the best mother to you that I can be. If I had been half the woman then that you are now, that's what I would have done. For what I put you through, you turned out to be an incredibly strong individual with a whole lot of faith. Even though I had nothing to do with it, I'm proud of the person you've become."

Lynnette walked over to where Rose was standing. "Do you remember what you told me after we first met when we were talking about the surgery?"

Rose thought for a moment. She'd said so much. "What?"

"You said that what doesn't kill us makes us stronger."

"Oh. Yes."

"We all have things happen in our lives, and they can either make us or break us. It's up to us to decide what we're going to do about it. I had to make up my mind that I was going to overcome my obstacles, but you're right. I didn't do it alone. God helped me through it all, and so did my family and friends. As for today, Simone came in after you left, and I let her talk me into going to lunch with her. I'm sorry if I hurt you."

Rose sighed. "I know you've been having a difficult time adjusting to all this chaos. I can't and I shouldn't expect you to act as though you can just overlook what I did and pretend everything is okay. For the rest of my life, I will have to live with what I did to you. As much as I want it to, my walking into your life at this point is not going to automatically make everything all right."

"No, it's not," Lynnette agreed, "but it's a start. The past is over and done with, and now we have to try to move on. With that said, I hope you'll change your mind and stay for supper. Robert, the kids, and I would love to have you. After all, we really are family now."

"Yes, I'd like that." Lynnette was right. They really were family, and Rose would never forsake them again.

Chapter 29

By November, the work on the children's home was still coming along nicely. Lynnette and Rose had gone on a few shopping sprees, selecting furniture and other furnishings.

Rose had even started attending worship services with Lynnette and her family. She had finally confided to Lynnette that because she felt God was displeased with her for abandoning her child, it had been years since she'd stepped foot in a place of worship. However, she had managed to sit through the brief memorial service for Thurgood in the funeral home chapel.

It had been a little over a month since Lynnette had been in the hospital. It was Thursday, and her surgery was scheduled for the next morning. She and Robert had to be at the hospital at seven o'clock.

For the past month, she had been constantly reminding Robert of things she felt were of importance, things she believed he needed to know. Just in case. She didn't say it, but he knew her reason for doing so. They were both nervous about the surgery. They prayed together before they went to bed.

As they laid in bed wrapped in each other's arms, Lynnette felt the urge to speak from her heart.

"Whatever happens tomorrow, remember I love you. This has been a tough year for all of us. You and I have had some rocky moments. I'm sorry for all the stress I added to our lives. I love you so much, and I want you to be happy. If I don't make it—"

Robert interjected, "Don't say that. You'll make it. We have to believe that."

Lynnette looked into Robert's face. "I have to say this. Please let me. I know it's painful and you don't want to hear it. I don't want to say it, but I have to because I love you. Sometimes we have to let ourselves go through a painful moment in order to make things right.

"If I don't make it through the surgery, I don't want you to spend the rest of your life grieving over me. I know you'll be sad, but you have to go on—for your sake and for Josh and Randa's. They need you. Be happy and live your life. And when the time comes, I'll see you all again."

Lynnette rested her face against Robert's cheek.

It had been a while since Robert had allowed his wife to see him shed any tears. The last time had been at his mother's funeral. But at this moment, he didn't mind her seeing his pain because he loved her so, and the thought of losing her crushed his spirit.

Lynnette felt the wetness of his tears against her face. She whispered, "Everything will be all right."

Lynnette said a silent prayer. *Tomorrow's the day. If I don't make it, please take care of my family.*

* * *

The hospital waiting room was packed with Lynnette's family and friends. Dr. Mandell was performing a vaginal hysterectomy on Lynnette. Compared to an abdominal one, this type of procedure required a shorter hospital stay and recovery time. She should be home in a day or two and would be able to return to work in a couple of weeks.

When Dr. Mandell finally stepped into the waiting area, all eyes were glued to him. Robert jumped up and rushed to him. He didn't give the doctor an opportunity to speak.

"How is she?" he asked quickly.

Dr. Mandell smiled. "She's doing great. Everything went fine. She's in recovery. As soon as she comes around, we'll put her in a room, and you can all see her."

Everyone present stood, smiles beaming across their faces. Robert grinned and shook Dr. Mandell's hand. "Thank you so much."

The doctor grinned back. "You're welcome." Then he turned and walked away.

After Lynnette was brought into her room, Robert was the first to see her. He pulled up a chair close to the bed and sat down. "Hey there, beautiful."

Lynnette slowly opened her eyes. As they began to focus, she saw the most handsome face. "Hey, handsome. I made it."

Robert grabbed her hand. "You made it." He stood, leaned down, and kissed her on her lips.

Lynnette commented, "I must look a mess."

"You're beautiful," Robert assured her. "I'm gonna get Josh and Randa. Then Rose wants to see you. There's a waiting room full of people who can't wait to see you. Are you up to it?"

"Of course."

"Okay. Hang on." Robert left the room.

Joshua and Miranda walked in. Lynnette reached out both arms to them. One went on one side of the bed and one on the other. Both leaned down and kissed a cheek. They visited for a few minutes and left. Then Rose came in.

Rose stood beside the bed holding Lynnette's hand. Lynnette looked up into her face and smiled. "I'm so glad you're here, Mama."

Mama. This was the first time Rose had heard Lynnette call her by the sentiment. It felt good. It sounded good.

Tears welled up in Rose's eyes, and she said, "I wouldn't be anywhere else but here by your side."

Rose pulled up a chair, sat down, and proceeded to tell Lynnette about the day she was born.

Afterward, James and Carla visited. Then Simone. Later in the afternoon, the Dotsons, other congregation members, and Beverly came to visit.

Later that evening when Lynnette had a brief moment alone in her room and all was quiet, she thanked God for seeing her through the surgery. She had put it off for almost a year because she had been so scared. But once she had put her life completely in His hands, her faith in Him had allowed her to make it through the whole scary ordeal. A measure of faith. Robert said that's all that was needed. But she had so much more than that.

It was Saturday. Two weeks after Lynnette's surgery. She was recuperating well. The tumors were benign. She and her family were preparing for one of the most exciting days of their lives.

As Lynnette checked the roast in the oven, she mumbled under her breath. "I'm so nervous." She closed the oven door and turned around to face Robert as she wiped her hands on the blue-and-white apron she was wearing.

"You'll be fine," he reassured her.

"What if I can't think of anything to say to them?"

Robert grunted and laughed at the same time. "Humph. That'll be a first. I've never known you to be at a loss for words, especially when it comes to giving me a piece of your mind."

Lynnette put a playful smirk on her face. "Ha, ha. Very funny."

Robert put his arms around her and pulled her close. "I'm just kidding. I told you you'll be fine."

Lynnette leaned back and looked at Robert. "I hope they like pot roast."

He laughed again. "Well, the way Rose talks, Greg eats everything. Let's just pray we made enough."

Lynnette laughed and leaned her head against Robert's chest. "You are so bad."

"They're here!" Joshua and Miranda yelled as they made their way to the kitchen.

Lynnette quickly removed herself from Robert's embrace and turned her back to him. "Honey, untie me." Robert untied her apron, and she hastily pulled it over her head.

Robert, Joshua, and Miranda had already decided among themselves to stay back at first and let Lynnette have her moment. Lynnette was nervous, but she was mostly excited. She didn't even notice that her family remained behind as she walked quickly out the door to the van in the driveway.

She caught sight of Rose getting out of the vehicle and a very pretty young woman behind her. Next, she saw an extremely handsome man, the spitting image of Rose, getting down from behind the wheel of the van. Lynnette approached him with tears in her eyes. If this was any indication of what the resurrection would be like, she was going to need a ton of tissues.

All Lynnette could say was his name. "Greg."

Greg smiled. "Lynn."

They took hold of each other's hands at first, just staring into the other's face as though they were attempting to obtain an indelible image in their brains of the face looking back at them. Before either of them knew it had happened, they were enclosed in each other's arms as if clinging for dear life. Neither was able to contain their tears. Greg lifted Lynnette off the ground and held her tight as he swung her around. When he put her back down, neither one could let go.

Nearby, Rose and Sheree stood side by side with their arms around each other, tears streaming down their faces as they smiled at the happy reunion.

After a moment, Greg looked at Rose and Sheree and motioned for the two to join them. They almost ran to them and formed a bigger circle. When Greg caught sight of Robert, Joshua, and Miranda standing nearby, he motioned for them to join their circle of love. All seven of them stood in the circle, hugging, laughing, and crying.

Chapter 30

The December air was cool. Only a few more weeks and the children's home would be complete. Open house was scheduled for the first week in January, just five days into the new year.

Lynnette, Rose, Greg, and Sheree walked throughout each room as Robert and his crew worked busily. The smell of fresh paint and cedar filled their nostrils. Lynnette and Rose couldn't believe their eyes. The house looked nothing like it did when Lynnette and Robert had initially seen it a year before. Greg and Sheree were impressed. Rose's face lit up like the moon as she took in the sight. Lynnette was delighted that she and Robert had a part in it.

In the kitchen, Rose admired the island cooking center, built-in pantry, and double-door closet for dishes, silverware, and linens. The recessed lighting above the island, sink, and cabinets were a hit with Greg and Sheree.

Lynnette explained, "This lighting here is good for this area of the kitchen because it provides illumination and improves safety." She stopped in front of the sink. "For instance, when washing or cutting up meats, fruits, and vegetables, it's important that you have the proper amount of lighting. It cuts down on accidents."

On their way upstairs, Lynnette pointed along the wall and said to Rose, "Those unframed landscape pictures we found at the flea market will go great along this wall. Of course, that's only a suggestion. Greg, you and Sheree may prefer something else here."

Greg answered, "No, I think the landscapes will look good." He turned to Sheree and asked, "What do you think, hon?"

Sheree nodded her approval. "I agree. I think they'd look really good arranged in a stair-step fashion."

Lynnette smiled. "That's a great idea, Sheree. I like your style."

When they reached the top of the stairs, Lynnette offered suggestions on adorning the hallway. "Some potted plants, trees, and floral arrangements will dress this hall up nicely and make it come to life."

Rose was getting an idea. She pressed her index finger up against the side of her mouth. "Greg. Sheree. I have just the thing at home to help liven up this area."

"What is it, Mama?" Greg asked curiously.

Before Rose answered her son, she asked, "Lynn, do you remember that old worn-out table we found at a yard sale?"

"Sure," Lynnette said. "We refinished it and stained it. Isn't it in your hallway at home?"

"Yes, but it would look great up here, don't you think?"

Lynnette had to agree. "It would look good."

The two women looked at Greg and Sheree, hoping to see some evidence of their approval.

Sheree asked, "Is it the one downstairs in the hallway between the living room and the den?"

Rose smiled as she shook her head. "Yes."

Sheree said, "It's gorgeous, but are you sure you want to part with it, Mama Rose?"

Rose laughed. "Honey, you've seen my house. I've got so much stuff, it's not like I can't stand to get rid of a few things."

"That's Mama for you," Greg added. "She never did believe in throwing anything away. Daddy used to get mad at her because she was always bringing somebody's junk home wanting him to try to fix it up."

They all began laughing, and Rose playfully swatted her son's hand. They surveyed the remainder of the house.

The following Saturday, Simone stopped by to see Lynnette. Since her surgery, Lynnette had not been spending as much time with Simone as she had in the past. She still loved Simone dearly and always would. Finally, after all she'd been through the past year, she could see clearly the negative effect Simone was having on her family life.

Lynnette felt horribly guilty every time she thought about how she had treated Robert—staying out late and not calling, being belligerent and arguing with him. It was as though she had lost all her mental capacities.

As she and Simone sat in the den talking, Lynnette was getting fed up with her friend's strong sentiments. Simone had been a good friend to her, but that did not give her the right to try to force her ideas on her. She listened to Simone ramble on.

"Lynn, you know you really should consider opening a store in Atlanta. Just think of all the money you could make. All the big-name celebrities you'd have as clients. Why be satisfied with the one little store you have here? Start a chain of stores. First Atlanta, then out of state. Hey, what about Chicago?"

Simone was getting carried away with all her big ideas. Once she got started, she didn't know when to stop. Lynnette felt as though she was belittling her business with her suggestions that she was not faring as well as she would in a bigger city. And as far as her clientele, she already had clients all over the world, many of whom were celebrities. She just didn't go around bragging about it.

Simone continued, "And another thing. I just don't understand your philosophy on not opening your store on Saturday. I don't see how you've stayed in business all these years with that concept. You should extend your hours of operation."

Finally, Lynnette told Simone, "I like my store where it is. I don't want a chain. I'm happy with just the one store. And I have a family. I'm not going to extend my hours."

Simone was disappointed in her friend's complacent attitude. When they were young, they had big dreams. She admitted that Lynnette was a successful businesswoman, but all she seemed to want to do was please Robert. He had brought her from the city to this little country town they lived in, and Lynnette was acting as though she liked it. Lynnette didn't like this little town any more than she did. Simone felt she was living Robert's dream, not her own.

Simone said, "Lynn, you've changed. You used to be so outgoing. So full of life. What happened?"

"Simone, don't start. People change. I'm not you. I love my life, believe it or not. Why is that so hard for you to believe?"

"The Lynn I used to know never would have left the only home she'd ever known for some man."

Lynnette felt like giving Simone a piece of her mind. A very huge chunk. She couldn't do it though. Simone and

Simone's mother had been there for her when no one else was. She simply gave her a playful warning. "Simone, I think we better change the subject before I lose my cool."

Simone wasn't worried about that. Lynnette had never lost her temper with her except for the time they'd gone to the club in Columbus. Even then, they had patched things up quickly. Lynnette would never get seriously agitated with her. That was why Simone pushed her as hard as she did.

In the past, even if it was something she didn't necessarily want to do, Lynnette usually gave in to Simone's desires. This situation was no different. It would just take some time considering the hold Robert had on Lynnette, but Simone was determined to have her friend back and have things the way they used to be.

Simone was in the midst of bragging about how she loved the city life when she began to manipulate the conversation again. "Just take your house for instance. You and Robert built this big, beautiful home out here in the middle of nowhere. You grew up in Chicago, one of the largest cities in the world. Then you meet Robert and let him bring you way down here to a place nobody ever heard of.

"How do you stand it here? I'd go crazy. Your house should be in the city. We were happy in Chicago. Why'd you have to leave? Where was Robert when we were growing up? Probably somewhere living in the lap of luxury. We had to struggle. Has he ever had to struggle? He probably had everything handed to him on a silver platter."

Lynnette had heard enough. It was one thing for Simone to disrespect her, but she would not sit there and allow her to disrespect her husband.

"Simone, I love my life. And I love Robert."

"Well, I didn't say you didn't," Simone interjected. "But—"

"But nothing," Lynnette spat out. "You know, you've never liked Robert. You've given him nothing but grief since the day you met him. Maybe if you'd stay out of other people's business and try to take care of your own, you'd still have a husband."

Lynnette's words were shocking even to herself. She had never spoken to her friend in that manner. She had not meant to make that last comment. Too late. It was out, and she didn't care how Simone took it. She was fed up with her.

Simone stood. "Well, if that's the way you feel, maybe I should leave."

Lynnette remained seated. With a disgusted look on her face, she refused to even look at Simone as she spat out, "Maybe you should. You know the way out." She was tired, too, of Simone always complaining about her family living in the country, so she added, "Hope you don't run into any bears."

Simone grabbed her purse and stormed away. She almost knocked Robert down as he was coming in through the kitchen door.

"Hey, Simone, where are you going in such a hurry?" he asked.

Simone did not utter a word but ran straight to her car, got in, and sped away.

Robert found Lynnette in the den and inquired, "What's wrong with Simone? She was running outta here like a chicken with its head cut off."

Lynnette started ranting and raving about how Simone was nothing but a busybody, always trying to run everybody else's life when she needed to mind her own business. Robert had never seen Lynnette like this when it came to her friend. He asked several times what Simone had done to upset her so. She wouldn't say. All she did was storm around the room talking about how she never wanted to see or speak to her again.

The thought occurred to Robert that this was his chance to get rid of Simone once and for all. After all, she wasn't crazy about him, and she wasn't exactly his cup of tea either. This was his chance to get Lynnette to give her the boot, hopefully for good. However, the more he thought about it, the more his conscience reminded him that he couldn't do it.

Robert told Lynnette, "You and Simone have been friends for a long time. Are you sure you want it to end just like that?"

Lynnette stopped pacing long enough to gaze at her husband. "What are you saying? You want me to stay friends with her? Neither one of you can stand the other."

"What I'm saying is you should talk to her and try to patch things up. Life is too short to be holding grudges. Look at all you've been through this year. Do you think God brought you this far just to have you get mad at Simone and write her off as no-account?"

Lynnette thought about how truly blessed she was to have Robert as her husband. He could easily have used this opportunity to his advantage to break her friendship with Simone, but he didn't.

Joshua interrupted Lynnette's thoughts when he ran into the room. "Mom, I just saw a car wreck down the road. It looks just like Ms. Kirkland's car. Was she here?"

Robert and Lynnette ran to their son.

"Yes," Lynnette answered. "Where'd you see the car?"

"Just down the road a piece. There were some other people there trying to help. The car went down an embankment."

Robert, Lynnette, and Joshua jumped into the Suburban and sped out of the driveway. As they got a little farther down the road, they could see a crowd. A light mist of rain had begun to fall. It had been raining earlier in the day, and the road was slippery. As they got closer, they could see Simone's Mustang sitting in a field.

The emergency medical technicians had already arrived. Lynnette jumped out of the vehicle and ran down the embankment. She slipped on the grass, falling on her hands and buttocks, and slid down. Robert was not far behind. He helped her up, and they went over to Simone's car. Simone was still inside, but medical personnel were assisting her. There was a small scrape across her forehead.

"Simone!" Lynnette screamed. "Are you all right?"

"Yeah," Simone answered. "I just bumped my head."

The technicians freed Simone from the car and helped her onto the stretcher. They couldn't get her to lie down so she sat up while they gave her medical attention and applied a bandage to her injury. They wanted to take her to the emergency room, but she refused to go. They warned her, however, that she would probably be sore the next day and if the pain became bothersome, she should seek medical attention.

There was some minor front fender damage to Simone's car. After the police obtained a report of the accident, Robert got her keys and pulled the vehicle onto the side of the road. He instructed Lynnette and Joshua to let Simone ride back to their house with them while he drove Simone's car.

Back at the house, Simone cried profusely as she apologized to Lynnette and Robert for all the grief she had caused them.

She said, "You know, Lynn, you were right about what you said this afternoon. I never liked Robert."

Robert was stunned. He'd always felt that Simone didn't like him, but actually hearing her say it did something to him. He stood. "Maybe I should leave."

Simone stayed his arm. "No, Robert, don't leave. This is your house. I have something I need to say to you. When I went down that embankment, I thought I was dead. Your life really does flash before your eyes. And there are a lot of things in mine that aren't too pretty. I haven't liked you from the day I met you and saw how head over heels in love with you Lynnette was and still is.

"I never gave you a chance. I saw you as the enemy because Lynnette was the best friend I ever had, and in my eyes, you took her from me. I'm so sorry for the way I've treated you. You've been nothing but kind to me ever since I've known you, and all I did was think negatively of you."

Robert did not know what to say. All those years, he never knew the pain Simone was going through over his and Lynnette's relationship. His heart went out to her. "That's okay, Simone. I'm just glad you're all right."

Simone looked down at her hands. "I have another confession to make. I didn't divorce Marshall. He divorced me. I was never there for him. I was always too busy trying to live my own life. He got fed up."

Lynnette was shocked, but Robert wasn't. He had figured as much but had never said anything to Lynnette.

Simone looked at her friend. "Lynnette, I'm so sorry for what I did to you. I could tell I was causing problems in your marriage, but I didn't care. I guess I wanted us to be the way we used to be."

Lynnette got up and went over to sit beside Simone. She took hold of her hands. Her tone was gentle. "It's all in the past. You didn't make me do anything at the time I didn't want to do, so it's just as much my fault as it is yours. You know, Simone, we're not kids anymore. We did have some good times, but we can't go back to the way we used to be. Something we can do though is make some new memories together.

"I love you, but I have to tell you that things can't go back to the way they were with you trying to force your ideas on me. I have some apologies to make, too. I'm sorry about what I said this afternoon about your marriage. No matter what you said to me, I was out of line, and I shouldn't have said it. Will you forgive me?"

Simone smiled. "Of course." The two friends hugged.

Simone had a revelation. Was God telling her she had better get her life in order? Was He trying to teach her a lesson? That she should value life, family, and friendships because tomorrow is not promised.

Epilogue

January

The group was all smiles as they posed for the photographer on the lawn in front of the Rose-Lynn Children's Home. Rose had wanted all her family and close personal friends in the photograph. In the back were Robert, Greg, James, Joshua, and Beverly. Lynnette, Sheree, Carla, Miranda, and Rose stood in front of them.

Open house had gone exceptionally well. People had come from all over the county and surrounding areas, even from some nearby states such as Alabama, Tennessee, and Florida. Afterward, back at the Montgomery house, there was a family gathering.

"Mama, are you okay?" Lynnette queried. She strolled over to join her mother on the window seat in the den.

Rose smiled, "I'm fine, dear." She paused. "So this is where you come to do all your serious thinking?"

Lynnette returned her mother's smile. "Yes. It's nice, isn't it?"

Rose breathed in deeply. "It certainly is. I was just sitting here thinking about how happy I am to have all my family together." As an afterthought, she added, "Finally."

"I know," Lynnette agreed. "It's nice."

"Yes, God has truly blessed us."

"He has."

"Here you two are." Greg popped his head in. "We were wondering where you ran off to."

Lynnette smiled at her brother. "Sorry, Greg. We didn't mean to be antisocial." She took Rose by the hand. "Come on, Mama. Let's join the rest of the family."

Sheree announced to her husband, "We see you found them."

"Yeah. I didn't have to look too far. They were all huddled up in the den. You know how you women are when you get to talking."

Everyone laughed.

Rose playfully popped her son on his hand. "Watch yourself now. You're still not too big for me to put you over my lap," she threatened.

Robert laughed as he said, "Mama Rose, I'd love to see that. Greg with his big, grown self laying across your li'l lap."

Laughter filled the room again.

Rose shook her finger at Robert and laughed. "You better watch yourself, or I'll have you over here, too."

Sheree warned, "Don't get Mama Rose started."

"I know that's right," Rose concurred and winked at Robert.

Robert leaned down and kissed Rose's cheek. "You know I love you."

Rose patted Robert's cheek. "I love you, too."

After a few minutes of everyone talking and laughing, Rose grabbed Lynnette's hand. "Come on. We have a surprise for you."

"I knew you guys were up to something," Lynnette exclaimed. "What have you done?"

"Come on," Rose repeated. "Close your eyes, and no peeking."

It was like the parting of the Red Sea as everyone else stood off to the side while Rose led Lynnette out and stopped her at the bottom of the staircase. "Now you can open your eyes."

When Lynnette opened her eyes, she caught sight of the most beautiful quilt that she had ever seen on the staircase wall. The recessed lights in the ceiling shone on it brilliantly. The quilt was made up of a few small items of baby clothes, family photographs, and exquisite pieces of fabric.

"I think she likes it, Grandma," Miranda said as she leaned over and whispered in her grandmother's ear.

Rose smiled and nodded.

Lynnette was speechless. She placed her hands over her mouth and took a few steps up to get a better view. Everyone followed. "Mama, it's beautiful. I don't know what to say. You made this, didn't you?"

"Yes." Rose beamed.

Lynnette threw her arms around Rose's neck. "It's beautiful. Thank you."

"I call it the Jiles-Alexander Family Quilt. The baby clothes are yours."

"You kept them after all these years?"

"I sure did."

Joshua was at the top of the stairs. "Look, Mom, there's a switch up here, too." He flipped the switch to turn off the recessed lighting above the quilt, then flipped the switch back on.

"That's neat," Lynnette said.

Rose informed Lynnette that some of the cloth on the quilt had come from clothing that had belonged to Lynnette's parents and grandparents. Everyone else decided to go back downstairs and give the two women some privacy. As they left, Rose was giving Lynnette the remaining history of the different portions that made up the quilt.

After everyone had gone home, Lynnette was wiping off the kitchen counter when Robert slipped up behind her and grabbed her around her waist. "Hey," he whispered in her ear.

"Hey."

"You've had a very busy day."

Lynnette let out a happy sigh. "Yes. We all have."

"Are you tired?"

"Not really. I'm too excited to be tired. I can't stop thinking about the quilt Mama gave me. It's so beautiful."

"Yes, it is."

"Now I know the real reason you and Josh were installing those recessed lights last week."

"Well, it was hard keeping it from you." Robert squeezed her. "You're so inquisitive."

Lynnette laughed. "That sounds like a very polite way of saying I'm nosy, but I'll let you get away with it this time." She folded the towel and placed it across the dish rack.

Robert flipped off the light as they left the kitchen with their arms around each other. When they got to the stairs, Lynnette suggested, "Honey, you go ahead. I'll be up in a minute."

"Okay, but don't be long."

"I won't. I love you."

"I love you, too."

They shared a kiss before Robert headed upstairs.

Lynnette went to the den to take a few moments to reflect.

As she paced, her thoughts became clear. Yes, things certainly had changed a lot. She recalled the day she came home from the doctor's office all upset about the possibility of surgery, thinking and feeling like it was the end of her world. How, in her mind, she just would not be the same woman. She realized she wasn't the same. Not because of the surgery, but because her faith had made her stronger. Yes, she had been dealt changes in her life for which she was not prepared. But she had also been given the opportunity to have a change of heart.

As she walked to the top of the stairs, Lynnette looked at the quilt once more and smiled. Then she turned off the lights.

Her life was now complete. Her family and her faith had accomplished that. When one phase of her life had ended, a new one was just beginning.

Dear Readers

I hope you enjoyed reading *A Measure of Faith* as much as I enjoyed writing it. As many of you know, this is my first inspirational novel. I would love to hear your thoughts about the characters, how they dealt with their fears, and what they learned in finally facing up to them.

Please enclose a self-addressed, stamped envelope with your letter and mail to: Maxine Billings, P. O. Box 307, Temple, GA 30179. Feel free to e-mail your comments to maxinebillings@yahoo.com. Please visit my website also at www.maxinebillings.com.

From my heart to yours,
Maxine

"**SAVED IN THE CITY** is a refreshing novel that delves into the heart of friendship, faith and making dreams become a reality."
—*Rawsistaz Reviewers*

Essence bestselling author

JACQUELIN THOMAS

New York City's elite Emerald Model Management is having an open call, and among the hopefuls are three beautiful women with big dreams—and the faith that they'll come true. But in a fast-paced town filled with temptation, is faith enough to keep them out of harm's way?

SAVED IN THE CITY

Coming the first week of April, wherever books are sold.

Visit us at www.kimanipress.com

KPJT0280407